# HIGH HEAT

**ALSO BY WALDY MALOUF:**

*The Hudson River Valley Cookbook*

**ALSO BY MELISSA CLARK:**

*Sylvia's Family Soul Food Cookbook: From Hemingway, South Carolina,
to Harlem* (with Sylvia Woods)

*Caviar and Champagne*

*The Modern Vegetarian Kitchen* (with Peter Berley)

*The Nantucket Restaurants Cookbook: Menus and Recipes from the
Faraway Isle* (with Samara Farber Mormar)

*The Last Course: The Desserts of Gramercy Tavern* (with Claudia Fleming)

# High Heat

### GRILLING & ROASTING YEAR-ROUND
### WITH MASTER CHEF WALDY MALOUF

## Waldy Malouf & Melissa Clark

BROADWAY BOOKS

NEW YORK

Broadway Books titles may be purchased for business or promotional use or for special sales. For information, please write to: Special Markets Department, Random House, Inc., 1745 Broadway, New York, NY 10019.

PRINTED IN CHINA

BROADWAY BOOKS and its logo, a letter B bisected on the diagonal, are trademarks of Broadway Books, a division of Random House, Inc.

Visit our website at www.broadwaybooks.com

Book design by Elizabeth Rendfleisch

Photography by William Meppem

Library of Congress Cataloging-in-Publication Data

Malouf, Waldy.
     High heat : grilling and roasting year-round with master chef Waldy Malouf /
Waldy Malouf and Melissa Clark.
        p.   cm.
     Includes index.
     1. Barbecue cookery.   2. Roasting (Cookery)   I. Clark, Melissa.   II. Title.
TX840.B3 M33 2003
641.5'784—dc21          2002027940

ISBN 0-7679-1070-2

10 9 8 7 6 5 4 3 2 1

While we were writing this book, a tragedy occurred that took the lives of many friends and colleagues. It was a failed attempt to quash our ability to enjoy freedom and to love life but has in fact strengthened our resolve to live life to its fullest.

It is to this bold spirit that we dedicate this book.

Cook well, eat well, live well.

# *Acknowledgments*

We would like to gratefully acknowledge the many people who helped bring *High Heat* into the world. The first are our wonderful agents, Angela Miller and Janis Donnaud, both of whom believed in our vision from the start. Then there is our dedicated editor at Broadway Books, Jennifer Josephy, and her whole team, who turned our manuscript into a beautiful book.

Of course the book wouldn't be nearly so good-looking without the talents of our photographer, William Meppem, and his assistant, Steven Kessler, and the food styling help of Babette Audant. And thanks to Elizabeth Rendfleisch for the terrific design.

Testing the recipes would not have been as painless, or in fact as fun, without recipe testers Karen Rush and Zoe Singer. We can be sure these recipes work thanks to their exactitude and excellent taste!

The Beacon family also deserves many, many thanks for supporting us during this endeavor. This includes the Emil family, partners at Beacon, for their encouragement and love of high-heat cooking. Beacon's chefs de cuisine, Mario Landaverde and Mark LeMoult, were invaluable, helping us develop and flesh out recipes and of course holding down the fort. Thanks also to Carlos "Carlito" Beach, who steadfastly delivered ingredients to the wilds of Brooklyn via the Q train, rain or shine.

Things could never have gone so smoothly without the organizational help and love of Dalila Mercado, who kept Waldy focused and sane and also kept him from throwing a pot at the computer.

*High Heat* is a better book thanks to Karen Schloss and Frank Diaz, because they're always there as good friends, constantly challenging and motivating. Grilling is a pleasure thanks to Viking Range, which contributed some of the best grills and ovens ever made. We were also endlessly pleased by the performance of one of Frontgate's world-class gas grills. And we're grateful to J. B. Prince for providing us with beautiful pots and pans for the photo shoot.

Most of all, we owe gratitude to our families. Thanks to Paul, who put up with many long trips to Connecticut for recipe testing and even traveled to another state to buy beer on a Sunday. And Meg, Max, and Merrill, Waldy's wife and children, for inspiration, love, support, and tasting everything, whether they liked it or not.

# Contents

# Introduction

I've always loved playing with fire, ever since I incinerated my first marshmallow over a campfire as a kid. As I grew up, this fascination stayed with me, from the oyster roasts and barbecues of my high school and college years to the more refined techniques of brûléing and roasting in cooking school. No matter how the fire is applied, it seems to me that food cooked with very high heat always tastes best.

I think most people would agree that there are few foods as compelling as a piece of meat or fish charred over open flames. Something almost magical happens: the skin contracts and crisps, turning crackling and brown; the juices drip and run; the flesh becomes sweet and intensely flavored. More than the complex sauces, seasonings, rubs, and techniques of my training as a chef, searing temperatures unlock the boldest characteristics of foods, whether it's the savory crunch and flavorful juices of a roasted chicken, the musky taste of a grilled steak, or the melting sweetness of caramelized onions.

Another thing I love about cooking with high heat is that it's sexy and exciting, especially compared to more moderate techniques like poaching. There is something primal and innately satisfying about cooking foods this way. In our hands-off, information-based culture, cooking food over an open fire brings people together. And given the omnipresence of outdoor and indoor grills and a national move toward simpler, more healthful foods, it's exactly how people today want to eat.

Since these are the flavors I love the most, writing *High Heat* was a natural and very personal process. This kind of cooking is the basis of the menu at my two Beacon restaurants, and more important, it's how my family likes to eat at home. High-heat cooking is ideally suited to home kitchens and backyards. And it's also a very fast way to prepare any kind of meat, fish, vegetable, or even fruit, which is key when making dinner comes at the end of a long day and everyone's hungry (and isn't that always?). The methods here are simple, developed with the home cook in mind, and I made sure to test every recipe in a home kitchen and backyard.

These recipes are an easy way to incorporate fresh, flavorful ingredients into your everyday cooking, especially since most are adapted for use either indoors or out. That flexibility means you can make any dish at any time. It's important to me that home cooking feel comfortable and natural. I see no need to crank up the oven if you're throwing a dinner party in July, and there's no reason why making a nice winter meal indoors should be any more involved than flipping some chops on the grill. Whether food is roasted or grilled, it has a similar flavor profile. These recipes were all developed with the charred, caramelized flavors of high heat in mind, so most have dual instructions, since they are easily adapted for both roasting and grilling.

In keeping with the easy cooking style of this book, my ingredient lists are pretty much limited to standard supermarket items. But just because the ingredients are accessible doesn't mean they are dull or timid. I use robust, intense seasonings to enhance the rich, charred flavors of the fire. They add a lot to the taste of a dish—and they do it fast. Every recipe features vivid elements, like the tang of pickled vegetables, the saltiness of olives, capers, and anchovies, the bright flavors of fresh herbs, the heat of fresh and dried chiles, the pungency of blue cheese, the aromatic depth of unsweetened cocoa, the bitterness of citrus zest . . . the list goes on. And since these ingredients pack a punch, I often use them singly and in small quantities—to enhance what I'm cooking without overpowering it.

A lot of these recipes and flavor choices speak of my heritage, particularly my Sicilian and Lebanese grandparents. I have reconnected with Italian and Middle Eastern cuisines at various points in my life, and they are essential to how I think about food. My cooking style speaks of the various influences on my cooking throughout my career, but it is most essentially influenced by my early experiences with food.

I grew up in Palm Harbor on the west coast of Florida, near Tarpon Springs. At the time that area was very rural. The food I ate growing up was a part of the beaches, orange groves, and cattle ranches we lived among. Big events were oyster roasts and barbecues—definitely rural southern cooking. Since my grandparents on my father's side were Lebanese and Sicilian, there was also a very strong connection in our house to ethnic, mostly Mediterranean food. My mother came from a New England farming family and brought with her farm food: stewing, roasting, canning, and putting things up.

None of this cooking was sophisticated, so when I started working at the French restaurant of a newly opened country club nearby, my parents had to expand their idea of a cook beyond the image of the guy slinging hash in a local diner. I started as a dishwasher when I was thirteen, to save up enough money to buy a motorcycle. As soon as I discovered that I could make a little more money as a cook's apprentice, I went to work for the two French chefs at the restaurant, who were used to hiring thirteen-year-old boys as apprentices in the European style. And all of a sudden I started to realize that I really liked doing this. I truly enjoyed cooking.

I got the motorcycle when I was fourteen and had wrecked it by the time I was fifteen, but I kept working at the restaurant. I was a pretty hyperactive, energetic kid, and I worked almost full-time all through high school. Of course, even though I was receiving a classical chef's training, it never occurred to me that this could be my career. My father is a lawyer, and my mother is a teacher and college professor, and at that time you didn't go into cooking in this country. I was learning about cooking at a very high level, but I didn't realize that becoming a chef was an option.

After high school I continued to work in restaurants, while taking prelaw courses first in Tampa and then in Tallahassee. I worked under a few European chefs, in restaurants and country clubs. By the time I was finishing my second year of college I knew I didn't want to be a lawyer. I decided to visit the Culinary Institute of America (CIA) in upstate New York. When I got there, I was impressed by the imposing gray stone building on the shores of the Hudson River that houses the CIA, and I enrolled. It felt like an exciting leap into a world that most people didn't even know existed.

In the early seventies the CIA was a very disciplined, almost militaristic school. When I arrived, I had hair down to my shoulders and was a little too wild for my own good. Being in an environment where uniforms were worn, shoes had to be shined, and fingernails were checked for cleanliness was actually very good for me. Cooking school really gave me focus.

Then, right before graduating, I won a cooking competition. The prize was a twenty-four-day cruise in the Mediterranean. I flew there, boarded the cruise ship, and learned that I was supposed to spend most of my time in the galley, working with the crew. After the first four hours I decided that the galley of the ship was not where I wanted to be. We would anchor at ports all along the Mediterranean, and I became much more interested in going to the markets, walking around, and soaking up other cultures. I didn't spend much more time in the galley.

What I saw in Europe sparked a keen interest in the foods of different cultures and how they are cooked. There was a tremendous amount of fresh regional produce, often grilled or roasted in huge community ovens. Open-fire cooking has maintained its predominance in so many warm parts of the world, from the coasts of Spain and Italy to the Mediterranean ports of the Middle East and northern Africa, Alexandria, Cyprus, Istanbul, Syria, and Israel to South and Central America. But aside from the occasional backyard hot-dog-and-burger cookout, this kind of cooking was not yet popular in the United States.

When the cruise was over, I decided not to fly back to America. I spent six or seven months weaseling my way into jobs in Greece, at the Olympics in Innsbruck, in London, and in Paris. Only after I ran out of money was I willing to take that return flight to New York. And because the CIA somehow owed me an $86 refund, I went directly there. While I was retrieving my $86, I got a temporary job as replacement banquet chef at the St. Regis hotel. I hadn't planned to go to New York, but after three months working there I was in love with the city. I never left.

I went on to work jobs in several hotel restaurants as a saucier, sous chef, executive sous chef, and then as the chef of a tiny restaurant in New York City called The Leopard. That's when something changed for me. The Leopard served forty meals at lunch and forty at dinner, and the menu was all prix fixe. Every day I came up with a few different options for each course and cooked them in the kitchen with no one around but the dishwasher. After all my training and travels, this was where I really developed. During the year I spent by myself in that kitchen I tried to draw on all my influences, experience, and education, to formulate a personal cuisine.

My next job was as the chef of a country French restaurant called La Crémaillère in Banksville, New York. This was in 1982, when French cuisine was really changing. Nouvelle cuisine was replacing classical cuisine, and regional peasant cuisines were also becoming popular. This meant I was able to use a lot of what I had developed at The Leopard, which was based on rustic Mediterranean cuisines. I just put a French spin on the kind of food I was interested in, and the upscale clientele was very receptive to it.

At La Crémaillère my cooking became ingredient driven, with an emphasis on celebrating regional and seasonal produce. This wasn't something that I came up with out of the blue; it's how people cook in most of the world, because they use whatever's growing outside their back door. But it wasn't how most restaurants presented food in the United States at that time. I wasn't alone. There was a small group of other chefs also tapping into this mentality, developing an awareness of seasonal, local ingredients. We were building relationships with farmers and producers all over the country. And that translated to the food on the table. Flavors got simpler because they were fresh enough to stand on their own, without a lot of sauces and other extras. As a result cooking techniques became less complicated as well, and for me roasting and grilling became more prominent.

Then I got the opportunity to help open a restaurant in lower Manhattan, where the whole concept would be regional, seasonal American cuisine. It would be called the Hudson River Club. I jumped at the chance. Of course there is no specific Hudson Valley or New York cuisine, and nothing really to emulate, so it was a unique opportunity for me to present my cuisine, which is American because I'm American. My cooking is a sort of melting pot of the different influences on me, and at the Hudson River Club I simply shifted my focus to Hudson River Valley products and produce and cooked to follow the seasons of the Hudson Valley. It was a success that culminated in *The Hudson River Valley Cookbook*.

After seven years at the Hudson River Club I was ready to move on, and it happened that the owners of New York's Rainbow Room were at that point looking to develop a new food program for the restaurant. They wanted to revitalize the dining aspect of the Rainbow Room, turning the menu into the epitome of American cuisine, served in a glamorous setting. By the time their lease would run out two years later, they hoped to have changed the reputation of their food for the better so that they could sign a new lease based on their successful new approach. They needed new ideas and energy, and I accepted the job as a challenge.

Reinvigorating the food at the Rainbow Room was good for me and for the restaurant. But when the lease ran out, a deal couldn't be arranged with the building, and the Rainbow Room owners asked me to move with them. When they asked me what kind of restaurant I wanted to cook in, I told them I wanted to open a casual restaurant with an open kitchen that relied on open-fire cooking. This kind of cooking was rare in New York, but it was beginning to catch on in other places around the country. It's where I thought people's tastes were going, and it was food that I loved to cook. The idea of an open kitchen appealed to me, not as a bastion of haute cuisine, although it would be a sophisticated New York restaurant, but as a casual way to interact with diners and involve them in the immediacy of open-fire cooking.

What we ended up with was Beacon Restaurant, first in Manhattan and then in Stamford, Connecticut, as well. I would describe it as a chef-driven steak house, but one where the techniques of cooking with a wood-burning oven, grill, and rotisserie lend intense flavors to every dish. In addition to these techniques, I rely on nothing more than a collection of side dishes, rubs, herbs, and spices to enhance the main ingredients. This style comes naturally to me, as a culmination of my training and experience.

*High Heat* takes my approach one step further by translating these flavors for the home cook. These are the foods that I cook for my family and friends. They are simple to make, yet they speak the same language and have the same influences as my cooking at Beacon. The book feels like an organic step to me, since this kind of cooking is based around little more than heating up your oven or grill, and it stems very much from the home cooking that is done in warm countries.

*High Heat* isn't about cooking like a restaurant chef. But once you've tried a few recipes I hope you'll find that they make good use of the influences and ideas that inspire me at Beacon, yet are easily brought home, into your kitchen and backyard. If this book can encourage a sense of comfort and community and an enjoyment of the primal urges and flavors of open-fire and high-heat cooking, then it's doing its job.

# Cooking with High Heat

### THE BASICS

## In the Oven or on the Grill?

You'll notice that in the recipes sometimes instructions for "In the Oven" are first and sometimes the instructions for "On the Grill" are first—this indicates my order of preference. Both methods will work wonderfully, although often the results are a little different. So on those days when you can't decide whether to cook inside or out, check to see which method is listed first.

### DONENESS

Through experience you'll know when a piece of meat or fish is done. I encourage you to touch the meat a little as it nears doneness, to develop a sense of this. You can always use an instant-read thermometer (see the doneness chart that follows), but in time you'll be able to tell just by touching the food. A common method used to explain how doneness feels is to press different parts of your hand between your forefinger and thumb. With a relaxed hand, raw or rare meat feels like the area close to the edge of your hand, and the farther you go back toward the muscle, the more well done it will feel. Really well done meat feels like the muscle of your hand in between your forefinger and thumb when you make a fist.

### KNOW WHEN TO STOP

Meat can go from the desired degree of doneness to overdone very quickly when the oven is at 450 or 500°F or the grill is hot. So it's important to keep a close eye on the meat's internal temperature. Take the meat out promptly, bearing in mind that the temperature continues to rise 5 to 20 degrees as the meat rests.

### RESTING TIME

Any chop more than an inch thick or roast should be given a rest time after it is taken out of the oven or off the grill. This allows the juices to redistribute throughout the meat, making it tender and moist. The thicker the meat, the longer the rest and the greater the continued rise in temperature. Generally, chops that are only about 1 inch thick or so and steaks should rest for 3 to 5 minutes, 2-inch-thick or more ones about 10 minutes, while a large roast can be left to rest for 30 to 40 minutes, covered in some foil to keep the outside from getting cold.

*These are the internal temperatures (°F) at which you want to remove the meat from the heat—the temperature will continue to rise as the meat rests. If a column is left blank, it's because I don't recommend cooking the item to that degree of doneness.*

| | RARE | MEDIUM-RARE | MEDIUM | WELL-DONE |
|---|---|---|---|---|
| BEEF | 110–120 | 125–130 | 135–140 | 160 |
| LAMB | 115–125 | 125–135 | 135–145 | 150 |
| VEAL | | 125–130 | 135–145 | |
| VENISON | 120–135 | 135 | 140 | 155 |
| PORK | | | 150 | 165 |
| POULTRY | | | 160 | 175 |
| FISH | 115–120 | 125–130 | 135 | |

RAW FOOD SAFETY

The food safety issue that pertains most to grilling or roasting (and especially grilling) is cross-contamination. This happens when you unwittingly put a piece of cooked meat, fish, or poultry onto a surface that held it in its raw state. Thus the platter you use to take the raw meat, fish, or poultry outside to the grill or to the oven shouldn't be used again when the food is cooked, unless you take adequate precautions. You can carefully line a platter with wax paper before placing raw food on it, then discard the wax paper before returning the cooked food. But your best bet is to have a separate, clean platter to hold the cooked food or to wash the platter that held the raw food while it's cooking.

## On the Grill

The bare essentials for grilling are really just heat and/or fire and some way to hold the food over it. From the very first days of cooking, people have been developing different methods to expose food to heat. Argentineans skewer a side of beef and cook it over a fire, while Native Americans would roast a whole salmon on a piece of wood angled in the sand by a fire. And traditional methods are still being used. Down South they make a fire in a pit, put a grate over it, dump oysters on top, and eat them as they open. At clambakes, New Englanders build a fire in a rock-lined pit in the sand and then steam seafood on seaweed in the pit. And at a Hawaiian luau, a 200-pound pig is buried in a pit with white-hot lava rocks. Of course, these days you can also opt to spend $5,000 for a stainless-steel gas grill.

For the purposes of this book, you'll be best off with a good solid grill that has enough surface area for the quantities you regularly cook. You should consider how you plan to use your grill before you buy one. Do you make burgers for two, or is it ribs and fish and chicken and steaks for a family of six plus friends? Beyond the fire pit or heat source and the grill surface, all you'll need is a cover, which is a standard feature on everything from a 12-inch hibachi to a 6-foot rotisserie.

If you cook outside a lot (more than twice a week), it's wise to invest in a high-quality grill. This is an area where you get what you pay for. If you have a good grill, you'll find yourself using it more and more, and you'll probably add on to your setup.

### WHERE TO GRILL

The more you cook outside, the more you will think of it as an outdoor kitchen. As budget allows, you may want to invest in lighting, electricity, refrigeration, counters, individual burners, rotisseries, places to keep platters, a sink and water source, and endless other amenities that make cooking outdoors convenient, versatile, and fun.

Unless your outdoor kitchen is already equipped with water, electricity, and refrigeration, you'll want to set the grill up as close to the kitchen as possible. Choose an open spot, since grilling creates carbon monoxide, which you never want in an enclosed space. And make sure it's level, so if somebody knocks into the grill it won't fall over. Also take into account where your guests will be sitting, so you don't smoke them out by placing the grill too close. And take care not to put the grill where a flare-up could catch a dry tree branch or falling ash could light something on the ground.

Grilling often goes on into the night, so it requires lighting, and holding a flashlight in one hand and tongs in the other is not a viable option. Unless an outdoor light of your home will illuminate the grill area, you should set up an outdoor lamp or some small clip-on lights.

The only other setup consideration is counter space. Grillers need a good surface to spread out platters and ingredients, be it a picnic table or cart or the fold-out counters of a large grill.

### GRILLING SAFETY

A grill is basically a kettle of fire, so the grill, cover, and anything touching them will be very hot. Cover your hands with reliable oven mitts, pot holders, or thick folded dish towels. Just as a precaution, I recommend keeping a fire extinguisher in the kitchen and a small one near your grill (these can be found at any hardware store).

### HANDLING FLARE-UPS

Of course, you don't need to douse your food with the fire extinguisher as long as the flames are in the grill. For small flare-ups, keep a spray bottle of water on hand. If the flames threaten to burn your food, take the food off the grill or move it to the side. If you're experiencing frequent flare-ups, it may be because the coals are too hot—rake some off to the side to cool the fire. High-fat foods like burgers or pork will drip fat onto the coals, which causes flare-ups, but since they are cooked in an open grill it is easy to monitor them, moving the meat and spraying the flames with water when necessary.

Another way to handle a flare-up is simply to cover the grill for a few minutes. Don't do this with quicker-cooking items, which may burn, but it's a good method for a thicker, longer-cooking ingredient.

### THE TEMPERATURE OF THE GRILL

You can always use a special grilling thermometer or oven thermometer (it needs to be able to register temperatures up to 500°F) to measure the heat of the grill, but experience will tell you when your grill is hot enough. A good rule of thumb is that the grill is at high heat when you can't hold your hand 6 inches over the grate for more than a couple of seconds. With gas grills you'll probably need to preheat the grill for about 5 to 10 minutes to warm up the metal diffuser that is under the grill grate.

For most of the recipes in this book you'll use the grill in a tempered way. Big flames are never necessary, and maximum heat is needed only for things like searing steak. For most of these dishes moderately high or indirect heat and a cover are more important than a raging fire.

### BEFORE YOU GRILL

Once your grill is hot, before you put food on the grill, get together everything you'll need (utensils, clean platters and boards, all ingredients and seasonings, oil and a brush, a water spray bottle, a drink, your recipe, etc.), because grilling is hard to walk away from.

## GAS OR CHARCOAL?

Used correctly, both charcoal and gas grills will work with all these recipes—you'll be fine using whichever you have. If you're shopping for a grill, set a budget and choose whichever seems more useful to you.

### GAS GRILLS

If you find it a real pain to build a fire and clean up the ashes, get a gas grill so that you'll use it more. Gas grilling is generally easier and more convenient, though the grills are also more expensive. With a gas grill you have greater temperature control but less of the smoky variables that make charcoal grilling both exciting and somewhat more flavorful. If you want to have your cake and eat it, too, you can use wood chips (page 8) on a gas grill to produce the smoke you need.

#### TIPS FOR BUYING A GAS GRILL

The first thing to do is to figure out what you want to spend (gas grills can be under $100 or over $5,000). Take into consideration how often you plan to use it and how large the groups are that you generally feed. You should always have enough room for all the things that you want to cook at the same time. I think gas grills with side burners are excellent for when you want to heat something in a pot or a pan—that way you can do all your cooking outside. However, you can always buy a separate side burner to use outdoors next to your grill.

I recommend gas grills with a stainless-steel body and either a stainless-steel or an iron grill grate. A convenient feature that's safer than matches is an electric starter, which is usually battery operated. If your grill doesn't have this feature, buy a lighting wand (a long lighter) at your local hardware store. Matches can be frustrating, especially in the wind.

#### BTUs

One of the big factors that differentiate gas grills is how many BTUs (British thermal units) they have. BTUs are a measure of energy, or heat given off. It used to be that gas grills could not produce the same kind of intense heat as charcoal grills, but today's grills are more powerful than those of old. BTUs for a gas grill can range from 8,000 to 100,000. You do want a grill that can produce a higher level of BTUs so that you can grill at searing temperatures when you need to. However, the size of the grill and how well it maintains heat are equally important. A compact, efficient grill is hotter than a more powerful grill if it is large and cannot retain heat. If you're buying a gas grill, you should look for one that is able to reach high temperatures, with a temperature control dial so that you can also cook at low temperatures.

### CHARCOAL GRILLS

These range from portable hibachis to 6-foot-wide kettle grills. If you like the idea of building fires, then you'll want a charcoal grill. I love the flavor that is created when fat drips onto hardwood charcoal. You can bring your grill to very high temperatures using charcoal, and you get more sear, but you are also much more liable to burn foods when cooking over charcoal. To avoid this, you have to wait until all your coals have burned down to white ash. If you cook over coals that are too hot, food is likely to scorch on the outside and remain raw in the middle. The best way to control this is to move the food around the grill, taking it away from the hottest parts (usually the center) and moving it toward the cooler areas (usually near the sides).

### FIRE STARTERS

A lot of cooks shy away from lighter fluid, and there is some debate as to whether the chemicals in it burn off or remain to taint the food. I find that some of the chemical flavor does remain. Instead, invest in a good-size chimney starter. This is a wide metal tube that you fill first with some newspaper, then with charcoal. You set the newspaper on fire at the base, and in 20 minutes the coals are ready to dump out, spread, and cook over. It's fast and clean, and the charcoal turns to white ash evenly and quickly.

The other option is an electric coil, but these don't heat as evenly, so you end up moving them around to start all the coals. And since they need to be plugged in, they aren't as convenient as a chimney starter, which doesn't require stretching an extension cord from the house to the grill!

Whichever method you use, keep in mind that when you spread the coals you'll want not only an even layer but also an empty border where the grill will stay cooler so that you can let food rest on the side of the grill as it is done or if it is cooking too fast.

## CHARCOAL

Charcoal has been used for cooking for millennia. The charcoal used for grilling is not coal from a mine but a processed wood product. The popularity of charcoal briquettes stems in large part from an innovation at the Henry Ford Auto Plant in Kingsford, Michigan. In 1924, Henry Ford opened a chemical plant to make use of the by-products of his Kingsford Model A and Model T parts manufacturing plant. The chemical plant turned scrap wood into Ford Charcoal Briquettes by grinding the wood into sawdust, forming it into briquettes using an adhesive, and then heating them until they turned to coal. When the Ford plant was closed, a group of workers bought the plant, renaming it the Kingsford Chemical Company and their major product Kingsford Charcoal Briquettes, as we know them today.

However, the adhesive and fillers in charcoal briquettes have fallen out of favor with many cooks, myself included, because they are more likely to lend foods a chemical flavor. I prefer hardwood lump charcoal, which is simply chunks of hardwood that have been burned slowly in a closed environment until they harden into coal. This kind of charcoal lends a nice wood-smoked quality to food.

In addition to using charcoal, you can add some wood chips for extra flavor. But charcoal should be the main substance of your fire, since it will burn longer and more evenly.

## WOOD CHIPS FOR SMOKE

Whether you are smoking in a gas or charcoal grill, it's advisable to use wood chips sold specifically for this purpose (small bags are available at many gourmet and hardware stores). Wood chips don't need to burn hot, so there's no need for mesquite or oak here. They should create a nice-flavored smoke. To give a slightly sweet taste to your smoked foods, use fruitwoods. Other nice choices are hickory and grapevines. Always avoid burning pine, because it gives off tar and resin flavors and can easily catch fire. Always soak wood chips before using (see pages 10–11 for more information on wood chip technique).

## EQUIPMENT AND ACCESSORIES

Whether or not you are planning to turn your grill into the center point of a deluxe outdoor kitchen, you'll need some basic tools for grilling.

### Tongs, Forks, and Spatulas

The most important utensil is a good pair of spring-loaded tongs, at least 8 inches and preferably 12 inches long. A barbecue set can be useful, since it usually comes with a good long-handled spatula, essential for turning wide, thin, or delicate foods; a long fork, which is great for quickly spearing sturdy foods; and perhaps a cleaning brush. But most barbecue sets lack spring-loaded tongs (they are likely to include the standard kind of tongs, which are a lot harder to wield).

### Thermometers

Another key gadget is an instant-read thermometer, for testing the doneness of meat or fish. You may also want a candy thermometer or special grill thermometer that you can stick through the top of the grill cover to gauge the temperature inside the covered grill.

### Brushes

In addition to a wire brush for cleaning the grill (see Cleaning the Grill, page 11), you should have one or two brushes for basting. Natural bristles will withstand heat better than nylon bristles, and like all grilling tools, the longer the handle the better. You may want to designate a brush for oil and another for nonoily sauces and glazes.

### Skewers

Large, sturdy metal skewers are great for main courses of kabobs or big pieces of meat or large vegetables. For smaller kabobs, hors d'oeuvres, or individual items, disposable wooden or bamboo skewers work well. You do need to soak them in water for an hour or overnight before you use them so they don't burn, but I get around this by keeping some in a jar of water, ready to go.

You can be creative with what you use as skewers, like rosemary branches (page 180). Since metal skewers retain heat, finger foods should be served on bamboo skewers.

To keep skewered items from spinning, stabilize them by using two skewers placed parallel to each other through the food.

### Grilling Baskets

Since the baskets are laid over the grill, there is a little more distance from the heat, and foods won't sear quite as well. But they are essential for small or loose items like shrimp or vegetables, fragile foods like fish, anything that might fall into the grate, and delicate foods that might stick to the grill or crumble, which includes burgers. They also give you more control, since you can pull the food off the heat instantly. Just keep in mind that if you use a grilling basket, the cooking time may be a few minutes longer than if you don't.

## GRILLING TECHNIQUES

### Searing

This is direct-heat cooking, on the hottest part of your grill, with the cover off. The point here is not to cook food through but to brown the outside very quickly, creating sear lines and often a crust. Once your food is seared, transfer it immediately to a cooler part of the grill to finish cooking if necessary. This technique is perfect for thinner foods and things that you want left rare in the center.

### Indirect Grilling

Indirect grilling (sometimes called *grill-roasting*) means cooking foods that are not placed over the hottest part of the grill and are usually cooked with the grill cover on. It's good for food that you want to cook slowly, like some kinds of fish, leaner cuts of meat, or a large cut like a whole pork shoulder. As a technique, indirect grilling can be used on its own or in combination with searing. Either way, the first order of business is to build a fire, then rake the coals over to one side of the grill, leaving the other side empty. Then the food is placed over the empty side of the grill, either after it's been seared on the hotter part of the grill or not, depending on the recipe.

Setting up your grill for indirect grilling is also good if you are cooking different kinds of food that require different degrees of heat, say veal chops and steaks, at the same time. The veal can be started on the hotter side of the grill, then finished on the cooler side while the steaks cook entirely on the hot side.

If you're using a gas grill, cooking over indirect heat is easy: heat the grill until it's very hot all over, then turn off the fire under one side of the grill. That's the side you'll use for indirect grilling.

### Hot Smoking

Hot smoking imparts a smoke flavor to the ingredient while it cooks. If you have a charcoal grill, you can create the smoke with either wood logs that you throw on the coals when they have burned down to white ash or wood chips. Wood chips need to be soaked in water before being used. I like to keep some wood chips in a bucket of water, ready to throw on the grill when I need them.

If you have a gas grill, you'll need a small metal pan to hold the wood chips. A disposable foil pan or pie tin is a good bet. Simply place the pan with the chips on the grill grate over direct heat, and soon the chips will start smoking. (If your gas grill has instructions for adding the wood chips, follow those.)

You will need to cover the grill when hot smoking to keep the smoke in.

### CLEANING THE GRILL

Your grill should be brushed, scraped, and kept in good condition after each use. Use a wire brush, preferably the kind with a blade on the sides of the brush that is shaped to scrape the sides of the grill bars. You can clean a cold grill, but it's easier to clean a warm one. Either way, scrape off any burned residue from the grate, then use a wet cloth (held with tongs) to wipe down the grate, followed by a lightly oiled cloth (be careful that oil is not dripping below the grate, or you risk flare-ups). I prefer to burn the grill for a while after the cooking is done, then scrape off the charred bits and do the rest of my cleaning and oiling when the grate has cooled down. When it's cool, you can soap the grate, then hose it off.

## In the Oven

Roasting at high heat involves most of the same skills that are used whenever you cook in your oven. High heat just speeds things up and creates a wonderfully browned, caramelized exterior. The only equipment you really need (in addition to an oven) is a roasting pan and rack, long reliable oven mitts, and an instant-read thermometer.

### EQUIPMENT AND ACCESSORIES

#### Roasting Pans

You can roast in any pan that will withstand 500°F temperatures. This includes metal pans, Pyrex glass pans, and some terra-cotta and ceramic dishes. If the pan is new, read the label to be sure that the handles are suitable for use at high heat. In general, avoid putting pans with plastic or rubber-coated handles in an oven above 350°F. Also, avoid pouring liquids into a nonmetal pan that is at very high temperatures, since this can shatter even a heatproof pan. It's unlikely, but I've seen it happen.

For extended broiling, especially when the pan is meant to be placed directly under the heat source, metal pans are your best bet. I recommend thick, rimmed baking sheets or jelly-roll pans.

Ceramic, terra-cotta, or enameled cast-iron gratin dishes are also handy, especially when you want to take the food to the table in its cooking vessel. They will withstand the broiler but aren't as large or versatile as rimmed baking sheets. It's good to have a few metal pans and gratin dishes in varying sizes on hand.

The basic tool for roasting is a large metal pan (look for stainless steel on the outside with a copper or aluminum core) that is sturdy enough to hold up even a heavy roast, with good upright handles. Flimsy metal pans may warp at high heat, which makes a loud cracking sound and causes liquids to collect at one side of the pan. Often pans "unwarp" when they cool, but heavier pans cook more evenly, let foods lie flat, and tend to be easier to clean. Choose a roasting pan that can hold a large roast but that doesn't have such high sides that they keep the hot air from circling freely around the food and browning it. And make sure your pan isn't so heavy that you can't lift it out of the oven once it is at 450°F and holding a sizzling hot turkey.

### Oven Mitts

When reaching into the oven to retrieve a hot pan, most home cooks use small square pot holders, and most chefs use folded-up kitchen towels. And just about all of us have gotten a nice stripe of burn from banging a forearm into the top of the oven, the upper oven rack, or the lip of a pan. The best way to avoid burns is to wear long oven mitts that really cover the bottom two thirds of your forearm. They are clumsy for other tasks, but for cooking with high heat, the bigger the mitt the better.

### Pizza Stones and Tiles

Many bread bakers will tell you that a preheated clay pizza stone is the best way to produce crackly browned crusts. Ceramic absorbs moisture, creating a really dry oven and producing really crisp breads. I find that lining the oven floor or lowest shelf with unglazed ceramic quarry tiles, a pizza stone, or ceramic oven liners also caramelizes the juices at the bottom of the roasting pan and generally keeps the oven at a more constant high heat. The stone needs an extra 20 minutes or so to preheat, so turn the oven on even earlier than you normally do. For pizzas and flatbreads, you can put the dough right on the stone, set on the lowest oven rack, or slide it onto the stone with parchment paper underneath (just trim the parchment so that only a thin border is exposed, or it will burn).

## ROASTING TECHNIQUES

### Preheating and Oven Thermometers

An important part of roasting at high heat is actually getting your oven to produce that heat. To do this, preheat for at least 20 minutes and use a reliable oven thermometer, since oven temperature often deviates by as much as 25 degrees from the temperature you have selected on the dial.

### The Blast Method

Occasionally I call for a method of roasting in which a blast of high heat is used initially, to brown the outside of the meat and create a crisp texture and rich, complex, savory flavors. Then I turn the oven down for gentler roasting, which helps the meat remain moist and tender. I call for this method for leaner or larger cuts of meat. I love the contrast of a darkly browned, caramelized exterior and meltingly tender, medium-rare meat.

### Broiling

If you're using the broiler in your oven, give it a few minutes to really heat up. You can control the process by keeping the food closer to or farther from the flames, although separate drawer-style broilers give you less flexibility in this regard and are best suited to quickly browning thinner foods. The broilers of electric ovens tend to have hot and cold spaces, so you may need to move the pan a few times while broiling to ensure even cooking.

CHARRED TUNA CARPACCIO
WITH BASIL OIL

ROASTED CLAMS WITH GARLIC,
LEMON, & RED PEPPER

ROASTED OYSTERS WITH
SHALLOTS & HERBS

CRISPY SQUID WITH ARUGULA &
GARLIC CROUTONS

SHRIMP WITH TOMATO-
HORSERADISH SALSA

MUSTARD SHRIMP WITH CAPERS

ARUGULA SALAD WITH
CRISP FINGERLING POTATO CHIPS

SPICY POTATO SALAD WITH SWEET
& HOT PEPPERS

SHIITAKE MUSHROOM & GINGERED
CRABMEAT SALAD

# 2 *Appetizers & Salads*

CHARRED FILET MIGNON TARTARE

GRILLED OR ROASTED ASPARAGUS
WITH SCALLIONS & FRIED EGGS

ENDIVE STUFFED WITH APPLES,
ROQUEFORT, & WALNUTS

ROASTED FENNEL & ORANGE SALAD
WITH ONION-BACON VINAIGRETTE

WATERCRESS SALAD WITH GRILLED
OR ROASTED RED ONIONS
& AGED CHEDDAR

MIXED HERB SALAD WITH ROASTED
TOMATO VINAIGRETTE

SWEET TOMATO &
BOCCONCINI SALAD
WITH SCALLIONS

BUTTER LETTUCE SALAD WITH
RED PEPPER VINAIGRETTE

# Charred Tuna Carpaccio with Basil Oil

Carpaccio is a classic Italian appetizer of thinly sliced raw beef, often served with arugula salad and Parmesan cheese. In my version I substitute sushi-quality tuna for the beef and give the outer edges a slight char on the grill. This lends a rich, smoky flavor to the fish without cooking it through. Bitter arugula and mushrooms round out the flavors, making this dish almost a salad. It's terrific as an appetizer or a light main course.

SERVES 6 AS AN APPETIZER, 2 TO 3 AS A MAIN COURSE

1/2 cup packed fresh basil leaves, plus additional sprigs for garnish

7 tablespoons plus 1 teaspoon extra virgin olive oil

Coarse sea salt or kosher salt, plus additional to taste

Freshly ground black pepper

10 ounces "grade A" sushi-quality tuna loin

1/4 cup dry white wine

2 cups coarsely chopped arugula

4 large white mushroom caps, thinly sliced

1 teaspoon freshly squeezed lemon juice

Shaved Parmesan cheese for garnish (see sidebar, page 23)

Chop enough of the basil to yield 1 tablespoon. Combine it in a shallow bowl or rimmed plate with 1 teaspoon of the olive oil and salt and pepper to taste. Add the tuna and turn until well coated. Cover with plastic wrap and refrigerate for 1 hour.

Lightly oil the grill grate and light the grill.

To make the basil oil, in the bowl of a blender or food processor combine the remaining basil leaves with 4 tablespoons of the remaining olive oil, the wine, 1 teaspoon salt, and pepper. Blend until smooth.

Grill the tuna for 1 to 2 minutes per side, charring the outside while keeping the center cold and red. Transfer to a board and let cool, then wrap the tuna in plastic and refrigerate for 1 hour or freeze for 20 minutes. This allows the fish to firm up enough to be sliced very thinly.

Transfer the tuna to a board and slice as thinly as possible.

In a bowl, toss the arugula with 2 tablespoons of the remaining olive oil. In another bowl, toss the mushrooms with the remaining tablespoon of olive oil, the lemon juice, and salt and pepper to taste. Mound some arugula in the center of each plate and surround it with slices of tuna. Scatter the mushrooms over all, drizzle with some of the basil oil, and garnish with shaved Parmesan and basil sprigs.

*Uses for Extra Basil Oil* Basil oil is a great addition to a salad dressing—just whisk in champagne vinegar or lemon juice and more olive oil and salt and pepper to taste. Or add some oil to the pan while scrambling eggs. As is, the oil makes a great sauce for pasta, fish (especially salmon), or chicken. It will keep for up to a week in the refrigerator.

# Roasted Clams with Garlic, Lemon, & Red Pepper

I think this dish picks up where old-fashioned stuffed clam dishes like Clams Oregano leave off. The mixture of bread crumbs, garlic, red pepper, and lemon slices is roasted around the clams instead of stuffed in them. It absorbs the juices from the clams but gets nice and crisp in the oven—unlike the soggy fillings in most stuffed clams. You still get clams and bread crumbs in each bite, but the flavors are much brighter, and the textures are perfect. This is a great way to serve clams to a crowd—you are limited only by how many clams will fit in your roasting pan.

SERVES 4 TO 6

1 $^1$/2 cups fresh bread crumbs (see sidebar)

$^3$/4 cup thinly sliced red bell pepper (about $^1$/2 large pepper)

6 garlic cloves, thinly sliced

1 teaspoon freshly ground black pepper

Coarse sea salt or kosher salt

1 lemon, halved lengthwise and thinly sliced, ends discarded

$^1$/3 cup extra virgin olive oil

24 live topneck or small cherrystone clams, scrubbed well in cold water

3 tablespoons chopped fresh mint for garnish

Preheat the oven to 500°F.

In a large bowl, toss together the bread crumbs, red pepper slices, garlic, black pepper, and salt to taste. Gently squeeze the lemon slices over the bowl, then add them and toss well. Drizzle the olive oil over all and toss to combine.

Lay the clams on a baking pan in a single layer, with their lips facing up. Sprinkle the bread crumb mixture over and around them. Roast until the clams open, about 10 to 12 minutes. Serve garnished with mint.

*Fresh Bread Crumbs* Fresh bread crumbs are moister and will absorb more liquid than the dried kind, making them perfect for soaking up the flavorful clam juice in this recipe. To make them, simply put cubes of fresh, sturdy bread (like a baguette, Italian loaf, or country-style loaf) in the food processor and process until it turns to crumbs.

*Clam Varieties* Several varieties of hard-shell clam are commonly used in cooking. They range in thickness (measured at their hinge) from over 3 inches to under 1 inch. In general, the smaller the clam the sweeter, and more expensive, it is. Quahogs (also called round or chowder clams) are the largest, and are often used for chowder or stuffed clam dishes, followed in size by cherrystone clams, topnecks, middlenecks, and littlenecks.

# Roasted Oysters with Shallots & Herbs

Roasting oysters on the half shell is a little different from cooking other things at high heat. The purpose isn't so much to char and brown them as it is to heat them through—just enough for them to release all their flavorful juices and firm up slightly. These oysters are topped with little spoonfuls of a shallot–white wine–butter sauce, which mixes with the oyster juices and reduces in the oven while the shallots get crisp. Six oysters make an impressive appetizer, or you can pass the oysters still in their baking dish (wear oven mitts) as an hors d'oeuvre.

To keep the oysters balanced while they roast, I line the baking dish with a layer of rock salt dotted with peppercorns. The salt and pepper makes a great presentation. You can buy rock salt at a hardware store. It's inexpensive, and one bag will last you forever!

SERVES 4

**6 tablespoons unsalted butter**

**1 cup thinly sliced shallots**

**$^1/_4$ cup dry white wine or dry vermouth**

**Coarse sea salt or kosher salt and freshly ground black pepper**

**$^1/_4$ cup chicken or vegetable broth (reduced-sodium if canned) or water**

**1 tablespoon snipped fresh chives**

**1 tablespoon chopped fresh flat-leaf parsley**

**Rock salt to roast the oysters on**

**3 tablespoons black peppercorns**

**24 oysters (see sidebar)**

**Lemon wedges for serving**

Preheat the oven to 500°F.

In a heavy saucepan over medium heat, melt 4 tablespoons of the butter. Reduce the heat to low and add the shallots and wine. Cover and cook until most of the liquid is absorbed, about 4 to 5 minutes. Season with salt and pepper and add the chicken broth and the remaining 2 tablespoons of butter. Bring to a simmer, then remove from the heat and stir in the herbs.

Cover the bottom of an ovenproof baking dish large enough to hold all the oysters with rock salt. Sprinkle the peppercorns evenly over the salt. Open the oysters, discarding the top shell. Loosen the oysters from the bottom shell, being careful not to spill their juices, and lay them in the baking dish. Stir the shallot mixture and spoon some over each oyster. Roast until the edges of the oysters just begin to curl, about 5 to 8 minutes. Serve on the baking dish with lemon wedges.

*Buying and Shucking Oysters* For this recipe you need to buy live oysters with unblemished shells. When opened, the meat should be pale (its color will vary, but avoid any that are pink, as this indicates they may be off), plump, and glossy and should smell like fresh seawater. If they smell off, discard them.

When you get the oysters home, scrub their shells in cold water with a brush. Store them flat on a baking sheet in the refrigerator, covered with a slightly damp paper towel, and use them within 2 days.

You can have your fishmonger shuck the oysters for you if you plan to use them immediately; just ask him to reserve the juice so you can take it home. Before roasting, strain the oyster juice and add a teaspoon of the juice to each oyster. To shuck live oysters yourself, insert a thin-bladed knife (or an oyster knife) into the joint or "foot" of the shell and twist the blade to loosen the shell. Being careful not to spill the liquid, slide the knife along the top of the shell (not deeply enough to cut the oyster). Discard the upper shell and cut through the muscle holding the oyster to the bottom shell.

# Crispy Squid with Arugula & Garlic Croutons

In this colorful, savory dish, squid are roasted or grilled with garlic and spicy red pepper flakes and served with a fresh summery salad of arugula and crunchy garlic croutons. Make sure not to over-cook the squid; they're done when they start to curl, the edges getting a little brown while the center stays tender and white. Buy small baby squid and have the fishmonger clean them for you.

If you don't have stale bread, you can fake it by putting slices in a low oven (about 200°F) and letting them dry out for an hour or so. If you want to, you can make the croutons in advance. They will keep in an airtight container for several days and can be recrisped in the oven if necessary.

SERVES 4 TO 6

**1 pound cleaned baby squid, tentacles separated and bodies halved lengthwise**

**$^1$/3 cup plus 3 tablespoons extra virgin olive oil**

**3 teaspoons minced garlic**

**Pinch of hot red pepper flakes**

**Coarse sea salt or kosher salt and freshly ground black pepper**

**$^1$/4 pound stale country or sourdough bread, cut into $^3$/4-inch cubes (about 4 cups)**

**2 tablespoons balsamic vinegar or to taste**

**2 bunches arugula (about 7 ounces), thick stems removed**

**Shaved Parmesan cheese for garnish (see sidebar)**

Light the grill or preheat the oven to 500°F.

In a large bowl, toss the squid with 2 tablespoons of the olive oil, 2 teaspoons of the garlic, and the red pepper flakes. Season with a generous pinch of salt and black pepper.

*On the Grill*    Lay the squid on the grill and cook, turning once, until curled and opaque (the ends will be browned), about 5 minutes.

*In the Oven*    Spread the squid out on a rimmed baking sheet and roast until curled and opaque (the ends will be browned), about 5 minutes.

To make the croutons, place 1 tablespoon of the remaining oil in a large pan over medium-high heat. When the oil shimmers, toss in the bread cubes and cook, stirring, until they are browned and toasted, about 5 minutes. Add the remaining teaspoon of minced garlic, season with salt and black pepper, and cook, stirring, for another 30 seconds. Transfer to a board or plate to cool.

To make the vinaigrette, in a small bowl season the balsamic vinegar with salt and black pepper. Whisking constantly, drizzle in the remaining $1/3$ cup of oil. Place the arugula in a large salad bowl, dress it with enough vinaigrette to coat the leaves, and toss well. To serve, divide the arugula salad among 4 plates and top with the squid. Garnish with the croutons and shaved Parmesan. Drizzle with the remaining vinaigrette.

---

*Shaved Parmesan* Fragile shavings of Parmesan cheese make a more dramatic garnish than the grated stuff and are more substantial to eat. Making them is easy. Use a vegetable peeler to make shavings from a wedge or block of cheese. The best Parmesan is the real thing, Parmigiano-Reggiano, with its dotted imprint on the rind, but grana or a good-quality domestic will do in a pinch. Other cheeses will also work, as long as they are hard and somewhat dry, like Romano or Asiago.

---

# Shrimp with Tomato-Horseradish Salsa

This is my version of shrimp cocktail. Instead of boiled shrimp and a thick, slightly sweet sauce, I grill or broil the shrimp and serve them with a robust tomato-horseradish salsa. It has all the spicy, intense flavors of a cocktail sauce but without the sugary stickiness of ketchup. Bright and fresh tasting, it's ideal to serve as a summer appetizer or as part of a buffet. And leftover salsa is excellent with chips!

SERVES 4

For the Salsa
- 2 large ripe tomatoes, finely chopped
- $1/4$ cup minced red onion
- 3 scallions, white and light green parts only, thinly sliced
- 3 tablespoons prepared horseradish
- 2 tablespoons minced fresh cilantro
- 2 teaspoons extra virgin olive oil
- $1/2$ jalapeño pepper or more to taste, seeded and minced
- Freshly squeezed lemon juice to taste
- Dash Tabasco sauce or more to taste
- Coarse sea salt or kosher salt and freshly ground black pepper

For the Shrimp
- 1 pound extra-large shrimp (about 20), peeled and deveined, tails left on
- 1 tablespoon prepared horseradish
- 2 teaspoons extra virgin olive oil
- Coarse sea salt or kosher salt and freshly ground black pepper
- Lemon wedges and lettuce leaves for serving

Light the grill or preheat the broiler.

Combine all the salsa ingredients in a bowl and set aside.

In a large bowl, toss the shrimp with the horseradish, olive oil, and salt and pepper to taste.

*On the Grill*   Place the shrimp in a grilling basket or on soaked skewers and grill, turning once, until they are opaque and browned on the edges, about 3 to 5 minutes.

*In the Oven*   Spread the shrimp on a baking sheet and place directly under the heat source. Broil, turning once, until the shrimp are opaque and browned on the edges, about 3 to 4 minutes.

To serve, spoon some salsa in a mound in the center of each plate and top with shrimp. Arrange lemon wedges around the shrimp. Or use the salsa as a dip. Make a bed of lettuce leaves on a platter and place the shrimp on the lettuce. Serve the salsa alongside in a bowl, garnished with lemon wedges. Serve hot or at room temperature.

# Mustard Shrimp with Capers

I came up with this dish when we were testing recipes one day and we had some shrimp left over from another dish. I poked around in the fridge and put together this flavorful combination of mustard, basil, jalapeño, and chopped capers that turned out to be a huge hit. This is a great dish to make at the last minute. Since you can coat the shrimp with the mustard mixture just before cooking, you don't need to plan much in advance. I like to serve it on skewers as an appetizer or even as a passed hors d'oeuvre for a cocktail party (then use just one shrimp per skewer or serve with toothpicks). It will also work as a main course to feed 2 (or double the quantities).

If you plan to use wooden or bamboo skewers, soak them for an hour before grilling.

SERVES 4 AS AN APPETIZER OR 2 AS A MAIN COURSE

**2 tablespoons Dijon mustard**

**2 tablespoons extra virgin olive oil**

**2 tablespoons chopped drained capers**

**2 tablespoons chopped fresh basil, plus additional sprigs for garnish**

**1 jalapeño pepper, seeded and chopped**

**16 jumbo shrimp, peeled and deveined, tails left on**

**Coarse sea salt or kosher salt and freshly ground black pepper**

In a large bowl, whisk together the mustard, olive oil, capers, basil, and jalapeño. Add the shrimp and a pinch of salt and pepper and toss to coat. If you have time, refrigerate for 1 to 4 hours, or use immediately.

Light the grill or preheat the broiler.

*On the Grill*  Thread the shrimp onto soaked skewers and grill until they turn opaque and the edges start to brown, about 2 to 4 minutes per side.

*In the Oven*  Lay the shrimp on a rimmed baking sheet and place directly under the heat source. Broil until they turn opaque and the edges start to brown, about 2 to 4 minutes per side.

Serve the shrimp garnished with the basil sprigs.

# Arugula Salad with Crisp Fingerling Potato Chips

Like croutons, these thin, crisp potato chips add a welcome crunch to salads. Fingerlings have a rich, earthy sweetness that sets off the bitter, fresh green flavor of arugula, and the mustard vinaigrette is a great contrast to the potatoes.

SERVES 6

**I pound fingerling potatoes, scrubbed and thinly sliced**
**$1/4$ cup extra virgin olive oil**
**Coarse sea salt or kosher salt and freshly ground black pepper**
**$2^1/2$ teaspoons white wine vinegar**
**I small shallot, minced**
**2 bunches arugula (about 7 ounces), thick stems removed**
**I ounce Parmesan cheese, shaved (see sidebar, page 23)**

Preheat the oven to 500°F or preheat the grill. In a large bowl, toss the potatoes with 2 tablespoons of the olive oil and salt and pepper to taste.

*In the Oven*  Spread the potatoes in one layer on a nonstick baking sheet (or one lined with a nonstick liner or parchment paper). Roast until browned on one side, about 9 minutes, then turn and roast until browned on the other side, about 5 minutes more.

*On the Grill*  Depending on the size of your grill basket, you will probably have to work in batches. Place as many of the potato slices as will fit in one layer in a grill basket. Grill, turning once, until browned on both sides, about 8 minutes. Repeat as necessary with the remaining potatoes.

In a small bowl, whisk together the remaining 2 tablespoons olive oil, vinegar, shallot, and salt and pepper to taste. Reserve about 18 potato slices for garnish. Place the rest of the potatoes in a large bowl, top with the arugula, and drizzle with the vinaigrette. Toss well and serve, garnishing each plate with the reserved potato slices and shaved Parmesan.

# Spicy Potato Salad
## with Sweet & Hot Peppers

Mayo-free and perfect on picnics, this couldn't be further from bland, starchy potato salads. Grilled potatoes are smoky and assertive enough to match the intensity of the grilled chiles and sweet bell peppers they're tossed with, not to mention the addition of capers, anchovies, and hard-cooked eggs. All this flavor packs a spicy Mediterranean punch, taking potatoes well beyond the realm of comfort food. If you're not an anchovy person, just leave them out.

SERVES 4 TO 6

$1^{3}/4$ pounds small red potatoes, quartered

7 tablespoons extra virgin olive oil, plus additional for brushing the peppers

Coarse sea salt or kosher salt and freshly ground black pepper

1 red bell pepper

1 green bell pepper

1 hot chile such as serrano, Thai bird, or Scotch bonnet

$1^{1}/2$ tablespoons red wine vinegar

2 scallions, finely chopped

2 hard-cooked eggs, chopped, for garnish

$1/4$ cup chopped black Moroccan oil-cured pitted olives for garnish

2 anchovies, chopped, for garnish (optional)

2 tablespoons chopped fresh flat-leaf parsley for garnish

Lettuce leaves for serving

Preheat the broiler or light the grill. In a large bowl, toss the potatoes with 2 tablespoons of the olive oil and season generously with salt and pepper.

*In the Oven*  Halve the bell peppers and chile lengthwise. Seed and stem them, then spread them, skin side up, on a baking sheet. Lightly brush the pepper skins with olive oil. Broil the peppers as close to the heat source as possible, until well charred, about 5 minutes. Immediately transfer the peppers to a large bowl and cover with a plate. Let steam for 5 minutes. Turn the broiler off and preheat the oven to 500°F.

Spread the potatoes in a single layer on a rimmed baking sheet and roast, turning every 5 minutes, until crisp on the outside and cooked through, about 20 minutes.

*On the Grill*  Lightly brush the whole bell and hot peppers with oil and grill them, turning, until charred on all sides, about 5 minutes for the chile and up to 15 minutes for the bell peppers. Immediately transfer the peppers to a large bowl and cover with a plate. Let steam for 5 minutes.

Spread the potatoes on the grill (or use a grilling basket) and cook them with the grill cover on, turning occasionally, until crisp on the outside and cooked through, about 15 minutes.

Peel the peppers using a spoon or your fingers. (Be sure to wear gloves while working with the chile.) Seed and stem the peppers if necessary and chop them into $1/2$-inch pieces.

In a small bowl, whisk together the vinegar, scallions, and salt and pepper to taste. Whisking constantly, drizzle in the remaining 5 tablespoons olive oil. In a large bowl, toss the warm potatoes with the peppers and enough of the dressing to coat the vegetables. Gently mix in the hard-cooked eggs, olives, and anchovies, if using. Taste and add more dressing and/or salt and pepper if desired. Garnish with parsley and serve warm or at room temperature on lettuce leaves.

# Shiitake Mushroom & Gingered Crabmeat Salad

Crab salad gets an Asian bent from grated ginger and grilled shiitake caps. Serve the crab on a bed of lettuce as a salad as I do here, or turn it into a fantastic hors d'oeuvre by piling it on endive leaves or cucumber slices. I think of this as a special-occasion recipe, since fresh lump crabmeat is expensive—but worth it. Get the best-quality crabmeat you can (choose quality over quantity) and go through it to make sure there are no bits of shell. This salad is at its best when made 30 minutes before serving. Let it rest at room temperature for the flavors to meld. Or make it a few hours ahead, refrigerate, then let it come to room temperature before serving.

SERVES 6

3/4 pound shiitake mushrooms, stems discarded

1/4 cup plus 2 tablespoons extra virgin olive oil

2 tablespoons plus I teaspoon minced fresh ginger

2 tablespoons plus I teaspoon minced shallots

Coarse sea salt or kosher salt and freshly ground black pepper

3 tablespoons freshly squeezed lemon juice

I pound fresh lump crabmeat, carefully picked over for small pieces of shell

2 teaspoons freshly grated lemon zest

I cup diced tomato

3 cups baby salad greens

1/2 cup sliced red radishes for garnish

Light the grill or preheat the oven to 500°F. In a bowl, toss the shiitake mushrooms with 2 tablespoons of the olive oil, 2 tablespoons of the ginger, 2 tablespoons of the shallots, and salt and pepper to taste.

*On the Grill*  Place the seasoned mushrooms in a grilling basket and grill for about 5 minutes on each side, until charred around the edges.

*In the Oven*  Spread the mushrooms in one layer on a baking sheet. Roast, tossing once, until browned, about 15 minutes.

Let the mushrooms cool slightly, then slice them.

In a small bowl, whisk 2 tablespoons of the lemon juice with $\frac{1}{2}$ teaspoon salt and pepper to taste. Whisking constantly, drizzle in the remaining $\frac{1}{4}$ cup olive oil.

Gently mix the crabmeat with the sliced mushrooms, the remaining ginger and shallots, the lemon zest, 2 tablespoons of the vinaigrette, the remaining tablespoon of lemon juice, and salt and pepper to taste.

Toss the diced tomato with 1 tablespoon of the remaining vinaigrette.

Toss the baby greens with the remaining vinaigrette. Divide among 6 plates and mound the crab salad in the center of the greens. Garnish with the radish slices and diced tomato.

# Charred Filet Mignon Tartare

This is a twist on the classic tartare of chopped raw beef. Here I add another level of flavor by charring the outside of the steak to create a great smokiness, while the inside remains raw. It's worth the time to chop the steak by hand with a really sharp knife or in a meat grinder (either the old-fashioned kind or a meat-grinding attachment on a mixer) to give it a really nice texture—a food processor will make it pasty. The meat is seasoned with the intense flavors of red onion, mustard, and capers and you can serve more of these ingredients as garnishes on the side. I also garnish the meat with chopped hard-cooked eggs, although if you want to be traditional you can mound the tartare, make an indentation on the top, and fill it with a very fresh, preferably organic egg yolk. Serve this as an appetizer, a buffet item, or a canapé topping for toast points.

SERVES 4 TO 6

**Two $1/2$-pound filets mignons, trimmed**

**Coarse sea salt or kosher salt and freshly ground black pepper**

**1 tablespoon extra virgin olive oil, plus additional for garnish**

**2 tablespoons Dijon mustard**

**1 tablespoon chopped drained capers, plus additional whole capers for garnish**

**2 minced anchovy fillets**

**1 tablespoon minced red onion, plus additional chopped red onion for garnish**

**2 teaspoons Worcestershire sauce**

**$1/2$ teaspoon freshly squeezed lemon juice**

**6 dashes Tabasco sauce or to taste**

**2 cups baby salad greens**

**1 hard-cooked egg, peeled and chopped, for garnish**

**Cracked black peppercorns for garnish**

Light the grill or preheat the broiler. Generously season the filets mignons with salt and pepper and drizzle them with olive oil.

*On the Grill*  Grill the meat, covered, until charred on all sides, about 2 minutes for the top and bottom plus another minute or two for the sides.

*In the Oven*  Place the filets on a baking sheet and position it directly under the heat source.

Broil the meat until it is charred on all sides, about 2 minutes for the top and bottom plus another minute or two for the sides.

Let the filets cool thoroughly. Wrap them in plastic wrap and refrigerate until cold, at least 2 hours.

Chop the meat finely or grind in a meat grinder and place in a large bowl. Season the meat with generous grindings of black pepper. Add the mustard, chopped capers, anchovy, minced red onion, Worcestershire sauce, lemon juice, and Tabasco. Taste and add more salt if desired.

Place the baby greens on a platter and mound the tartare over the greens. Garnish with the whole capers, chopped red onion, hard-cooked egg, and cracked peppercorns. Drizzle with a little olive oil.

# Grilled or Roasted Asparagus with Scallions & Fried Eggs

This is the perfect appetizer or luncheon entree to serve in the spring, when wild asparagus are in season. Light yet flavorful, the nuttiness of roasted or grilled asparagus is enhanced by the combination of fried eggs, soft, melting cheese, and crisp bread crumbs. As you break the yolk with your fork, it creates a creamy sauce that reminds me of hollandaise but is much simpler and not nearly as decadent. If you have some truffle oil in your pantry, use just a few drops here. It really brings another level of flavor to the dish—just be sure not to overdo it so the more subtle flavors aren't lost.

SERVES 4

1 bunch jumbo asparagus (about 1 pound), bottoms trimmed, lower stalks peeled

2 tablespoons extra virgin olive oil

1/2 teaspoon coarse sea salt or kosher salt, plus additional to taste

Freshly ground black pepper

1/3 cup dried unseasoned bread crumbs

2 tablespoons unsalted butter

2 scallions, minced

1/4 cup grated Bel Paese or white Cheddar cheese (about 1 ounce)

4 eggs

Truffle oil for garnish (optional)

Preheat the oven to 500°F or light the grill. Toss the asparagus with the olive oil, 1/2 teaspoon salt, and pepper to taste.

*In the Oven*  Spread the asparagus in a roasting pan and roast, shaking the pan halfway through, until the ends are crisp and the stalks are tender, about 10 to 12 minutes.

*On the Grill*  Place the asparagus on the grill (or use a wide grill basket) and grill, turning, until they are browned and tender, about 10 to 12 minutes.

Transfer the asparagus to an ovenproof gratin dish and set aside. In a large skillet over medium-high heat, toast the bread crumbs, stirring so they brown evenly, until golden, about 3 minutes. Transfer to a plate to cool. Place 1 tablespoon of the butter in the pan, let it melt, then add the bread crumbs, scallions, and salt and pepper to taste and toss to coat. Transfer to a bowl and stir in the cheese.

Preheat the broiler. Wipe the skillet out with a paper towel. Add the remaining tablespoon of butter to the pan and raise the heat to high. Break the eggs into the pan, season with salt and pepper, and fry until the whites are just firm but the yolks are still very soft. Gently slide the eggs onto the asparagus. Sprinkle the bread crumb mixture over the eggs and place the dish under the broiler until the topping is browned and crisp, about 1 minute. Divide the eggs and asparagus among 4 plates and garnish with a few drops of truffle oil if desired.

# Endive Stuffed with Apples, Roquefort, & Walnuts

Endive, blue cheese, and nuts are a classic, winning combination of flavors and textures. I combine raw endive with halved heads of endive that have been stuffed with blue cheese and walnuts and roasted or grilled. The soft cooked endive is offset by the crunch of raw endive, tart red apple, and nuts, and the salty richness of Roquefort brings it all together. This makes a substantial winter salad or accompaniment to simple grilled meats or roast chicken. You can also serve it after the meal, as a combined salad and fruit and cheese course.

SERVES 4

**Coarse sea salt or kosher salt**

**5 heads Belgian endive, trimmed**

**$1/3$ cup crumbled Roquefort (about 1$1/4$ ounces), plus additional for garnish**

**2 tablespoons chopped toasted walnuts, plus additional for garnish**

**6 tablespoons extra virgin olive oil**

**1 tart red apple, such as Cortland**

**2 tablespoons freshly squeezed lemon juice**

**$1/2$ tablespoon Dijon mustard**

**2 tablespoons minced fresh chives**

**Freshly ground black pepper**

**$1/4$ cup chopped fresh cilantro**

Preheat the oven to 500°F or light the grill. Bring a large pot of salted water to a boil. Place 4 of the endives in the boiling water and blanch for 2 minutes. Drain and cool under cold running water. Halve the blanched endives lengthwise and core them.

In a small bowl, combine the Roquefort with the toasted walnuts and mix well. Stuff the endive halves with this mixture, then drizzle them with 2 tablespoons of the olive oil.

*In the Oven*  Place the stuffed endives on a baking sheet, stuffed sides up, and roast until the cheese is bubbling and brown, about 8 to 10 minutes.

*On the Grill*  Place the stuffed endives in a grilling basket, stuffed sides up, and grill, covered, until the cheese is melted and the endives have begun to brown, about 5 to 10 minutes.

Trim the remaining endive, halve it lengthwise, and slice it into $1/4$-inch sticks. Quarter and core the apple (unpeeled) and slice it lengthwise $1/4$ inch thick, then cut the slices into $1/4$-inch sticks.

In a small bowl, whisk together the lemon juice, mustard, chives, and salt and pepper to taste. Drizzle in the remaining 4 tablespoons olive oil, whisking well to combine. Place the sliced apple and endive in a bowl and add the cilantro. Toss with the vinaigrette and divide among 4 plates. Place two grilled endive halves on top of the salad and garnish with additional crumbled Roquefort and walnuts.

# Roasted Fennel & Orange Salad with Onion-Bacon Vinaigrette

I say you can never have enough bacon. Here bacon is combined with onion in a savory vinaigrette that balances the sweetness of caramelized fennel and fresh orange wedges. The fennel is roasted or grilled in wedges so that the outside browns while the inside remains crunchy, then it is sliced and tossed with bright, juicy chunks of orange and colorful bell peppers and garnished with fennel fronds. Substantial and beautiful, this is a terrific salad course. It can also be served as a side with meat, chicken, fish, or lobster dishes, or it could be turned into a main-course seafood salad, topped with lobster or shrimp. It's a good alternative to slaw at a picnic since it gets even better when made in advance (just omit the lettuce leaves).

SERVES 8 TO 10

4 large fennel bulbs, trimmed and quartered, fronds chopped and reserved

1/4 cup extra virgin olive oil, plus additional for brushing the fennel

3 navel oranges

1 small red bell pepper, very thinly sliced

1 small green bell pepper, very thinly sliced

1/4 pound sliced bacon, cut into 1/2-inch pieces

1 medium red onion, thinly sliced

1/2 cup white wine vinegar

1 teaspoon freshly squeezed lime juice

Coarse sea salt or kosher salt and freshly ground black pepper

Lettuce leaves for serving

Preheat the oven to 500°F or light the grill. Brush the fennel all over with olive oil.

*In the Oven*   Place the fennel on a baking sheet and roast in the lower third of your oven for 18 to 20 minutes, turning to brown on all sides.

*On the Grill*   Place the fennel in a grilling basket or directly on the grill and cook until browned on all sides, 15 to 25 minutes, turning once or twice.

Cut the top and bottom off each orange and stand it up on a cutting board on one of the flat sides. Using a small knife, cut away the peel and white pith, following the natural curve of the fruit, so that the flesh is completely exposed. Working over a bowl to catch the juices, cut the segments of fruit away from the membranes that connect them. The segments will also fall into the bowl.

When the fennel is cool enough to handle, core and thinly slice it. In a salad bowl, combine the fennel, peppers, and oranges with their collected juices.

Warm the $1/4$ cup of olive oil in a large skillet over medium-high heat. Add the bacon and onion and cook, stirring, until browned, about 5 minutes. Toss the fennel salad with the vinegar and lime juice. Pour the onion-bacon mixture over the salad, including the oil and fat. Toss well, season with salt and pepper, and serve on lettuce leaves, garnished with about 2 tablespoons of the fennel fronds.

# Watercress Salad with Grilled or Roasted Red Onions & Aged Cheddar

The peppery freshness of watercress is one of the best accompaniments to the charred flavors that high heat imparts. That's why it's the standard garnish for meats in steak houses around the country. But in this salad I skip the meat altogether and substitute grilled or roasted tomatoes and onions. Brief exposure to intense heat brings out the sweetness of the onions and concentrates the sugar and acidity in the tomatoes, making them the perfect foil for the watercress and the pronounced flavor of aged Cheddar. Serve this as a salad course or pair it with grilled meats as a brightly flavored side dish.

SERVES 6

1 red onion, sliced $^1/_2$ inch thick

7 tablespoons extra virgin olive oil

Coarse sea salt or kosher salt and freshly ground black pepper

1 pint cherry, grape, or pear tomatoes

3 tablespoons freshly squeezed lemon juice

2 teaspoons Dijon mustard

$^3/_4$ teaspoon prepared horseradish

2 large bunches watercress, thick stems removed

$^1/_4$ cup grated aged Cheddar cheese (about 1 ounce)

Preheat the oven to 500°F or light the grill. Brush the onion slices with $^1/_2$ tablespoon of the oil and season with salt and pepper to taste, using tongs to turn them without breaking apart the rings. Place the tomatoes in a bowl and toss them with another $^1/_2$ tablespoon of the oil, then season with salt and pepper.

*In the Oven*   Lay the onion slices in a single layer on a rimmed baking sheet. Spread the tomatoes in a single layer on another rimmed baking sheet. Roast the onions for 12 to 15 minutes, turning once, until they are golden brown around the edges. Roast the tomatoes until lightly charred, about 8 to 10 minutes, tossing every few minutes.

*On the Grill*   Place the onion slices on the grill or in a grilling basket without breaking them apart and grill until sear lines appear, about 5 minutes per side (turn them carefully so they don't fall apart). Transfer the onions to a plate to cool. Place the tomatoes in a grill basket and grill, shaking occasionally to turn the tomatoes, until softened and charred yet not collapsed, about 5 minutes.

In a small bowl, whisk together the lemon juice, mustard, and horseradish. Season with salt and pepper, then gradually whisk in the remaining 6 tablespoons of olive oil.

Place the watercress in a large bowl and toss with most of the vinaigrette, reserving some for drizzling. To serve, place mounds of watercress on each plate. Top with some onion slices and some of the tomatoes, drizzle with a little more vinaigrette, and sprinkle with the cheese. Serve at once.

*Tiny Tomatoes* These days supermarkets and vegetable shops offer all different kinds of tiny tomatoes, in an array of reds, oranges, and yellows. Cherry tomatoes are the largest and easiest to find and taste best when you can buy them still attached to the stem. Grape tomatoes have been gaining popularity recently and are often a little sweeter than the cherries. And pear tomatoes, which look like miniature pears in shape, are the most delicate of the lot. You can use them interchangeably in this recipe (and in most), though the cherry tomatoes might need a minute longer on the heat. In general the red tomatoes have a slightly more intense flavor than the yellow ones, which tend to be milder and less acidic.

# Mixed Herb Salad with Roasted Tomato Vinaigrette

Roasted or grilled tomato is sweet and concentrated, giving this vinaigrette enough muscle to stand up to a highly flavorful herb salad. Whole herb leaves tossed in with the lettuce add a fresh, zesty character and a surprise element to what looks like an ordinary mix of greens.

SERVES 4

2 large tomatoes, sliced $1/2$ inch thick, seeds discarded

3 tablespoons sherry vinegar

1 tablespoon chopped shallot

$1/2$ teaspoon coarse sea salt or kosher salt, plus additional to taste

$1/4$ teaspoon freshly ground black pepper, plus additional to taste

$1/4$ cup plus 1 tablespoon extra virgin olive oil

$1/4$ cup plus 1 tablespoon grapeseed or canola oil

1 head Boston or Bibb lettuce, torn

1 cup fresh basil leaves

1 cup fresh flat-leaf parsley leaves

$1/2$ cup fresh mint leaves

$1/2$ cup fresh chives cut into 2-inch pieces

Light the grill or preheat the broiler.

*On the Grill*   Lay the tomatoes in a grilling basket or directly on the grill and cook, turning once, until both sides are well charred, about 3 to 5 minutes.

*In the Oven*   Lay the tomatoes in a pan and place directly under the heat source. Broil, turning once, until both sides are well charred, about 3 to 5 minutes.

Place half the tomatoes in the bowl of a blender or food processor and add the vinegar, shallot, and salt and pepper. Puree until smooth. With the motor running, drizzle in both oils until well combined. Salt and pepper to taste.

Chop the remaining tomatoes. In a large bowl, toss the lettuce and herbs with enough vinaigrette to coat the leaves. Divide the salad among 4 plates. Surround each mound with chopped tomatoes drizzled with additional vinaigrette.

# Sweet Tomato
# & Bocconcini Salad
# with Scallions

This is my miniaturized, robust revision of the popular Italian salad of sliced tomatoes, red onion, and mozzarella. It's particularly pretty to combine the green scallions and white cheese with a mix of red and yellow pear tomatoes. Grilling or roasting the scallions softens them and brings out their sweetness. If bocconcini are not available, substitute larger balls of fresh mozzarella cut into 1-inch cubes. This summery salad makes an elegant appetizer.

SERVES 6

**2 bunches scallions, white and light green parts only (about 6 inches of each)**
**2 1/2 tablespoons extra virgin olive oil**
**Coarse sea salt or kosher salt and freshly ground black pepper**
**1 pint pear, cherry, or grape tomatoes, halved**
**3/4 pound fresh mozzarella bocconcini**
**1/4 cup chopped fresh mint leaves**

Light the grill or preheat the oven to 500°F. Place the scallions in a large bowl, toss them with 1 tablespoon of the oil, and season with salt and pepper to taste.

*On the Grill*    Spread the scallions on the grill and cook, turning once, until they are charred yet still firm at their centers, about 6 minutes.

*In the Oven*    Place the scallions on a rimmed baking sheet and roast, turning once, until they are charred yet still firm at their centers, about 6 to 7 minutes.

Let the scallions cool slightly, then slice them in half lengthwise.

In a salad bowl, toss the scallions with the tomatoes, mozzarella, and mint. Drizzle with the remaining 1 1/2 tablespoons of oil and season with salt and pepper.

# Butter Lettuce Salad
## with Red Pepper Vinaigrette

This roasted red pepper vinaigrette is so delicious and intense that you'll want to dip bread in it and eat it all by itself. Leftovers have a lot of wonderful uses, from topping grilled vegetables or potatoes to marinating chicken or fish or serving as a dip. Here I pair the vinaigrette with an assortment of light, crunchy vegetables, including tender lettuce, strips of red pepper, and crisp cucumbers. The clean, bright sweetness of this salad really perks up the appetite when served before the meal or between courses.

SERVES 4

**2 red bell peppers**

**$1/2$ cup extra virgin olive oil, plus additional for brushing the pepper**

**3 tablespoons sherry or white wine vinegar**

**I tablespoon chopped shallot**

**$1/2$ teaspoon coarse sea salt or kosher salt, plus additional to taste**

**$1/4$ teaspoon freshly ground black pepper, plus additional to taste**

**I large head butter lettuce, torn**

**I cup fresh flat-leaf parsley leaves**

**I cucumber, peeled, halved, seeded, and sliced**

**2 ounces crumbled feta cheese (about $1/2$ cup) for garnish (optional)**

**2 scallions, thinly sliced, for garnish (optional)**

Light the grill or preheat the broiler.

*On the Grill*   Brush one of the peppers with oil and grill it, turning frequently, until the skin is charred and blistered all over, about 15 minutes.

*In the Oven*   Halve one of the peppers lengthwise and discard the seeds and stem. Lay the pepper skin side up on a baking sheet, brush it lightly with olive oil, and place it directly under the heat source. Broil until the skin is charred and blistered all over, about 3 minutes.

Immediately transfer the pepper to a deep bowl and cover with a plate to trap the steam. Let steam until cool, about 5 minutes, then rub the skin off the pepper using your hands or a metal spoon. Remove the seeds and stem if necessary and coarsely chop the pepper.

In the bowl of a blender or food processor, combine the roasted pepper, vinegar, and shallot. Puree until smooth. With the motor running, slowly drizzle in the $1/2$ cup olive oil. Season with salt and pepper.

Seed the remaining pepper and cut it crosswise into very thin strips.

Place the lettuce in a salad bowl. Toss the lettuce with the parsley and cucumber, drizzle with $1/2$ cup of the vinaigrette, and toss to coat lightly. Garnish the salad with the pepper strips and the feta and scallions if desired.

# 3 *Soups*

# Charred Yellow Tomato Soup

This smooth chilled soup is a great warm-weather starter. Yellow tomatoes are slightly sweeter than red tomatoes, with less moisture and lower acidity, which makes them ideal for high heat. When grilled or roasted, their sugars begin to caramelize and their tomato flavor is concentrated. With its refreshing taste and vivid, sunny color, this soup needs little more to enhance it—I season it simply with some onion, garlic, coriander seeds, and lemon juice. Then I top it all off with a cilantro onion relish featuring more assertive versions of the flavors in the soup: diced red tomatoes, red onion, fresh cilantro, and lime juice.

If you can't find yellow tomatoes, you can substitute red tomatoes for a more intense version of this soup. Whatever tomatoes you use, if they are ripe the soup will be excellent.

SERVES 6

**For the Soup**
**6 large yellow tomatoes**
**2$^1/_2$ tablespoons extra virgin olive oil**
**I teaspoon coarse sea salt or kosher salt, plus additional to taste**
**I cup chopped onion**
**2 garlic cloves, minced**
**I teaspoon coriander seeds**
**$^1/_2$ teaspoon cumin seeds**
**I tablespoon freshly squeezed lemon juice**
**$^1/_2$ teaspoon freshly ground black pepper**

**For the Cilantro-**
**Onion Relish**
**I medium red tomato, seeded and diced**
**$^1/_2$ cup finely chopped red onion**
**$^1/_4$ cup chopped fresh cilantro**
**I tablespoon freshly squeezed lime juice**
**I tablespoon extra virgin olive oil**
**I teaspoon minced jalapeño pepper**
**Coarse sea salt or kosher salt and freshly ground black pepper to taste**

Light the grill or preheat the oven to 500°F. Place the tomatoes in a bowl and toss them with 1$^1/_2$ tablespoons of the olive oil and salt to taste.

*On the Grill* Grill the tomatoes, turning, for 10 to 15 minutes, until the tomatoes are charred.

*In the Oven*     Place the tomatoes in a roasting pan and roast for 10 minutes. Turn the tomatoes over and roast for another 5 minutes.

Transfer the tomatoes to a bowl and let cool slightly. Core and roughly chop them, reserving their juices. Heat the remaining tablespoon of oil in a large pot over medium heat. Add the onion and garlic and cook, stirring, until they are translucent, about 5 minutes. Do not let them brown (if they start to color, add a tablespoon of water).

Meanwhile, in a small skillet, toast the coriander and cumin seeds over medium-high heat until they are fragrant and lightly browned, shaking the pan so the spices don't burn, about 2 minutes. Add them to the pot, along with the tomatoes and their liquid and 1 1/2 cups water. Stir in 1 teaspoon salt.

Bring the tomato mixture to a boil over high heat, then reduce the heat and simmer for about 15 minutes.

Turn off the heat and let the soup cool slightly. Puree the soup either with an immersion blender or in batches in a blender or food processor. Strain through a coarse strainer and discard the solids. Chill the soup until cold, at least 4 hours.

Meanwhile, in a bowl, stir together all the ingredients for the cilantro-onion relish.

Season the soup with lemon juice, salt to taste, and the pepper. Serve garnished with a spoonful of the cilantro-onion relish.

# Charred Onion Soup

Intense, with a smooth texture and a sweet, smoky flavor, this is a refined and elegant onion soup without the gloppy cheese cap of the usual kind. Instead, the charred onions give the soup an amber color and real depth of flavor. The addition of 7 heads of garlic sounds potent, but after it is blanched the garlic contributes a mellow sweetness that rounds out the onion flavor. Each bowl is garnished with crunchy toasts topped with just a sprinkle of cheese.

SERVES 8

Coarse sea salt or kosher salt

I pound garlic, about 7 large heads, halved crosswise, plus I clove, peeled, for croutons

3 large Spanish onions, peeled

$1/4$ cup plus 3 tablespoons extra virgin olive oil

Freshly ground black pepper

$1/2$ cup dry white wine

10 cups chicken broth (reduced-sodium if canned)

$1/2$ small baguette, halved lengthwise

$1/4$ cup shredded Gruyère cheese (about I ounce)

$1/4$ cup grated Parmesan cheese (about I ounce)

I teaspoon chopped fresh flat-leaf parsley

I tablespoon very finely minced shallot

$1/2$ teaspoon fresh thyme leaves

Preheat the oven to 400°F or light the grill (use a low setting on a gas grill). Bring a large pot of salted water to a boil, add the halved heads of garlic, and boil for 5 minutes. Drain and let cool. Squeeze the garlic cloves out of their skins.

*In the Oven*  Slice each onion into 6 wedges. Lay the onions and garlic in a 9 × 13-inch roasting pan and pour $1/4$ cup of the olive oil over all. Season with salt and pepper to taste and roast, turning occasionally, until the onions are browned and tender, about 45 minutes. Transfer the vegetables to a stockpot. Place the roasting pan on the stove over medium heat. Add the white wine to the pan and stir, scraping the bottom and sides of the pan to loosen all the cooked-on bits of onion and garlic. Pour the wine mixture into the stockpot and add the broth.

*On the Grill*  Slice the onions in half crosswise. Brush with 2 tablespoons of the olive oil and season with salt and pepper. Drizzle 2 tablespoons of the remaining olive oil over the garlic, season with salt and pepper, and wrap in foil. Lay the onions in a grill basket and place, along with the foil-wrapped garlic, on the grill. Cook, turning occasionally, until tender, about 1 hour. Transfer the onions and garlic to a stockpot and add the wine and broth.

Bring the soup to a boil over medium-high heat, then reduce the heat to medium and simmer, uncovered, for 1 hour.

Puree the soup using a food mill (set over a clean pot), food processor, blender, or immersion blender. Return the soup to the stockpot over medium heat and bring to a simmer. Simmer for 15 minutes, stirring occasionally. Push the soup through a strainer, using a wooden spoon to force the solids through. Refrigerate for at least 8 hours. Reheat and adjust the seasonings before serving.

Preheat the oven to 300°F or light the grill. Using a garlic press, crush the remaining garlic clove into a small bowl and combine it with the remaining 3 tablespoons of olive oil (alternately, mince the garlic and add it to the bowl with the oil). Brush over the cut sides of the baguette. Grill or toast the bread cut sides up in the oven until well browned, about 5 minutes, then season lightly with salt.

Just before serving, in a small bowl, mix together the cheeses, parsley, shallot, and thyme. Spoon this mixture onto the garlic toast. Lay the baguette halves, cut side up, on the grill or place on a cookie sheet in the oven until the cheese has melted. Slice the baguette halves on the diagonal into 4 pieces each. To serve the soup, float a crouton on each bowl.

# Asparagus Soup with Egg Mimosa

Asparagus Mimosa is a traditional spring dish in which steamed asparagus is topped with a mixture of bread crumbs and hard-cooked eggs. I like the symbolic images of rebirth that green asparagus and eggs evoke, as well as their springtime flavors. In this recipe I turn that combination into a soup. It has a lot of flavor—the high-heat roasting or grilling caramelizes the asparagus and condenses it. Then I simmer the asparagus with meaty mushrooms and onions and puree the mixture into a smooth, creamy soup. A topping of hard-cooked egg and a dollop of chive cream add just a touch of richness, while the red pepper flakes liven it all up. It's perfect for those cool spring nights when something hot really hits the spot.

SERVES 4 TO 6

**3 pounds asparagus, trimmed**

**1/4 cup extra virgin olive oil**

**1 1/2 teaspoons coarse sea salt or kosher salt, plus additional to taste**

**2 tablespoons unsalted butter**

**1/2 pound white mushrooms, sliced**

**2 medium onions, chopped**

**6 cups chicken or vegetable broth (reduced-sodium if canned)**

**Freshly ground black pepper**

**1/2 cup heavy cream, whipped, for garnish**

**1 tablespoon chopped fresh chives for garnish**

**2 hard-cooked eggs, chopped, for garnish**

**1 tablespoon chopped fresh flat-leaf parsley for garnish**

**Hot red pepper flakes for garnish (optional)**

Light the grill or preheat the oven to 500°F. In a large bowl, toss the asparagus with the olive oil and 1 teaspoon of the salt.

*On the Grill*     Lay the asparagus on the grill (or use a grilling basket) and grill, turning, until browned and tender, about 10 to 15 minutes.

*In the Oven*     Spread the asparagus in a single layer on a rimmed baking sheet and roast, shaking the pan to toss them every 5 minutes, until the asparagus are browned and tender, about 10 to 15 minutes.

Cut the top inch off the asparagus and set aside the tops for garnish. Melt the butter in a soup pot over medium heat. Add the mushrooms, onions, and the remaining $\frac{1}{2}$ teaspoon salt and cook, stirring frequently, until the onions are translucent, about 10 minutes. Roughly chop the asparagus stalks and add them to the pot. Add the broth and, if necessary, enough water so that the liquid covers the vegetables by $1\frac{1}{2}$ inches. Bring to a simmer. Cook, covered, for 45 minutes.

Puree the soup either with an immersion blender or in batches in a blender or food processor and transfer it to a large bowl. Rinse out the soup pot. Strain the soup back into the pot through a coarse strainer, using a wooden spoon to press on the solids to extract all the liquid. Discard the solids. (Alternately, puree the soup through a food mill into a bowl, then return it to the rinsed pot.) If the soup seems too thick, thin it with a little water. Season the soup with salt and pepper to taste.

Just before serving, warm up the soup over medium heat. Season the whipped cream with salt and pepper to taste and fold in the chives. To serve, garnish the soup with the reserved asparagus tops, hard-cooked eggs, parsley, and red pepper if desired. Pass the chive cream at the table.

# Caramelized Cauliflower Soup

If cauliflower soup sounds pale and bland to you, you're probably thinking of the taste of steamed or boiled cauliflower. But once you roast cauliflower, its sweetness and rich nutty flavors really stand up for themselves. This soup has an intense flavor on its own, but garnishing it with crisp cauliflower florets that have been broiled with cinnamon sugar adds a terrific crunchy spiciness. If you don't want to bother with the florets, just garnish each bowl with a sprinkling of cinnamon sugar. It really brings out the caramelized taste of the cauliflower and makes a huge difference.

SERVES 8 TO 10

2 tablespoons unsalted butter, melted

1 large head cauliflower, trimmed and cut vertically into $^1/_2$-inch slices

Coarse sea salt or kosher salt

1 medium Spanish onion, halved lengthwise and thinly sliced

2 medium Idaho potatoes, peeled and diced

1 fresh sage sprig

7 cups chicken or vegetable broth (reduced-sodium if canned) or water

Freshly ground black pepper

2 teaspoons sugar

1 teaspoon ground cinnamon

1 cup crème fraîche (or use heavy cream mixed with 1 teaspoon lemon juice)

$^1/_4$ cup snipped fresh chives for garnish (optional)

Preheat the broiler. Brush a large baking sheet with melted butter and lay the cauliflower slices on it in a single layer. Brush the slices with more butter, sprinkle with salt, and broil directly under the heat source until brown, 3 to 5 minutes. Use a spatula to carefully turn the cauliflower slices over. Add the sliced onion to the baking sheet, brush with more butter, and continue to broil until nicely browned, another 3 to 5 minutes. Set aside 16 nice cauliflower florets from the slices to use as a garnish.

Place the rest of the cauliflower and the onion in a large soup pot and add the potatoes and sage. Pour in the broth, adding water if necessary to cover the vegetables with liquid by 1 inch. Bring the liquid to a boil, then reduce the heat and simmer, partially covered, for 45 minutes, until the vegetables are completely soft.

Remove the sage and puree the soup, either with an immersion blender or in batches in a blender or food processor. Return the soup to the pot and season with pepper to taste and additional salt if desired. If the soup seems too thick, add a little water to thin it.

Just before serving, combine the sugar and cinnamon in a small bowl. Lay the reserved cauliflower florets on a baking sheet and dust them with the cinnamon sugar, turning to coat them evenly. Broil until toast colored, glossy, and caramelized, about 2 minutes per side (watch carefully so they don't burn).

Gently reheat the soup over medium heat. Whisk the crème fraîche or cream and lemon juice mixture into the soup and ladle it into warm soup bowls. Garnish with the caramelized florets and chives if desired.

# Roasted Butternut Squash & Pear Soup

Perfectly autumnal, with the rich, dense texture of butternut squash complemented by the lightness of pear, this creamy broth features two fruits of the fall. Although you might think that the pear, squash, and crystallized ginger would make for a pretty sweet soup, dry white wine and spicy fresh ginger temper this tendency. Instead the flavors are savory and mellow with a hint of spices, while the garnish of candied ginger adds just the right spark.

SERVES 6 TO 8

- 1 large butternut squash (about 3 pounds), peeled, seeded, and cut into 1-inch pieces
- 2 carrots, cut into 1-inch pieces
- 2 tablespoons extra virgin olive oil
- Coarse sea salt or kosher salt and freshly ground black pepper
- 3 leeks, white and light green parts only, sliced
- 2 Bosc pears, peeled, cored, and cut into 1-inch pieces
- 1/2 cup dry white wine
- 1/4 cup brandy
- 7 cups chicken or vegetable broth (reduced-sodium if canned) or water
- 1 large fresh thyme sprig, plus additional leaves for garnish
- One 1-inch piece fresh ginger, peeled and grated
- 1/4 cup crème fraîche or sour cream for garnish (optional)
- 1 tablespoon chopped crystallized ginger for garnish

Preheat the oven to 450°F. Place the squash and carrots in a roasting pan large enough to hold them in one layer (or use 2 pans) and toss with the oil and salt and pepper to taste. Roast for 10 minutes, then add the leeks and pears. Toss to combine and continue to roast for another 30 minutes, until the vegetables are tender and browned.

Remove the pan from the oven and immediately add the wine and brandy, using a wooden spoon to scrape the vegetables and fruit and their caramelized juices from the sides and bottom of the pan. Transfer the vegetables, pears, and liquid to a large soup pot. Pour in the broth or water, adding water if necessary to cover the vegetables with liquid by 1 inch. Add the thyme sprig and grated ginger and bring the liquid to a boil. Reduce the heat and simmer, partially covered, for 1 hour.

Remove the thyme sprig and puree the soup, either with an immersion blender or in batches in a blender or food processor. Transfer the soup to a medium-mesh strainer set over another pot. Use a rubber spatula to press the solids through the strainer. If the soup seems too thick, thin it with a little water. Season with salt and pepper.

Just before serving, warm the soup over low heat. Serve in warmed bowls, drizzled with crème fraîche or sour cream, if desired, and garnished with the crystallized ginger and a sprinkling of fresh thyme leaves.

# Roasted Parsnip & Celery Root Soup

Two root vegetables that people don't use nearly enough are featured in this unusually delicious winter soup. They are easy to work with, inexpensive, and I think more flavorful than many other, more common root vegetables. Parsnips are simultaneously sweeter and more complex than carrots, while celery root has an herbal celery flavor with a round, deep richness. Together they make a sweet, earthy soup that is creamy and surprising. A quick garnish of celery leaves and a little celery seed oil adds freshness and spice.

SERVES 6

2 large celery roots, trimmed and cut into 1-inch cubes

4 large parsnips, peeled and cut into 1-inch chunks

2 large carrots, peeled and cut into 1-inch chunks

6 tablespoons extra virgin olive oil

Coarse sea salt or kosher salt and freshly ground black pepper

2 tablespoons unsalted butter

2 celery stalks, chopped, leaves reserved for garnish

1 Spanish onion, chopped

1 leek, white and light green parts only, sliced

6 cups chicken or vegetable broth (reduced-sodium if canned) or water

1 fresh sage sprig or 4 large fresh sage leaves

1 teaspoon celery seed

1 whole clove

Preheat the oven to 500°F. Spread out the celery roots in one layer on a rimmed baking sheet and spread the parsnips and carrots out on another baking sheet. Drizzle each pan with 1½ tablespoons of the olive oil and season with salt and pepper to taste. Toss to coat. Roast the vegetables until browned, stirring halfway through, about 15 to 20 minutes.

Meanwhile, melt the butter in a large heavy soup pot over low heat. Add the celery, onion, and leek and cook, stirring, until the vegetables are translucent, about 10 minutes (do not let them brown).

When the roasted vegetables are ready, reserve ½ cup of the roasted celery root for garnish. Add the rest of the roasted vegetables to the soup pot. Pour in the broth or water, adding water if necessary to cover the vegetables with liquid by 1 inch. Add the sage and salt and pepper to taste. Simmer the soup over medium heat, partially covered, until the vegetables are soft, about 45 minutes.

Pluck out the sage and discard it. Puree the soup, either with an immersion blender or in batches in a blender or food processor. If the soup seems too thick, add a little more water. Season with additional salt and pepper if desired.

Dice the reserved roasted celery root and set aside for garnish. In a small pan over medium-high heat, toast the celery seed and clove until fragrant, about 3 minutes. Remove from the heat and let cool. Add the remaining 3 tablespoons of oil to the pan with the cooled spices and bring to a simmer over medium heat. Cook for 5 minutes, then strain the oil through a cheesecloth-lined strainer and discard the spices. Gently reheat the soup and serve garnished with celery root cubes, celery leaves, and a drizzle of the spice oil.

# Creamy Mushroom Soup

Simple and elegant, this creamy soup is an easy way to impress your guests. Mushrooms condense at high heat until their flavor becomes deep and lingering. Spiked with a little sherry, smoothed with cream, and garnished with chopped mushroom toast points, this soup has great flavor and texture and a lot of character. You can take the flavor even further by using some wild mushrooms, mixing and matching varieties as you like.

SERVES 4 TO 6

1/2 pound portobello mushrooms

1/2 pound white mushrooms

I onion, sliced 1/2 inch thick

3 tablespoons extra virgin olive oil

Coarse sea salt or kosher salt and freshly ground black pepper

2 garlic cloves, peeled

2 tablespoons unsalted butter

I fresh thyme sprig, plus additional leaves for garnish

I quart chicken or vegetable broth (reduced-sodium if canned) or water

Six 1/2-inch-thick baguette slices

3 tablespoons freshly grated Parmesan cheese

I cup heavy cream

1/4 cup dry fino sherry

Preheat the oven to 450°F or light the grill.

*In the Oven*   Cut the portobellos into 1/2-inch slices and halve the white mushrooms. In a large bowl, toss the mushrooms and onion with 2 1/2 tablespoons of the oil and salt and pepper to taste. Spread the mushrooms and onion in a single layer on a rimmed baking sheet or two. Roast, tossing once, until browned, about 15 minutes.

*On the Grill*   Brush the mushrooms and onion with 2 1/2 tablespoons of the oil and sprinkle with salt and pepper to taste. Place the mushrooms and onion in a grilling basket and grill, turning once, until browned, about 15 minutes. Let the mushrooms cool slightly and cut the portobellos into 1/2-inch slices.

Mince one of the garlic cloves. Melt the butter in a large pot over medium heat. Add the mushrooms, onion, minced garlic, and thyme sprig. Cook, stirring, until the vegetables are tender, about 5 minutes. Use tongs to transfer 4 of the portobello slices to a board, finely chop them, and set aside to use as garnish. Pour the broth into the pot, adding water if necessary to cover the vegetables with liquid by 1 inch. Bring the liquid to a boil. Reduce the heat and simmer, uncovered, for 45 minutes, until the vegetables are completely soft.

Meanwhile, brush the baguette slices with the remaining $\frac{1}{2}$ tablespoon olive oil. Toast them on both sides on the grill, under the broiler, or in a toaster oven. Halve the remaining garlic clove and rub the cut sides over the toasts. Top each toast with some of the reserved chopped portobellos and sprinkle with the cheese. Just before serving, broil the mushroom toasts to melt the cheese.

Remove the thyme sprig from the soup, add the cream and sherry, and puree, either with an immersion blender or in batches in a blender or food processor. Return the soup to the pot and warm it up gently. If the soup seems too thick, thin it with a little water. Season with salt and pepper to taste. Ladle the soup into warmed bowls and top each with a mushroom toast and a sprinkling of thyme leaves.

# Sweet Potato Soup with Spicy Red Pepper Aïoli

This sweet potato soup isn't mellow and sweet, and it doesn't taste like pumpkin pie. Instead it combines regular white potatoes with the sweet potatoes for a creamy texture and not-too-sweet flavor, while a topping of spicy, garlicky aïoli made with hot and sweet peppers gives it a real punch. Toasted almonds make a crunchy garnish to contrast with the smooth broth. Serve as a vibrant starter for a fall or winter meal.

SERVES 8 TO 10

2 tablespoons unsalted butter

I cup finely chopped leek (white parts only)

I large onion, finely chopped

1$\frac{1}{4}$ teaspoons coarse sea salt or kosher salt, plus additional to taste

3 medium Idaho potatoes, peeled and cut into I-inch chunks

3 sweet potatoes, peeled and cut into I-inch chunks

5$\frac{1}{2}$ cups chicken or vegetable broth (reduced-sodium if canned) or more as needed

2 star anise pods

Freshly ground black pepper

I red bell pepper

$\frac{1}{4}$ cup extra virgin olive oil, plus additional for brushing the pepper

$\frac{1}{4}$ cup fresh white bread cubes

I tablespoon freshly squeezed lemon juice

I garlic clove, peeled

Large pinch of hot red pepper flakes

$\frac{1}{4}$ cup sliced almonds

Crème fraîche or sour cream for serving

Light the grill or preheat the broiler. In a soup pot over medium-low heat, melt the butter. Add the leek, onion, and $\frac{1}{2}$ teaspoon of the salt. Cook, stirring, over low heat without browning until the vegetables are softened, about 10 minutes. Add all the potatoes, broth, and star anise and bring to a simmer over medium heat. Simmer, covered, for 30 minutes.

Uncover the pot and continue to simmer the soup until the potatoes are tender, about 20 minutes more. Remove and discard the star anise and puree the soup, either with an immersion blender or in batches in a blender or food processor. Return it to the pot. Bring to a boil over medium heat and season with salt and pepper to taste. If the soup seems too thick, thin it with some additional broth or water.

*On the Grill*   Brush the pepper with oil and grill, turning frequently, until the skin is charred and blistered all over, about 15 minutes.

*In the Oven*   Halve the red bell pepper lengthwise, discarding the seeds and stem. Lay the pepper skin side up on a baking sheet and brush lightly with olive oil. Place directly under the heat source and broil until the skin is charred and blistered all over, about 3 minutes.

Immediately transfer the pepper to a deep bowl and cover with a plate to trap the steam. Let steam until cool, about 5 minutes. Rub the skin off the pepper using your hands or a metal spoon. Remove the seeds and stem if necessary and coarsely chop the pepper.

In a blender or food processor, puree the red bell pepper with the bread cubes, lemon juice, garlic clove, red pepper flakes, remaining $3/4$ teaspoon salt, and black pepper to taste. With the motor running, drizzle in the $1/4$ cup olive oil and puree until smooth.

Heat a heavy skillet over medium heat and add the almonds. Toast, shaking and tossing the almonds constantly, until they are fragrant and browned, about 3 to 4 minutes. Immediately transfer the almonds to a plate to cool.

To serve, gently reheat the soup if necessary. Ladle it into bowls and pass the red pepper aïoli, crème fraîche or sour cream, and almonds on the side.

# Garlic & Egg Chicken Soup

I first tasted this hearty soup early in the morning at a fish market in San Sebastian, Spain. I was on a trip with a group of chefs, and we'd been out eating and drinking until the wee hours the night before a 5:00 A.M. tour of the market. I saw several of the fishmongers eating this porridgelike soup, made of fried eggs and garlic bread moistened with boiling water, and was told it was a hangover cure. It definitely made me feel better, but maybe just because I loved the intense garlic flavor. When I got back to Beacon, I came up with this slightly more refined version using a rich, garlicky chicken broth poured over grilled sourdough toast points and a fried egg. It's become my signature version of chicken soup—not only will it heal what ails you; it'll also keep the vampires away.

SERVES 4

**Coarse sea salt or kosher salt**

**1 head of garlic, halved crosswise, plus 1 tablespoon sliced garlic**

**2 teaspoons extra virgin olive oil**

**1 quart chicken broth (reduced-sodium if canned)**

**Freshly ground black pepper**

**8 slices good-quality sourdough bread**

**Unsalted butter, melted, or extra virgin olive oil for the eggs and toast**

**4 eggs**

**1 medium tomato, seeded and diced (about 1 cup)**

**1/4 cup chopped fresh flat-leaf parsley**

Preheat the oven to 400°F or light the grill (use a low setting on a gas grill). Bring a small pot of salted water to a boil. Add the halved garlic head and simmer for 5 minutes. Drain the garlic.

*In the Oven*  Place the blanched garlic in a small ovenproof dish and drizzle with the olive oil. Season with salt and pepper to taste. Cover the dish with foil and roast for 5 minutes, then reduce the oven to 350°F and continue to roast until the garlic is completely tender, about 35 to 45 minutes. Let cool slightly, then squeeze the garlic from its skin into a small bowl and set aside.

*On the Grill*  Place the blanched garlic on a sheet of foil and drizzle with the olive oil. Season with salt and pepper to taste. Wrap the foil around the garlic and grill over low heat (or at the edge of the grill if using a charcoal grill) until tender, about 30 minutes. Let cool slightly, then squeeze the garlic from its skin into a small bowl and set aside.

Place the broth in a large pot and season with salt and pepper to taste. Bring the stock to a boil, then add the roasted or grilled garlic puree and the sliced fresh garlic. Reduce the heat to medium-low and simmer for 5 to 10 minutes.

Lightly brush the slices of bread with melted butter or oil and grill or toast them on both sides in the oven, in a toaster, or on the grill.

When the soup is almost ready, place a large skillet over medium-high heat. Add a little butter or oil to the pan and fry the eggs, sunny side up, seasoning them with salt and pepper to taste.

To serve, lay 2 slices of toast in each soup plate. Place an egg on top of the toast, then ladle simmering soup over the egg. Garnish with tomato and parsley and serve immediately.

# Shrimp & Fennel Soup with Pernod

With a good shot of licorice-flavored Pernod mixed into a tomatoey broth, plus plenty of chopped fennel and sweet, smoky shrimp, this soup evokes the flavors of Provence. I like to serve this before roasted or grilled lamb or Chicken with Cipollini (page 106). If you really want to gild the lily, serve the soup as a main course, accompanied by skewers of additional grilled shrimp.

SERVES 10

**2 pounds large shrimp**

**3 tablespoons extra virgin olive oil**

**Coarse sea salt or kosher salt and freshly ground black pepper**

**3 tablespoons unsalted butter**

**I cup finely chopped celery**

**I cup finely chopped fennel bulb**

**I cup finely chopped onion**

**I cup finely chopped green bell pepper**

**I cup finely chopped leek (white and light green parts only)**

**2 tablespoons all-purpose flour**

**I quart chicken or vegetable broth (reduced-sodium if canned)**

**I quart fish broth (reduced-sodium if canned)**

**I cup dry white wine**

**2 tablespoons tomato paste**

**I cup long-grain white rice**

**1/4 cup Pernod**

**Chopped fennel fronds for garnish**

Light the grill or preheat the oven to 500°F. In a large bowl, toss the shrimp with 2 tablespoons of the olive oil and salt and pepper to taste.

*On the Grill*    Place the shrimp in one layer in a grilling basket or on skewers and grill, turning once, until the shells are pink, about 3 to 4 minutes. When the shrimp are cool enough to handle, peel them and reserve the shells.

*In the Oven*    Lay the shrimp in a single layer on a baking sheet and roast for 3 to 4 minutes, until the shells are pink. When the shrimp are cool enough to handle, peel them and reserve the shells.

Warm I tablespoon of the butter with the remaining tablespoon of olive oil in a large stockpot over medium-high heat. Add $1/2$ cup each of the celery, fennel, onion, green pepper, and leek and season with salt and pepper to taste. Cook, stirring, until the vegetables have begun to brown, about 6 minutes. Sprinkle the flour over the vegetables and continue to cook, stirring, until the flour is browned, about I to 2 minutes. Add the reserved shrimp shells, the broths, white wine, tomato paste, and I quart water. Simmer, uncovered, for 45 minutes.

Warm the remaining 2 tablespoons of butter in a large heavy pot over medium heat. Add the remaining $1/2$ cup each of celery, fennel, onion, green pepper, and leek and season with salt and pepper to taste. Cook, stirring, until the vegetables wilt, about 5 minutes. Line a fine-mesh strainer with 2 layers of cheesecloth and strain the shrimp stock into the pot of vegetables. Add the rice and simmer for 25 minutes. Chop the shelled shrimp into $1/2$-inch cubes and add them to the pot along with the Pernod. Simmer for another 5 minutes, until the shrimp are warmed through. Adjust the seasonings and serve garnished with the chopped fennel fronds.

# Smoky Corn & Cod Chowder

This is a light yet creamy chowder with a nice smokiness that comes from grilled corn. Serve it at the end of summer when the nights begin to grow cold, as an appetizer or first course, or with bread, cheese, and salad as the centerpiece of a light meal. Cod, potatoes, and milk make it comforting, while sweet corn and a topping of tomatoes add freshness. Scallops, other white fish, or even cooked lobster meat can be used in addition to or in place of the cod.

SERVES 4 TO 6

**4 ears of corn**

**1 to 2 small jalapeños, to taste**

**4 slices bacon, diced**

**3 celery stalks, diced, leaves reserved for garnish**

**2 medium Idaho potatoes, peeled, halved lengthwise, and sliced**

**1 Spanish onion, diced**

**3 cups chicken or vegetable broth (reduced-sodium if canned)**

**3 cups whole milk**

**Coarse sea salt or kosher salt and freshly ground black pepper**

**1/2 pound skinless, boneless cod fillets, cubed**

**1 cup diced tomato**

Light the grill or preheat the oven to 450°F. Cut the tops and bottoms off the corn.

*On the Grill*    Place the unhusked corn and the jalapeño on the grill. Cover the grill and cook for 15 minutes, turning once.

*In the Oven*    Place the unhusked corn and the jalapeño on a rimmed baking sheet and roast for 15 minutes, turning once.

Let the corn cool slightly, but shuck it while still warm. Holding the shucked corn in a large bowl, slide a sharp knife along the cobs to cut away all the kernels, then scrape the back of the knife along the cobs to scrape the liquid into the bowl. Set aside. Seed and chop the jalapeño.

In a large heavy pot, cook the bacon over medium-high heat until crisp, about 5 minutes. Use a slotted spoon to transfer the bacon to a paper towel–lined plate. Reduce the heat to medium and add the jalapeño, celery, potatoes, and onion to the pot (if there is too much bacon fat and the vegetables seem greasy, spoon off some of the fat). Cook, stirring, until the vegetables are soft, about 10 minutes. Add the corn kernels and their liquid to the pot, add the broth and milk, and season with a large pinch of salt and pepper. Bring the liquid to a boil, then reduce the heat and simmer for 15 minutes, stirring occasionally.

Add the cod to the pot and simmer over low heat, partially covered, for 15 minutes. Add the diced tomato and cook for 1 minute longer.

Serve the soup in bowls, garnished with celery leaves and diced bacon.

# 4 Pasta, Rice, & Polenta

# Crisp Penne with Ricotta, Roasted Tomatoes, & Herbs

There's not much more than cheese, pasta, and some tomato in this recipe, but it's just one of those dishes that's somehow better than the sum of its parts. You could say it's my version of baked ziti, but instead of cooking the tomatoes into a sauce, I quickly caramelize them. The pasta is tossed with fresh herbs, creamy ricotta, sharp nutty Asiago, and then the sweet, smoky bits of succulent tomato. When the whole thing comes out of the oven, the top is crunchy, the herbs have given their flavors to the pasta and cheese, and the ricotta has turned into a delicate white sauce. You may never make regular baked ziti again!

SERVES 6

**Coarse sea salt or kosher salt**

**1 pound penne pasta**

**2 pounds plum tomatoes (10 to 12), halved lengthwise**

**3 tablespoons extra virgin olive oil**

**Freshly ground black pepper**

**1 1/4 cups fresh ricotta cheese**

**1/4 cup plus 1 tablespoon heavy cream**

**1/4 cup plus 2 tablespoons grated Asiago cheese (about 1 1/2 ounces)**

**1/4 cup plus 2 tablespoons grated Bel Paese cheese (about 1 1/2 ounces)**

**1 tablespoon chopped fresh flat-leaf parsley**

**2 tablespoons chopped fresh oregano or marjoram or a combination**

Preheat the oven to 500°F or light the grill. Bring a large pot of salted water to a boil. Cook the penne in the boiling water until it is just barely al dente.

*In the Oven*    Lay the tomatoes cut side down on a rimmed baking sheet, drizzle them with the olive oil, and season them with salt and pepper to taste. Place the baking sheet in the oven and roast until the tomatoes are soft and their skins are browned and peeling, about 10 minutes.

*On the Grill*    In a bowl, toss the tomatoes with the olive oil, salt, and pepper. Lay the tomato halves skin side down on the grill and grill until they are soft and charred, about 10 minutes (do not turn).

Preheat the oven to 475°F. When the tomatoes are cool enough to handle, remove their skins and chop them. In a bowl, whisk together the ricotta and cream. In a large bowl, toss the drained penne with the ricotta mixture, then stir in $1/4$ cup each of the Asiago and Bel Paese cheeses. Mix in the herbs and season with salt and pepper to taste.

Add half the tomatoes to the pasta and toss. Spread the pasta mixture in a 9 × 13-inch baking dish or large gratin dish and top with the remaining tomatoes. Sprinkle with the remaining 2 tablespoons each of Asiago and Bel Paese and additional pepper to taste. Bake until the top is crisped, about 15 minutes. Serve immediately, while hot.

# Rigatoni with Roquefort & Corn

This unusual pasta dish features the surprising combination of piquant, salty blue cheese and sweet grilled corn. A tangy buttermilk dressing brings the flavors together, accented with fresh summer herbs and crunchy slices of radish. Served warm or at room temperature, it makes a vibrant, satisfying dish for an end-of-summer al fresco meal.

SERVES 4 TO 6

**3 ears of corn**

**Coarse sea salt or kosher salt**

**1 pound rigatoni**

**3/4 cup crumbled Roquefort cheese (about 3 ounces)**

**1 cup buttermilk**

**1 tablespoon minced red onion**

**Freshly ground black pepper**

**6 radishes, sliced**

**1/3 cup chopped fresh basil, plus additional sprigs for garnish**

**2 tablespoons snipped fresh chives**

**Mesclun or baby salad greens for serving (optional)**

Light the grill. Place the unshucked corn on the grill. Cover and grill the corn for 15 minutes, turning once. Let the corn cool slightly, but shuck while still warm. Holding the ears upright, slide a sharp knife along the cobs to remove the kernels. Place the kernels in a large salad bowl.

Bring a large pot of salted water to a boil and cook the rigatoni until al dente.

Meanwhile, in a bowl, whisk together the Roquefort, buttermilk, and onion and season with pepper and salt if desired.

When the pasta is done, drain it and place it in the salad bowl with the corn. Add the radishes, basil, and chives and toss well. Pour the dressing over all and toss to coat. Serve the pasta as is or on a bed of greens, garnished with basil sprigs.

# Cremini Mushrooms with Chive Pasta

With a bright green color and intense meaty, herbal flavor, this beautiful pasta dish is a true crowd pleaser. The technique is fast and simple. While the mushrooms cook, spaghettini is dressed with an instant sauce of oniony chives blended with olive oil. Then cremini are tossed in, adding texture and a satisfying earthy flavor. As an added bonus, this pasta can sit out for an hour or two without any loss of flavor, making it perfect for a buffet.

SERVES 4

**Coarse sea salt or kosher salt**
**I pound cremini mushrooms, trimmed**
**$1/2$ cup plus 2 tablespoons extra virgin olive oil**
**Freshly ground black pepper**
**I cup roughly snipped chives (2 to 3 bunches)**
**I pound spaghettini or angel hair pasta**
**Freshly grated Pecorino Romano cheese for serving**

Light the grill or preheat the oven to 500°F. Bring a large pot of salted water to a boil for the pasta. In a bowl, toss the mushrooms with 2 tablespoons of the olive oil and generous pinches of salt and pepper.

*On the Grill*  Place the mushrooms in a grill basket. Grill, turning once, until tender and browned, about 8 minutes. When cool enough to handle, cut the mushrooms into quarters.

*In the Oven*  Spread the mushrooms in a single layer on a rimmed baking sheet. Roast, turning once, until tender and browned, about 10 minutes. When cool enough to handle, cut the mushrooms into quarters.

In a food processor or blender, combine the remaining $1/2$ cup olive oil, the chives, and a generous pinch of salt and pepper. Process until pureed.

Cook the spaghettini until al dente. Drain, reserving 2 tablespoons of the cooking water if you plan to serve the pasta hot. In a large serving bowl, toss the pasta with the mushrooms and chive oil. If serving immediately, toss with 1 to 2 tablespoons of the reserved cooking water. Otherwise, let the pasta cool to room temperature. Serve with the cheese.

# Roasted Shells with Potatoes & Cheese

Stuffing pasta shells with mashed potatoes may seem weird, but serve this substantial wintry dish at a party and kids and adults alike will attest to its success. The combination makes sense along the lines of potato gnocchi, pierogi, and potato ravioli—and it couldn't be simpler to make or more fun to eat. These stuffed shells are my take on manicotti—I find that potato lightens the cheese filling and smooths its texture. Melting more cheese on top of the pasta creates a crispy contrast and a sharp bite.

SERVES 6

**Coarse sea salt or kosher salt**

**1$^1$/2 pounds Yukon Gold potatoes, peeled and cut into 2-inch chunks**

**1 cup plus 2 tablespoons whole milk**

**1 cup plus 2 tablespoons heavy cream, plus additional if necessary**

**3 garlic cloves, smashed with the side of a knife and peeled**

**3 tablespoons unsalted butter**

**One 12-ounce box large pasta shells**

**1 cup grated Pecorino Romano cheese (about $^1$/4 pound)**

**$^1$/4 cup plus 2 tablespoons fresh goat cheese (about 3 ounces)**

**$^1$/4 cup plus 2 tablespoons minced shallot**

**Freshly ground black pepper**

Preheat the oven to 450°F. Bring a large pot of salted water to a boil for the pasta. In another pot, put the potatoes in enough water to cover them by 2 inches. Salt the potato water well and bring to a boil. Boil, uncovered, until the potatoes are tender, about 15 to 20 minutes.

Meanwhile, in a saucepan over medium heat, combine the milk, cream, and garlic cloves and bring to a simmer. Simmer for 10 minutes, then use a slotted spoon to remove the garlic. Pour 1$^1$/2 cups of the cream mixture into a heat-proof measuring cup and set aside. Add the butter to the pot with the remaining milk and cream and let it melt.

When the pasta water comes to a boil, add the shells and cook until al dente, about 1 to 2 minutes less than the package indicates. Drain the pasta and let cool slightly.

Drain the potatoes and return them to the pot. Turn the heat to low. Use a potato masher or fork to mash the potatoes, stirring until they are smooth and dry. Turn off the heat. Add the milk mixture to the potatoes and stir until smooth. Stir in $1/2$ cup of the Romano, the goat cheese, and the shallot and season with salt and pepper to taste.

Use a spoon to stuff the shells with the potato mixture. (Or transfer the potato mixture to a large resealable plastic bag, snip one corner off, and pipe it into the shells.) Arrange the shells side by side in a large gratin dish or baking pan and pour the reserved milk and cream mixture into the bottom of the pan to reach $1/2$ inch up the sides, adding more cream if necessary. Sprinkle the remaining $1/2$ cup of Romano over the top and bake until crisp and golden, about 15 to 20 minutes.

# Roasted Winter Squash Ravioli with Sage & Walnut Butter

This is a rich and warming dish. Stuffing the pasta requires some advance preparation, but the results are special enough for a fall or winter dinner party. Roasting squash gives it a caramelized flavor and a dry, smooth texture that is ideal for filling ravioli. Wonton skins eliminate the need to make fresh pasta yourself—unless you want to. If you make these ahead and freeze them, you'll be able to prepare the sage and walnut butter in the time it takes to boil the ravioli. And don't be put off by the idea of a butter sauce—a small amount of nicely browned butter is flavorful enough to go a long way.

If you can't find sugar or cheese pumpkins, which will be available at many farm stands in the fall, don't substitute the regular jack-o'-lantern type. The flesh is much too watery. Use a butternut squash instead.

SERVES 4 TO 6 AS AN APPETIZER OR A SIDE DISH

I sugar pumpkin or $^1/_2$ small cheese pumpkin or butternut squash
(about I pound), halved and seeded

$^1/_4$ cup ricotta cheese

I large egg white

$^1/_2$ teaspoon coarse sea salt or kosher salt, plus additional to taste

$^1/_4$ teaspoon freshly ground black pepper, plus additional to taste

All-purpose flour

One 12-ounce package wonton skins

$^1/_2$ cup (I stick) unsalted butter

$^1/_2$ cup roasted chopped walnuts (see Note)

I bunch fresh sage

Juice of $^1/_2$ lemon or to taste

$^1/_4$ cup vegetable broth or water, plus additional if needed

Preheat the oven to 450°F. Lightly oil a rimmed baking sheet and place the pumpkin or squash on it, cut side down. Roast until tender when pierced with a knife, about 35 to 60 minutes.

While the pumpkin is roasting, line a strainer with cheesecloth and set it over a small bowl. Place the ricotta in the strainer and let drain.

When the pumpkin is cool enough to handle, scoop out its flesh. Pass the pumpkin flesh through a food mill or strainer. You should have about $3/4$ cup. Whisk the drained ricotta and egg white into the pumpkin and season with the salt and pepper.

Line 2 baking sheets with parchment or wax paper. Sprinkle the paper and a work surface lightly with flour. Lay a wonton skin on the work surface and place I heaping teaspoon of pumpkin filling on it. Brush the edges of the wonton skin with water, then lay another wonton skin on top and press from the filling outward to push any air out before sealing the ravioli. Use a 3-inch round cookie cutter or a glass to cut the ravioli into rounds and lay them on the baking sheets. Repeat until all the filling has been used. Sprinkle the ravioli with a little more flour, cover them with parchment or wax paper, and refrigerate until ready to use, up to 8 hours.

When ready to serve, bring a large pot of salted water to a boil. In a large heavy skillet over medium heat, melt the butter. When the butter starts to foam, add the nuts and cook, stirring occasionally, until the butter is brown and has a nutty aroma, about 6 to 8 minutes.

Meanwhile, reserve some sage leaves for garnish and chop the remaining sage. Add the sage and lemon juice to the butter and nuts and season with salt and pepper to taste. Add enough broth or water to thin the sauce. When the ravioli water is boiling, slide the ravioli into the pot and cook until they float, I to 2 minutes. Use a skimmer or slotted spoon to transfer the ravioli to the butter mixture. Toss the ravioli and cook them in the butter sauce over medium heat for I minute. Serve garnished with the reserved sage.

NOTE     To roast walnuts, spread them on a baking pan and roast them at 325°F for about 10 minutes, stirring once or twice, until they are browned around the edges.

# Grilled Summer Vegetable Risotto

This colorful risotto is a great way to showcase summer vegetables. Consider the recipe a guide—feel free to add other grilled vegetables like peppers or asparagus or to use this as a formula for a single-vegetable risotto using all zucchini, all eggplant, or whatever is most abundant. It makes a fine first course or a vegetarian main course.

SERVES 4 TO 6

2 small zucchini, sliced crosswise $1/4$ inch thick

2 small yellow squash, sliced crosswise $1/4$ inch thick

I Japanese eggplant, sliced crosswise $1/4$ inch thick

3 tablespoons extra virgin olive oil, plus additional for the tomatoes

Coarse sea salt or kosher salt and freshly ground black pepper

I large ripe tomato, halved and seeded

I tablespoon balsamic vinegar

5 to 6 cups vegetable or chicken broth (reduced-sodium if canned)

2 tablespoons unsalted butter

$1/4$ cup minced shallot

I large garlic clove, minced

2 cups Italian risotto rice such as Arborio, Vialone, or Carnaroli

$1/2$ cup dry white wine

$1/2$ cup grated Parmesan cheese, plus additional for serving

$1/4$ cup chopped fresh basil, plus sprigs for garnish

Light the grill. In a bowl, toss the zucchini, yellow squash, and eggplant slices with 2 tablespoons of the olive oil and a large pinch of salt and pepper. Brush the tomato halves all over with oil and season the cut sides with salt and pepper.

Lay the vegetables on the grill (or use a grill basket), placing the tomato halves skin side down. Grill, turning once, until charred and tender, about 10 to 15 minutes. Transfer the tomatoes to a cutting board. Transfer the other vegetables to a bowl and drizzle with half the balsamic vinegar.

When the tomato halves are cool enough to handle, dice them into $1/2$-inch cubes. Drizzle with the remaining balsamic vinegar.

In a saucepan, bring the broth to a boil, then reduce the heat to low and keep the broth just below a simmer.

In a large saucepan over medium heat, warm the butter and remaining tablespoon of olive oil. Stir in the shallot and garlic and cook, stirring occasionally, until tender, about 3 minutes. Add the rice and cook, stirring, for 2 more minutes.

Pour the wine into the pan and stir until it is absorbed. Add the broth, $1/2$ cup at a time, stirring after each addition until the liquid is practically absorbed. After 20 minutes, taste a grain of rice. Continue to add broth and cook, if necessary, until the rice is tender and creamy yet still slightly firm at the center. The total cooking time should be about 25 minutes. Stir in half the grilled vegetables, the cheese, and the chopped basil and season with salt and pepper to taste. Remove from the heat.

Serve the risotto topped with the remaining vegetables and basil sprigs and pass grated cheese alongside.

# Roasted Winter Vegetable Risotto

Adding roasted seasonal vegetables turns risotto into a substantial and warming main course. The creamy rice is a nice foil for the hearty flavors of sage, nutty roasted Brussels sprouts, and caramelized butternut squash. All together the vegetables make this a particularly robust and richly hued risotto.

SERVES 4 TO 6

$^1/_2$ small butternut squash, peeled, seeded, and cut into $^1/_2$-inch cubes (about 2 cups)

1 pint (about 10 ounces) Brussels sprouts, trimmed and quartered

$3^1/_2$ tablespoons extra virgin olive oil

Coarse sea salt or kosher salt and freshly ground black pepper

3 large carrots, peeled and sliced crosswise $^1/_4$ inch thick

1 medium onion, diced

5 to 6 cups vegetable or chicken broth (reduced-sodium if canned)

2 tablespoons unsalted butter

2 cups Italian risotto rice such as Arborio, Vialone, or Carnaroli

$^1/_2$ cup dry white wine

$^1/_2$ cup grated Parmesan cheese, plus additional for serving

$^1/_4$ cup chopped fresh flat-leaf parsley

2 tablespoons chopped fresh sage

Preheat the oven to 500°F. In a large rimmed baking pan, toss the butternut squash and Brussels sprouts with $1^1/_2$ tablespoons of the olive oil and a large pinch of salt and pepper. Spread them out in one layer. Put the carrots and onion in 2 separate baking pans (pie plates or cake pans will also work well here) and toss each with $^1/_2$ tablespoon of the olive oil and salt and pepper to taste. Spread the pieces out in one layer.

Place all the vegetables in the oven and roast, tossing them every 5 minutes, until browned and tender. This should take about 12 minutes for the onion, 15 minutes for the Brussels sprouts and squash, and about 20 to 25 minutes for the carrots. Transfer the pans with the vegetables to wire racks to cook.

In a saucepan, bring the broth to a boil, then reduce the heat to low and keep the broth just below a simmer.

In a large saucepan over medium heat, melt the butter with the remaining tablespoon of olive oil. Add the rice and cook, stirring, for 2 minutes.

Pour the wine into the pan and stir until it is absorbed. Add the broth, $1/2$ cup at a time, stirring after each addition until the liquid is practically absorbed. After 20 minutes, taste a grain of rice. Continue to add broth and cook, if necessary, until the rice is tender and creamy yet still slightly firm at the center. The total cooking time should be about 25 minutes. Stir in half the roasted vegetables, the cheese, and the herbs and season with salt and pepper to taste. Remove from the heat.

Serve the risotto topped with the remaining vegetables and pass grated cheese alongside.

# Grilled or Roasted Shrimp Risotto

Firm, smoky shrimp and cubes of juicy ripe tomato turn a simple risotto into a very elegant first or main course. If there should be leftovers, form them into patties, dredge them in flour, and pan-fry them to make out-of-this-world risotto cakes.

SERVES 6

24 large shrimp (about 1 1/2 pounds), peeled and deveined, tails left on

2 tablespoons extra virgin olive oil

Coarse sea or kosher salt and freshly ground black pepper

6 cups chicken or vegetable broth (reduced-sodium if canned)

1 tablespoon fresh thyme leaves

3 tablespoons unsalted butter

1/2 cup chopped onion

1 large garlic clove, minced

2 cups Arborio rice

1/2 cup dry white wine

1 large ripe tomato, seeded and diced

1/2 cup grated Parmesan cheese

1/2 cup chopped fresh flat-leaf parsley

Light the grill or preheat the oven to 500°F. Toss the shrimp with 1 tablespoon of the olive oil and a pinch of salt and pepper.

*On the Grill*   Place the shrimp in a grilling basket in one layer and grill until the shells turn pink, about 2 minutes on each side.

*In the Oven*   Place the shrimp in one layer on a baking sheet and roast until the shells turn pink, about 2 minutes on each side.

Roughly chop 12 of the shrimp, leaving the other 12 whole. Cover to keep warm.

In a saucepan, bring the broth and thyme to a boil, then reduce the heat to low and keep the broth just below a simmer.

In a large saucepan over medium heat, melt the butter. Add the onion and garlic and cook, stirring, until softened but not colored, about 5 minutes. Add the rice, turn the heat to medium-high, and continue to cook and stir for 1 to 2 minutes, stirring to coat the grains well.

Pour the wine into the pan and stir until it is absorbed. Add the broth, $1/2$ cup at a time, stirring after each addition until the liquid is practically absorbed. After 20 minutes, taste a grain of rice. Continue to add broth and cook, if necessary, until the rice is tender and creamy yet still slightly firm at the center. The total cooking time should be about 25 minutes. Stir in the chopped shrimp, tomato, and cheese and season with salt and pepper. Remove from the heat.

Place the remaining 12 whole shrimp in a skillet with the remaining tablespoon of olive oil and cook, stirring, over high heat until warmed through, about 2 minutes.

Divide the risotto among 6 bowls and garnish each with 2 whole shrimp and the chopped parsley. Serve immediately.

# Seared Polenta Squares with Spicy Broccoli Rabe

Squares of firm cornmeal polenta really benefit from a quick sear on the grill or in the oven. The squares crisp and caramelize at the edges, while the centers remain soft and creamy. Here I top them with a spicy, slightly bitter sauté of broccoli rabe and plenty of garlic, with a shower of grated mozzarella cheese. It's a terrific combination of flavors and makes a very substantial side dish. In fact this recipe could also serve as the main attraction for any vegetarians at the table (just remember to cook the polenta in vegetable broth or water!). If you're deciding between the 2 polenta dishes in the book, keep in mind that this one is more hearty and pungent, while the corn and scallion polenta is sweeter, and its mild corn flavor gets a tang from melted Parmesan.

SERVES 6

I quart chicken or vegetable broth (reduced-sodium if canned) or water

I cup instant polenta (see Note)

1 1/2 cups grated Parmesan cheese

1/2 teaspoon coarse sea or kosher salt, plus additional to taste

1/4 teaspoon freshly ground black pepper, plus additional to taste

1 1/2 pounds broccoli rabe, trimmed

3 tablespoons extra virgin olive oil

3 garlic cloves, thinly sliced

1 1/2 teaspoons hot red pepper flakes or to taste

2 tablespoons unsalted butter, melted, or extra virgin olive oil

I cup grated fresh mozzarella cheese (about 1/4 pound)

Bring the broth to a boil in a medium saucepan. Turn the heat down to medium and add the polenta in a thin stream, stirring constantly with a whisk. Continue cooking, whisking all the while, until the polenta is quite thick, about 5 minutes. Remove from the heat, stir in 1/2 cup of the Parmesan, and season with the salt and pepper (add extra salt to taste if using water to cook the polenta). Pour into a 9 × 13-inch baking pan, smoothing the top with a rubber spatula, and allow to cool, about 30 minutes. At this point the polenta can be covered with plastic wrap and refrigerated for up to 2 days.

Bring a large pot of salted water to a boil. Fill a bowl with water and ice. Blanch the broccoli rabe in the boiling water until crisp-tender, about 1 minute. Drain and cool in the ice water. Drain well and coarsely chop.

Warm the olive oil in a large pan over medium heat. Add the garlic and cook until fragrant, about 30 seconds. Add the broccoli rabe and red pepper flakes and toss to coat with the oil. Add $\frac{1}{2}$ cup water and simmer, covered, for 2 minutes. Uncover and continue to simmer if the broccoli rabe is too soupy. Season with salt to taste.

Light the grill or preheat the broiler. Cut the chilled polenta into 6 portions and brush them with the melted butter.

*On the Grill*   Lay the polenta out on the grill and cook until sear lines appear, about 2 to 3 minutes. Use a spatula to flip the polenta and cook until seared on the second side, about 2 minutes longer.

*In the Oven*   Lay the polenta on a baking sheet and broil, 5 inches from the heat source, turning once, until the polenta is golden and slightly crisp on the outside and thoroughly warmed, about 10 minutes.

Combine the remaining cup of Parmesan with the mozzarella. Lay the polenta in a large pan and top with the broccoli rabe mixture. Sprinkle the cheeses over all and return to the broiler or a covered grill until the cheese is melted and bubbling.

**NOTE**   You can buy instant polenta in many large supermarkets and gourmet shops. If you can't find it, substitute fine yellow cornmeal.

# Seared Polenta Squares with Corn & Scallions

This polenta dish has the same crisp-around-the-edges, soft-in-the-center appeal of the previous one, but with a mellower topping of succulent summer corn, scallions, and tangy Parmesan cheese.

SERVES 6

**I quart chicken or vegetable broth (reduced-sodium if canned) or water**

**I cup instant polenta (see Note, page 87)**

**$^3/_4$ cup grated Parmesan cheese (about 3 ounces)**

**$^1/_2$ teaspoon coarse sea or kosher salt, plus additional to taste**

**$^1/_4$ teaspoon freshly ground black pepper, plus additional to taste**

**4 tablespoons unsalted butter, melted, or extra virgin olive oil**

**I cup corn kernels, scraped from 2 ears**

**$^1/_2$ cup sliced scallion**

**$^1/_4$ cup shredded fresh basil or mint**

Bring the broth to a boil in a medium saucepan. Turn the heat down to medium and add the polenta in a thin stream, stirring constantly with a whisk. Continue cooking, whisking all the while, until the polenta is quite thick, about 5 minutes. Remove from the heat, stir in $^1/_2$ cup of the Parmesan, and season with the salt and pepper (add extra salt to taste if using water to cook the polenta). Pour into a 9 × 13-inch baking pan, smoothing the top with a rubber spatula, and allow to cool, about 30 minutes. At this point the polenta can be covered with plastic wrap and refrigerated for up to 2 days.

Light the grill or preheat the broiler. Cut the chilled polenta into 6 portions and brush them with 2 tablespoons of the melted butter.

*On the Grill*　　Lay the polenta out on the grill and cook until sear lines appear, about 2 to 3 minutes. Use a spatula to flip the polenta and cook until seared on the second side, about 2 minutes longer.

*In the Oven*　　Lay the polenta on a baking sheet and broil, 5 inches from the heat source, turning once, until the polenta is golden and slightly crisp on the outside and thoroughly warmed, about 10 minutes.

Meanwhile, in a small skillet over medium heat, melt the remaining 2 tablespoons butter and add the corn and scallions. Season with salt and pepper to taste and cook, stirring, for 1 to 2 minutes. Serve the polenta squares topped with the corn and scallions and sprinkled with the remaining $1/4$ cup Parmesan cheese and fresh basil or mint.

CHILI-RUBBED CHICKEN FINGERS WITH
MOLASSES & BRANDY DIPPING SAUCE

CHOPPED CHICKEN SALAD WITH
GRILLED OR ROASTED VEGETABLES

HERBED CHICKEN SALAD WITH
BASIL-CHIVE VINAIGRETTE

ROASTED CHICKEN WITH
TOMATO & TARRAGON

ROASTED CHICKEN WITH TEN HERBS

# 5 *Poultry*

CRISP SPICY CHICKEN WINGS

ROASTED SPICE-RUBBED
CHICKEN UNDER A BRICK

CHICKEN WITH CIPOLLINI

CHICKEN BREASTS WITH CIDER GLAZE
& GRILLED APPLES

CHICKEN BREASTS WITH GRAINY
MUSTARD, ALMONDS, & THYME

HOT-SMOKED CHICKEN BREASTS
WITH BALSAMIC MARINADE
& ONION-PARSLEY RELISH

QUAIL WITH BACON, SAGE,
& CAMEMBERT

DUCK BREASTS WITH TANGERINE &
ARUGULA SALAD

TURKEY BREAST PAILLARDES WITH
BLACK PEPPER, SAGE, & GARLIC

# Chili-Rubbed Chicken Fingers with Molasses & Brandy Dipping Sauce

Sweet and a little spicy, these sataylike skewers are a fun main course or the perfect party hors d'oeuvres that everyone will love, including kids. Make sure you use fresh chili powder so they have some oomph.

If you use wooden skewers, don't forget to soak them for at least an hour before cooking.

MAKES ABOUT 30 SKEWERS, SERVING 4 TO 6 AS A MAIN COURSE

$3^1/_2$ pounds boneless, skinless chicken breasts

1 tablespoon ground cumin

1 tablespoon chili powder

$^1/_2$ teaspoon coarse sea salt or kosher salt, plus additional to taste

Freshly ground black pepper

$^1/_2$ cup light molasses

3 tablespoons brandy

2 bunches scallions, trimmed and sliced into 6-inch lengths

1 tablespoon extra virgin olive oil

Rinse the chicken and pat dry with paper towels. Cut the chicken breasts lengthwise into $^1/_2$-inch-thick strips.

In a medium bowl, combine the cumin, chili powder, salt, and a good amount of pepper. Add the chicken breast strips and toss until thoroughly coated. Cover the bowl with plastic wrap and refrigerate for at least 1 hour and preferably 4 hours or overnight.

Light the grill or preheat the broiler. In a small saucepan, bring the molasses and brandy to a boil, stirring. Thread the chicken strips onto skewers using 1 skewer per strip. Brush them all over with the molasses mixture.

Put the scallions in a bowl and toss them with the olive oil and a pinch of salt and pepper.

*On the Grill*  Spread the scallions and skewered chicken on the grill and cook until they both are browned around the edges and the chicken is cooked through, about $1\frac{1}{2}$ minutes per side.

*In the Oven*  Spread the scallions in a pan and place it 4 inches away from the heat source. Broil until browned and tender, about $2\frac{1}{2}$ minutes. Remove from the oven and tent with foil to keep warm. Put the skewered chicken in a pan and broil, turning once, until it is cooked through and browned around the edges, about 3 minutes.

Serve the chicken with the scallions, drizzling additional molasses-brandy glaze over all.

# Chopped Chicken Salad with Grilled or Roasted Vegetables

You'll find no mayo in this colorful, brightly flavored chicken salad. A takeoff on Cobb salad, studded with avocado, bacon, and blue cheese, it's dressed with a zesty lemon and mustard vinaigrette. A great way to feed a crowd, this is also the perfect dish if you like to get your cooking done in advance, since the chicken and vegetables can be grilled or broiled up to a day ahead of time. Serve this as a main course or part of a buffet for brunch or lunch.

SERVES 6

3 boneless, skinless chicken breast halves (1$\frac{1}{2}$ to 2 pounds)

$\frac{1}{2}$ cup plus 2 tablespoons extra virgin olive oil, plus additional for basting

Coarse sea salt or kosher salt and freshly ground black pepper

2 medium red onions, cut into $\frac{1}{2}$-inch slices

1 large bunch asparagus (about 1 pound), trimmed

$\frac{1}{2}$ pound bacon, diced

3 tablespoons freshly squeezed lemon juice

2$\frac{1}{4}$ teaspoons Dijon mustard

1 head romaine lettuce, tough outer leaves removed and the rest chopped

4 cups mesclun salad mix ($\frac{1}{4}$ pound)

1 avocado, halved, pitted, and diced

$\frac{1}{2}$ cup crumbled Roquefort cheese (about 2$\frac{1}{2}$ ounces)

2 large ripe tomatoes, diced

Preheat the oven to 500°F or preheat the grill. Rinse the chicken and pat dry with paper towels. Lay the chicken breasts on a rimmed baking sheet, brush them on both sides with 2 tablespoons of the oil, and season with salt and pepper to taste. Place the onion slices on a baking sheet, brush them on both sides with $\frac{1}{2}$ tablespoon of the oil, and season with salt and pepper to taste. Toss the asparagus with 1$\frac{1}{2}$ tablespoons of the olive oil and season with salt and pepper to taste.

*In the Oven*  Roast the chicken breasts on the baking sheet, basting with additional olive oil and turning once until they are cooked through, about 15 minutes. Roast the onion slices on the baking sheet, turning once carefully, using tongs to keep the rings intact, until they are charred at the edges and crisp, 10 to 15 minutes. Spread the asparagus out in one layer in a rimmed baking sheet and roast, shaking the pan halfway through, until they are tender and browned at the edges, about 8 to 10 minutes.

*On the Grill*  Place the chicken breasts on the grill and cook, turning once and basting with additional olive oil, until sear lines appear and the chicken is cooked through, about 12 to 15 minutes. Place the onion slices on the grill (or use a grill basket) and cook, turning once carefully, using tongs to keep the rings intact, until sear lines appear, about 8 to 10 minutes. Place the asparagus on the grill (or use a grill basket) and cook, turning once, until they are browned and can be pierced with a knife, about 8 minutes.

When the chicken is cool enough to handle, chop it into $^3/_4$-inch pieces.

Cook the bacon in a large pan over high heat until crisp. Use a slotted spoon to transfer the bacon to a paper towel–lined plate.

In a small bowl, whisk together the lemon juice and mustard. Season with a pinch of salt and pepper and drizzle in the remaining 6 tablespoons oil, whisking constantly. Add more salt and pepper to taste if necessary.

Toss the romaine and mesclun with enough vinaigrette to coat the leaves, then divide among 6 plates. Lay the asparagus, onions, chicken, bacon, avocado, Roquefort, and tomatoes across the salad greens. Drizzle with additional vinaigrette and serve.

# Herbed Chicken Salad with Basil-Chive Vinaigrette

This refined chicken salad incorporates plenty of salad greens and an intense, bright green herb vinaigrette. The grilled chicken works really well in this recipe, but you can also use the vinaigrette as a sauce or marinade for other grilled meats, fish, or poultry or as a dressing on other salads or on grilled vegetables. If you like, toss this salad with any of the following: cherry tomatoes, avocado, bell pepper, bacon, cheese, croutons, or nuts.

SERVES 4

**4 boneless, skinless chicken breast halves (about 2$^{1}$/4 pounds)**

**$^{3}$/4 cup plus 2 tablespoons extra virgin olive oil**

**1 large shallot, thinly sliced**

**Grated zest and juice of 1 lemon**

**Coarse sea salt or kosher salt and freshly ground black pepper**

**1 cup fresh basil, all but the smallest leaves torn**

**$^{1}$/2 cup fresh chives in 2-inch lengths**

**1 garlic clove, peeled**

**4 cups arugula**

Rinse the chicken and pat dry with paper towels. Place the chicken in a large bowl and toss it with 2 tablespoons of the olive oil, the shallot, lemon zest, and salt and pepper to taste. Cover the bowl and let sit at room temperature for 30 minutes or refrigerate for 2 hours or overnight.

Light the grill or preheat the broiler. To make the vinaigrette, place $^{1}$/2 cup of the basil and $^{1}$/4 cup of the chives in the bowl of a blender or food processor. Add the lemon juice, garlic clove, and a large pinch of salt and pepper and puree until smooth. With the motor running, drizzle in the remaining $^{3}$/4 cup olive oil and puree until incorporated. Add more salt and pepper if desired.

*On the Grill*  Lay the marinated chicken breasts on the grill and cook, turning once, until they are well seared on both sides and cooked through, about 15 minutes.

*(continued)*

Roasted Oysters with
Shallots & Herbs, page 20

Grilled or Roasted Asparagus
with Scallions & Fried Eggs, page 34

Spicy Potato Salad with Sweet & Hot Peppers, page 28

Charred Yellow Tomato Soup, page 48

Creamy Mushroom Soup, page 60

Crisp Penne with Ricotta,
Roasted Tomatoes, & Herbs, page 72

Seared Polenta Squares with
Spicy Broccoli Rabe, page 86

Roasted Chicken
with Ten Herbs, page 100

Crisp Spicy Chicken
Wings, page 103

*In the Oven*  Place the marinated chicken breasts on the broiler pan and broil, 4 inches from the heat, turning once, until cooked through, about 15 minutes.

Slice the chicken diagonally into $1/4$-inch strips. Place the arugula in a large salad bowl with the remaining basil and chives and toss with enough of the vinaigrette to coat the leaves. Divide among 4 salad plates, top with the chicken slices, either warm or at room temperature, and drizzle with additional vinaigrette.

# Roasted Chicken with Tomato & Tarragon

This roast chicken has the compelling summery flavors of sweet tomatoes, herbs, and wine, mellowed with a little butter. It's different and a little lighter than your average roasted chicken, usually cooked with hearty winter root vegetables like carrots and potatoes. I like to make this in late summer or early fall if it's too rainy to cook outside.

SERVES 4

1 chicken (about 3$^{1}/_{2}$ pounds)

1 bunch fresh tarragon, leaves chopped and stems reserved

2 shallots, peeled

1 small head garlic, root end sliced off to expose the cloves

2 tablespoons unsalted butter, softened, plus 1$^{1}/_{2}$ tablespoons, cubed

Coarse sea salt or kosher salt and freshly ground black pepper

1 cup canned whole peeled tomatoes, chopped, liquid reserved

$^{1}/_{2}$ cup chicken broth (reduced-sodium if canned)

$^{1}/_{4}$ cup dry white wine

2 tablespoons tarragon vinegar

Preheat the oven to 500°F. Rinse the chicken and pat dry with paper towels. Stuff the chicken with the tarragon stems, shallots, and garlic. Rub the chicken with the softened butter, sprinkle with 2 teaspoons of the chopped tarragon, and season generously with salt and pepper.

Place the chicken breast up on a rack in a flameproof roasting pan and roast for 15 minutes. Reduce the temperature to 325°F and cook for another 30 minutes. Transfer the chicken to a plate, cover loosely with foil, and set aside. Turn the oven back up to 500°F.

Take the roasting rack out of the pan and set it aside. Skim the fat from the juices in the roasting pan and place the pan on top of the stove over medium-high heat. Add the tomatoes and their liquid, the broth, wine, tarragon vinegar, and 2 tablespoons of the remaining chopped tarragon and bring to a boil. Use a wooden spoon to scrape the bottom and sides of the pan, loosening the caramelized juices. Let boil until the mixture is thick and saucy, about 10 minutes.

Stir the cubed butter into the sauce. Place the roasting rack back in the pan and put the chicken back on the rack. Pour any juices that have collected on the plate into the pan. Return the pan to the oven for 15 minutes, basting every 5 minutes. Serve the chicken with the sauce, garnished with more of the tarragon.

# Roasted Chicken with Ten Herbs

This is the ultimate roast chicken, golden brown with a crackling skin. The herb butter permeates the meat and really infuses the bird with its intense flavor. Then, as the butter melts, it bastes the chicken, keeping it very moist.

You can roast the chicken by itself or throw in some vegetables for a one-pan meal. Bell pepper slices, onion wedges, halved fingerling potatoes, carrot coins, zucchini sticks, and fennel pieces are all great additions. Add them to the pan along with the chicken broth.

SERVES 4

**I chicken (about 3 1/2 pounds)**

**Coarse sea salt or kosher salt and freshly ground black pepper**

**1/2 cup plus 2 tablespoons Ten-Herb Butter (recipe follows), softened**

**Reserved herb stems from the Ten-Herb Butter**

**1/2 cup chicken broth (reduced-sodium if canned)**

**1/4 cup dry white wine**

**2 tablespoons chopped fresh herbs (use some of the same herbs used for the Ten-Herb Butter)**

Rinse the chicken and pat dry with paper towels. Season the chicken all over with salt and pepper. Place the chicken on its back. Using a small, sharp knife, make 6 incisions into the bird: one in the meaty part of each drumstick (go through the flesh), one at the joints of the thighs (go under the skin), and two under the skin of the breasts (one cut on each side). Turn the chicken onto its breast and make two more incisions, one on the upper part of each thigh going into the back of the chicken.

Place 1/2 cup of the herb butter in a heavy-duty resealable plastic bag. Snip off one corner of the bag and use it like a pastry bag. Squeeze the butter from the opening into the incisions in the chicken (try to use an equal amount in each incision). Massage the herb butter into the chicken.

Stuff the cavity with the reserved herb stems. Rub the remaining 2 tablespoons herb butter all over the outside of the chicken.

Using a piece of kitchen string, truss the chicken, beginning at the neck and ty-ing the legs together. Place the chicken in a bowl and cover. Let the chicken marinate in the refrigerator for at least 4 hours or overnight.

Preheat the oven to 450°F. Place the chicken on a rack in a roasting pan, breast side up. Roast the chicken for 25 minutes. Turn the oven down to 300°F and add the chicken broth and wine to the pan. Roast the chicken for another 25 to 30 minutes. Turn the oven off and let the chicken rest inside it for another 15 to 20 minutes.

Remove the chicken from the oven and pour the juices into a bowl. Skim the fat off the juices and reserve them.

Carve the chicken into 8 pieces. Garnish with the chopped fresh herbs. Serve with the pan juices.

## Ten-Herb Butter

Extra herb butter can be frozen. It's also great on pasta, vegetables, leftover chicken sandwiches, or you can save it for the next time you make Roasted Chicken with Ten Herbs. You don't have to use ten herbs here if you don't have them, but be sure to use at least five, including rosemary, basil, parsley, tarragon, and thyme.

MAKES 2 1/4 CUPS

**I pound unsalted butter at room temperature**

**1/2 cup chopped fresh flat-leaf parsley leaves, stems reserved**

**2 tablespoons snipped fresh chives**

**I tablespoon freshly squeezed lemon juice**

**1/2 tablespoon truffle oil (optional)**

**1/2 tablespoon chopped fresh chervil leaves, stems reserved**

**1/2 tablespoon chopped fresh cilantro leaves, stems reserved**

*(continued)*

$^1/_2$ tablespoon chopped fresh basil leaves

$^1/_2$ tablespoon chopped fresh mint

I teaspoon minced shallot

I teaspoon minced garlic

I teaspoon minced seeded jalapeño pepper

I teaspoon coarse sea salt or kosher salt

$^1/_2$ teaspoon freshly ground black pepper

$^1/_2$ teaspoon chopped fresh sage leaves, stems reserved

$^1/_2$ teaspoon chopped fresh tarragon leaves, stems reserved

$^1/_2$ teaspoon chopped fresh oregano leaves, stems reserved

$^1/_4$ teaspoon chopped fresh rosemary leaves, stems reserved

Place all the ingredients, except for the herb stems (reserve those for the chicken), in the bowl of a food processor. Process until well blended. Alternately, mix the ingredients together with a rubber spatula until smooth.

# Crisp Spicy Chicken Wings

These wings are a fusing of two inspirations—the more obvious Buffalo wings and also the salt-baked Chinese shrimp I love to eat as a snack, which are crisp and spicy and served on lettuce leaves. Here the spiciness comes from roasting the chicken wings with red pepper flakes, then tossing them with fresh sliced jalapeños. Rice vinegar and scallions offset the fire, and when you eat the crisp wings with lettuce leaves the sauce from the chicken dresses the leaves. I like to place a pile of lettuce leaves beside the wings so that people can pick the chicken up with the lettuce, using it as an edible napkin. Serve these as a snack or hors d'oeuvre or as part of a buffet, either hot or at room temperature. You can modify the spiciness by adding more or less red pepper flakes, and chile lovers can pick up a wing with a few more jalapeño slices, while others can always shake some of the chiles off.

SERVES 4

**4 pounds chicken wings**

**4 teaspoons extra virgin olive oil**

**2 teaspoons hot red pepper flakes**

**Coarse sea salt or kosher salt and freshly ground black pepper**

**$1/2$ cup chopped scallions (white and tender green parts)**

**4 jalapeño peppers, seeded and diced**

**$1/3$ cup rice vinegar**

**Romaine or iceberg lettuce for serving**

Light the grill or preheat the oven to 500°F. Rinse the chicken and pat dry with paper towels. Place the chicken wings in a large bowl and sprinkle with the olive oil, red pepper flakes, and a generous pinch of salt and black pepper. Toss well.

*On the Grill*   Lay the wings on the grill and cook for 10 minutes. Turn the wings over and grill until they are crisp and brown, about 10 minutes longer.

*In the Oven*   Spread the wings out in a single layer on a rimmed baking sheet and roast for 10 minutes. Turn the wings over and roast for another 10 minutes.

Transfer the wings to a large bowl. Add the scallions, jalapeños, and rice vinegar. Toss well, season with salt to taste, and serve on lettuce leaves.

# Roasted Spice-Rubbed Chicken Under a Brick

This chicken is incredibly crispy and intensely flavorful, making it an exciting alternative to milder roast chicken recipes. Weighting the chicken ensures that each piece is of the same thickness, so they cook quickly and evenly. The weight also causes the fat under the skin to render, melting out and leaving the skin deliciously crisp. But first the chicken marinates for 12 hours in a dry rub of cumin, cinnamon, allspice, and turmeric, and the spices permeate the meat so well that no sauce is necessary. I arrived at this mix of spices through trial and error, and it ended up with a Moroccan flavor that's great with steamed couscous. I also like to serve it with salad and plain polenta or, better yet, Seared Polenta Squares with Spicy Broccoli Rabe (page 86).

When you buy the chicken for this recipe, ask your butcher to remove the back and breast bones and halve the bird so that there is a drumstick and wing on each side. And don't worry if you can't find a brick—a big casserole on a baking sheet will work too.

SERVES 4

1 whole chicken (about 3 1/2 pounds), halved, back and breast bones removed (leave the rib bones)

1 tablespoon ground cumin

1 tablespoon coarse sea salt or kosher salt

1/2 tablespoon ground cinnamon

1/2 tablespoon ground allspice

1/2 tablespoon freshly ground black pepper

1/2 tablespoon ground turmeric

2 tablespoons extra virgin olive oil

Chopped fresh cilantro for garnish

Lemon wedges for serving

Rinse the chicken and pat dry with paper towels. In a bowl, mix together the cumin, salt, cinnamon, allspice, pepper, and turmeric. Pat the mixture onto the chicken and wrap it tightly in plastic wrap. Refrigerate for 12 hours.

Remove the chicken from the refrigerator 1 hour before cooking. Place a 14-inch skillet or heavy-duty roasting or baking pan in the oven, along with 2 foil-wrapped bricks, and preheat the oven to 500°F for 15 minutes.

Rub the chicken with the olive oil and press it flat. Wearing oven mitts, remove the pan from the oven and press the chicken, skin side down, on the pan. Place a brick on top of each chicken half. (Instead of the foil-wrapped bricks, you can preheat another baking sheet and/or a heavy heatproof object such as a thick cast-iron skillet to use as a weight. Place the baking sheet on top of the chicken and weigh it down with the weight.) Roast for 30 minutes. Garnish the chicken with cilantro and serve with lemon wedges.

# Chicken with Cipollini

Cipollini are like flat, slightly larger pearl onions, and they tend to have a stronger onion flavor. In tandem with herbs, the cipollini elevate roast chicken legs and thighs to a dish worthy of company. This is great any time of year—Marina, a five-year-old friend of Melissa's, would like to eat it every day of the year.

SERVES 4

4 chicken legs and 4 thighs (about 2$^{1}$/4 pounds)

$^{1}$/2 cup chopped fresh oregano, plus additional for garnish

2 tablespoons freshly squeezed lemon juice

4 garlic cloves, minced

Coarse sea salt or kosher salt and freshly ground black pepper

$^{1}$/3 cup extra virgin olive oil, plus additional for grilling

1 pound cipollini, peeled (see Note)

1 cup chicken broth (reduced-sodium if canned) or water

$^{1}$/2 cup dry white wine

Chopped fresh flat-leaf parsley for garnish

Rinse the chicken and pat dry with paper towels. In a large bowl, combine the oregano, lemon juice, and garlic and season with a large pinch of salt and pepper. Whisk in the olive oil. Add the chicken and cipollini to the bowl and toss to coat. Cover the bowl with plastic wrap and refrigerate for 2 to 4 hours.

Preheat the oven to 500°F or preheat the grill.

*In the Oven*  Place the chicken, skin side up, in a flameproof roasting pan. Scatter the cipollini around the chicken. Roast for 20 minutes. Add the broth and wine to the pan and roast for 10 minutes more. If the pan juices are too thin, remove the chicken and cipollini from the roasting pan, place the pan on the stove over high heat, and let the juices simmer until slightly thickened. Season with salt and pepper.

*On the Grill*  Place the cipollini in a grill basket. Lay the chicken and cipollini on the grill and cook, turning, until the cipollini begin to brown and the chicken is cooked through (about 10 minutes for the cipollini and 25 minutes for the chicken). Place the grilled cipollini in a saucepan and add the broth and wine. Bring the mixture to a simmer over medium heat and cook until reduced by half, about 10 minutes. Season with salt and pepper.

Serve the chicken and cipollini drizzled with the sauce and sprinkled with parsley and oregano.

NOTE    The easiest way to peel cipollini is to blanch them in boiling water for 30 seconds, drain, let cool, then slip off their skins.

# Chicken Breasts with Cider Glaze & Grilled Apples

Served with apples and cider simmered until syrupy, chicken is given a classic fall spin in this recipe. But unlike other dishes in this vein, the result isn't overly sweet, since the Granny Smith apples and cider vinegar contribute a forceful tang. Made on the grill, the apples gain a deep savory smokiness, whereas they are softer and sweeter when roasted—but either technique yields absolutely delicious results.

SERVES 4 TO 6

**6 cups apple cider**

**$^2$/$_3$ cup cider vinegar**

**I cinnamon stick**

**$^1$/$_4$ teaspoon freshly ground black pepper, plus additional to taste**

**3 whole chicken breasts**

**Coarse sea salt or kosher salt**

**3 Granny Smith apples, cored and peeled**

Preheat the oven to 500°F or preheat the grill. Combine the cider, vinegar, and cinnamon stick in a saucepan over medium-high heat and season with the pepper. Bring the liquid to a boil. Lower the heat and simmer until the liquid is reduced to 1$^1$/$_4$ cups and has a syrupy consistency, about 50 minutes. Discard the cinnamon stick.

Rinse the chicken and pat dry with paper towels. Place the chicken breasts in a bowl, season with salt and pepper, and drizzle $^2$/$_3$ cup of the cider glaze over them; toss to coat.

*In the Oven*　Place the chicken breasts, skin side down, in a large roasting pan. Cut the apples into eighths, toss with I tablespoon of the cider glaze, and arrange around the chicken. Roast for 15 minutes, then gently turn the chicken and apples over and brush the chicken with more of the cider glaze. Reduce the oven temperature to 400°F and roast for 15 minutes more, until the apples are tender and the chicken is crisp and cooked through.

*On the Grill*  Lay the chicken breasts on the grill, skin side down, and cook, covered, until well seared, about 8 to 10 minutes. Turn the breasts, brush them with more of the cider glaze, and grill for another 10 minutes, until crisp and cooked through. Meanwhile, slice the apples into $1/2$-inch rounds and brush them with glaze. Grill the apples, turning once, until they are tender, about 7 to 10 minutes.

To serve, bring the remaining cider glaze to a simmer and cook for 2 minutes. Halve the chicken breasts and serve them with some of the apples, drizzled with additional glaze.

# Chicken Breasts with Grainy Mustard, Almonds, & Thyme

What may at first seem like an unusual combination of mustard and almonds becomes a crisp, tasty crust that rivals the crunch of fried chicken. Using chicken breasts on the bone ensures that the meat will stay moist and flavorful as the skin browns.

SERVES 4 TO 6

1/4 cup whole-grain mustard

1/4 cup Dijon mustard

2 tablespoons fresh thyme leaves, finely chopped, plus additional sprigs for garnish

1/4 teaspoon freshly ground black pepper, plus additional to taste

1/2 cup extra virgin olive oil

3 whole chicken breasts

Coarse sea salt or kosher salt

1/2 cup sliced almonds, toasted (see sidebar), for garnish

In a very large bowl, whisk together the mustards, chopped thyme, and pepper with 2 tablespoons water. Whisk in the olive oil. Place the chicken breasts in the bowl and toss to coat. Cover the bowl and let sit at room temperature for 30 minutes (or refrigerate for 2 hours or overnight).

Preheat the oven to 500°F or light the grill. Rinse the chicken and pat dry with paper towels. Season the chicken with salt and pepper.

*In the Oven*  Lay the chicken breasts skin side down in a roasting pan. Roast for about 25 minutes, turning once and basting with marinade, until the chicken is crisp and cooked through.

*On the Grill*  Lay the chicken breasts on the grill, skin side down, and cook, covered, until well seared, about 8 minutes. Turn the breasts, brush them with more of the marinade, and grill for another 10 minutes, until crisp and cooked through.

To serve, halve the chicken breasts and serve them garnished with the almonds and thyme sprigs and sprinkled with salt.

*Toasting Almonds* An easy way to toast almonds is on top of the stove in a skillet. Spread $1/2$ cup almonds in a large skillet and place over high heat. Cook, stirring constantly, until the nuts are fragrant and browned, about 3 minutes. Immediately pour the almonds onto a plate to stop the cooking.

# Hot-Smoked Chicken Breasts with Balsamic Marinade & Onion-Parsley Relish

The sweet balsamic and bold smoky flavors permeating these moist, boneless chicken breasts defy their usual bland stereotype. This recipe uses hot smoking as a way to create a new level of flavor. Plus, cooking the chicken over indirect heat ensures that it will retain its juiciness, instead of becoming dry and rubbery. Leftovers are incredible in chicken sandwiches or on pasta salads or green salads.

SERVES 4

**For the Chicken**

**4 boneless, skinless chicken breast halves (about 2$^1$/4 pounds)**

**$^1$/2 Spanish onion, thinly sliced**

**3 garlic cloves, minced**

**$^3$/4 cup balsamic vinegar**

**$^1$/4 cup extra virgin olive oil**

**Coarse sea salt or kosher salt and freshly ground black pepper**

**For the Relish**

**I bunch fresh flat-leaf parsley, chopped**

**I medium red onion, thinly sliced**

**I teaspoon minced garlic**

**3 tablespoons balsamic vinegar**

**3 tablespoons extra virgin olive oil**

Rinse the chicken and pat dry with paper towels. To prepare the marinade, mix together in a bowl the onion, garlic, vinegar, olive oil, and generous pinches of salt and pepper. Add the chicken breasts and turn to coat them in the marinade. Cover and refrigerate for at least 2 hours and preferably 8 hours or overnight.

An hour before serving, prepare the relish. In a bowl, toss together the parsley, onion, garlic, vinegar, and olive oil. Let sit at room temperature for at least I hour.

If grilling over coals, light the grill using plenty of charcoal. If using firewood, add it now and let the wood and charcoal burn for about an hour, or until most of the firewood is burned up; you'll be left with some ash and the charcoal. If using wood chips, soak them for at least 20 minutes, then add them to the coals after they are completely gray. Let the chips burn for 10 minutes. Move the charcoal and wood over to one side of the grill for indirect grilling. If using a gas grill, preheat the grill thoroughly, adding soaked wood chips according to the manufacturer's instructions. When the grill is hot and smoky, turn off the fire under half of the grill.

Remove the chicken from the marinade and place on the grill over the side without the heat. Baste with marinade, cover the grill, and let smoke for 15 minutes. Baste again, turn, and grill for another 10 to 15 minutes, until the chicken is cooked through.

Serve the chicken with the onion-parsley relish.

# Quail with Bacon, Sage, & Camembert

Quail is a small bird that makes a big impression. It's got a sweet, mellow flavor that's slightly gamy and assertive enough to stand up to strong ingredients such as bacon, spices, and vinaigrettes. High heat accentuates the quail's sweetness, while a combination of bacon, sage, and cheese ensures that it stays moist and succulent. Stuffing a bit of creamy sheep's milk Camembert into the cavity, along with smoky bacon and a touch of fresh sage, is a simple way to add complexity. If you can't find sheep's milk Camembert, use cow's milk Camembert. It's a little milder than the sheep's milk kind but still sharp enough to do the trick.

SERVES 8 AS AN APPETIZER, 4 AS A MAIN COURSE

8 slices bacon, cooked crisp and drained

8 fresh quail (semiboneless), wing tips cut off (see Note)

1/4 pound ripe Camembert, preferably sheep's milk, cut into 8 pieces

8 large fresh sage leaves plus 1 teaspoon chopped fresh sage

6 tablespoons extra virgin olive oil

Coarse sea salt or kosher salt and freshly ground black pepper

2 teaspoons chopped shallot

3 tablespoons sherry vinegar

2 teaspoons chopped fresh flat-leaf parsley

1 cup diced tomato

Light the grill or preheat the oven to 500°F. Cut 4 of the bacon strips in half crosswise; reserve the other 4 for the vinaigrette. Rinse the quail and pat dry with paper towels. Stuff each quail with 1/2 strip of bacon, a piece of Camembert, and a sage leaf. Place the stuffed quail in a bowl and drizzle with 2 tablespoons of the olive oil. Season with salt and pepper to taste and gently mix to coat the quail.

Prepare the bacon vinaigrette. Chop the remaining bacon. Put the remaining 1/4 cup olive oil and the chopped bacon in a small sauté pan over medium heat. Cook, stirring, for 2 minutes. Add the shallot and cook for another minute. Add the vinegar, chopped sage, and parsley and remove from the heat. Season with salt and pepper to taste.

*On the Grill*    Grill the quail, breast side down, for about 4 minutes. Turn and grill for another 3 to 4 minutes, until the skin is crisp and the juices run clear. Transfer the quail to a platter and let them rest for 2 minutes.

*In the Oven*    Place the quail on a rack in a roasting pan and roast for 10 to 12 minutes, until the skin is crisp and the juices run clear. Transfer the quail to a platter and let them rest for 2 minutes.

Drizzle the quail with the vinaigrette. Garnish with the tomato and serve immediately.

**NOTE**    If you can't find quail in a shop near where you live, you can mail-order it from D'Artagnan, (800) 327–8246.

# Duck Breasts with Tangerine & Arugula Salad

Magrets are oversized duck breasts from the Muscovy duck, the type of duck raised for foie gras, which is fattened duck liver. The very large, meaty breasts are essentially a delicious by-product of the foie gras industry. The duck legs are also used, often for slow-cooked stews or confits, whereas the breasts can be prepared almost like steak, roasted or grilled and served rare.

I use a Japanese approach to flavor the duck in this recipe, combining fresh ginger, garlic, and soy sauce in the marinade, while the accompanying salad of sweet-tart tangerines and sharp arugula is a nod to the French duck à l'orange. Marinating allows these flavors to sink in a little so that when the breasts are cooked the skin gets crisp and the marinade almost caramelizes, creating a flavorful coating. The duck's thick layer of fat keeps the meat extremely moist—even after some of it is cooked out, there will be about 1/4 inch of fat remaining. I love this flavorful layer, but if it bothers you it's easy to remove once the duck is sliced.

If grilling, keep a spray bottle handy for flare-ups.

SERVES 4

2 tablespoons soy sauce

2 tablespoons grated fresh ginger

2 teaspoons minced garlic

1/2 teaspoon freshly ground black pepper, plus additional to taste

4 magret duck breasts

4 tangerines

1 bunch arugula, torn

1/2 teaspoon coarse sea salt or kosher salt

2 tablespoons freshly squeezed lemon juice

2 tablespoons extra virgin olive oil

In a bowl, whisk together the soy sauce, ginger, garlic, and black pepper. Rinse the duck and pat dry with paper towels. Lay the duck breasts in a nonreactive baking dish just large enough to hold them and pour the soy mixture over them. Cover with plastic wrap and let sit at room temperature for 30 minutes or refrigerate for 4 hours or overnight.

Meanwhile, prepare the tangerine salad. Cut the top and bottom off each tangerine and stand it up on a cutting board on one of the flat sides. Using a small knife, cut away the peel and white pith, following the natural curve of the fruit, so that the flesh is completely exposed. Working over a bowl to catch the juices, cut the segments of fruit away from the membranes that connect them. The segments will also fall into the bowl. Add the arugula and season the salad with the salt and black pepper to taste. Drizzle with the lemon juice and toss well. Drizzle the olive oil over all and toss once more. Let rest for 20 minutes.

Preheat the broiler or light the grill. Use a slotted spoon to transfer the tangerine salad to a serving bowl. Strain the liquid through a strainer into a saucepan.

Bring the liquid to a simmer over low heat and cook for about 12 minutes or until reduced by half.

*In the Oven*   Broil the duck breasts, skin side up, until the skin is crisp and brown and the meat is done to taste, about 5 to 7 minutes for rare.

*On the Grill*   Place the duck breasts, skin side down, on the hottest part of the grill and cook until sear marks appear, about 5 minutes. Move the duck breasts to a cooler spot on the side of the grill, turn them skin side up, and finish cooking with the grill covered (keep an eye out for flare-ups), until the meat is done to taste, about another 3 to 5 minutes per side for rare.

Transfer to a board and let rest for 3 to 4 minutes. Carve the duck breasts on a bias into $1/4$-inch-thick slices and arrange them on a platter. Drizzle the duck with the reduced tangerine sauce and serve with the salad.

# Turkey Breast Paillardes with Black Pepper, Sage, & Garlic

These turkey breasts are so thin that they cook in a flash. You can buy thin turkey cutlets precut or simply slice turkey breasts into cutlets, pounding them to an even thickness. The marinade of garlic, pepper, and sage makes them particularly savory, reminiscent of deconstructed turkey with sage stuffing. Get the rest of the meal ready to go before you grill or broil these, since overcooking will rob them of their succulence. I love to serve these with Spicy Potato Salad with Sweet and Hot Peppers (page 28).

SERVES 4

**Eight ¹/₂-inch-thick boneless, skinless turkey breast cutlets (¹/₄ pound each)**

**¹/₄ cup extra virgin olive oil**

**4 garlic cloves, thinly sliced**

**3 tablespoons chopped fresh sage**

**Coarse sea salt or kosher salt and freshly ground black pepper**

**2 tablespoons drained capers for garnish**

**8 lemon wedges for garnish**

Rinse the turkey and pat dry with paper towels. Combine the olive oil, garlic, sage, and a pinch of salt and pepper in a wide, shallow bowl. Mix together using the back of a fork to crush the garlic a bit and blend the flavors. Add the turkey breasts to the marinade and turn to coat. Cover the bowl and let sit at room temperature for 30 minutes or refrigerate for 2 hours or overnight.

Light the grill or preheat the broiler.

*On the Grill*   Lay the turkey breasts on the grill and cook, turning once, until well seared and done in the center, about 5 to 6 minutes.

*In the Oven*   Lay the turkey breasts under the broiler and cook, turning once, until well seared and done in the center, about 5 to 6 minutes.

Serve sprinkled with capers and garnished with lemon wedges.

# 6 *Beef, Pork, & Other Meats*

# Classic Grilled Hamburger with Homemade Ketchup

Call me a purist, but I believe that a great hamburger is nothing more than meat and a little salt. The meat should not just be good-quality beef but what's known as 80/20: ground shoulder or chuck that is 20% fat. Please avoid prepackaged 98% fat-free beef that tastes like cardboard. Hamburgers aren't health food, so if you're going to eat a burger, it should be the most flavorful burger you can get, and that wonderful flavor comes from fat. If you can't buy 80/20, you can have your butcher grind the meat with a little extra fat, putting it through the grinder twice so it is well combined.

For the best burger ever, you'll need a real roll, not the packaged kind. A kaiser roll or Portuguese roll from the bakery section of your supermarket is preferable. Then there's the ketchup, really the jewel of this recipe. It's a slightly sweet, spicy, intensely flavorful sauce that will elevate an already amazing burger to even greater heights. And once you've made it for the burger, you'll have it around to liven up everything from chicken breasts to plain potatoes. Used wherever you'd expect to find bottled ketchup, it will happily surprise everyone who tastes it. It will last several months in the refrigerator.

SERVES 4

**For the Ketchup**
$^1/_2$ cup red wine vinegar

$^1/_4$ cup light molasses

1 teaspoon anchovy paste

1 $^1/_2$ cups tomato juice

2 tablespoons finely chopped red bell pepper

2 tablespoons Dijon mustard

2 garlic cloves, finely chopped

**For the Burgers**
1 $^1/_2$ pounds ground beef

1 teaspoon coarse sea salt or kosher salt, plus additional to taste

$^1/_2$ teaspoon freshly ground black pepper, plus additional to taste

Tomato slices

Red onion slices

Portobello mushroom caps

Extra virgin olive oil

Hamburger rolls

**Slices of sharp Cheddar cheese (optional)**

**Pickles (optional)**

For the ketchup, in a heavy saucepan over medium heat combine the vinegar, molasses, and anchovy paste and bring to a boil. Simmer for 3 to 4 minutes. Add the tomato juice, red bell pepper, mustard, and garlic and bring to a boil. Simmer gently over medium-low heat, stirring and scraping the sides of the pot occasionally, until thick and shiny, about 1 1/2 hours.

Use an immersion blender or a food processor to puree the ketchup and store it in the refrigerator.

Light the grill. To make the burgers, season the meat with the salt and pepper and gently form it into 4 rounded 1 1/2-inch-thick patties. Lightly brush the tomato and onion slices and mushroom caps with olive oil and season with salt and pepper to taste.

Grill the burgers and vegetables until the burgers are done to taste, 4 to 5 minutes per side for rare, and the vegetables are charred, 2 minutes per side for the tomatoes, 4 to 5 for the onions, and about 8 for the mushrooms. Toast the rolls, melting the cheese on them if desired. Serve the burgers topped with the ketchup, vegetables, and pickles if desired.

# Flank Steak with Rosemary & Roasted Garlic

Flank steak cooks quickly, is inexpensive, and has great flavor—all it asks is to be served rare. It really doesn't even need a recipe since it tastes great on its own—just season with salt and pepper, sear the meat on both sides, then slice it on a diagonal against the grain. Marinating the steak overnight in a roasted garlic puree makes this cut even more flavorful, and then a quick rosemary-garlic mustard is all it needs to be the star of a meal or to be made into a sandwich on a roll. Either way, it's great for a crowd if you double the recipe and make two or serve this as part of a cookout with hot dogs and hamburgers going on the grill at the same time.

SERVES 4 TO 6

$1/2$ teaspoon coarse sea salt or kosher salt, plus additional to taste

3 heads garlic, halved

2 tablespoons extra virgin olive oil

Freshly ground black pepper

3 tablespoons chopped fresh rosemary leaves, plus additional sprigs for garnish

I flank steak (I to I $1/2$ pounds)

$1/2$ cup Dijon mustard

Preheat the oven to 400°F. Bring a small pot of salted water to a boil. Add the halved garlic heads and simmer for 5 minutes. Drain well. Place the garlic in a small ovenproof dish and drizzle with the olive oil. Season with salt and pepper to taste. Cover the dish with foil and roast for 5 minutes, then reduce the oven to 325°F and continue to roast until the garlic is completely tender, about 35 to 45 minutes. Microwave the garlic instead if you wish (see sidebar).

Let the garlic cool slightly, then squeeze the cloves from their skins into a small bowl. Use a fork to mash the garlic into a rough puree and stir in the chopped rosemary. Season with the $1/2$ teaspoon salt and plenty of pepper.

Using a sharp knife, lightly score the steak across the grain at $1/4$-inch intervals on both sides. Season the meat all over with salt and pepper. Set aside half of the rosemary-garlic paste and rub the rest all over the steak. Wrap the meat tightly in plastic wrap. If you are pressed for time, let the meat marinate at room temperature for 30 minutes or, preferably, refrigerate it for 4 hours or overnight.

Light the grill or preheat the broiler.

*On the Grill*   Place the meat on the grill and cook for 2 to 3 minutes on each side for rare.

*In the Oven*   Put the meat in a broiler pan and place it as close to the heat source as possible. Broil for 2 to 3 minutes, then turn and cook for another 3 to 5 minutes for rare.

Transfer the steak to a board and let rest for 5 to 10 minutes to allow the steak to reabsorb the juices. Meanwhile, in a small bowl, combine the remaining garlic-rosemary puree with the mustard.

Slice the meat into $1/4$-inch slices on a diagonal across the grain. Serve with the garlic-rosemary mustard, garnished with the rosemary sprigs.

---

*Microwave "Roasted" Garlic*  To microwave garlic, slice the top of the head off to reveal all the cloves. Place the heads in a small, deep microwave-safe dish and drizzle with 2 tablespoons extra virgin olive oil. Season with salt and pepper. Spoon 2 tablespoons water into the bottom of the dish, cover it with plastic wrap, and microwave at medium power for 7 to $7^1/2$ minutes. Let stand for a few minutes.

---

# New York Strip Steaks with Black Pepper, Onions, & Garlic

Strip or sirloin steaks are my favorite cut of beef. Meat cutters in Chicago dubbed them "New York cut" because they would ship so many here, but now they're popular across the country. Look for well-marbled steaks that ideally have been aged whole on the shell, then trimmed down. Any high-quality butcher can provide you with aged prime Black Angus or high-quality choice strip steak. When I cook a great piece of meat like this, I don't do much to it—black pepper, a little garlic, and some grilled onion heighten the flavor without masking it. Add a salad and/or some garlicky sautéed spinach (recipe follows), and you've got a superb meal.

SERVES 4

**1 cup dry red wine**

**2 tablespoons extra virgin olive oil, plus additional for brushing**

**2 garlic cloves, thinly sliced, plus 2 heads garlic**

**2 bay leaves**

**$^1$/$_2$ tablespoon black peppercorns, crushed**

**Two $^3$/$_4$-pound boneless New York strip steaks (1 $^1$/$_2$ inches thick)**

**2 medium onions, peeled and halved from root to stem**

**Coarse sea salt or kosher salt and freshly ground black pepper**

In a dish large enough to hold the steaks, combine the wine, oil, sliced garlic, bay leaves, and peppercorns. Lay the steaks in the dish, spooning the marinade over them, cover, and refrigerate for at least 4 hours or overnight.

Take the steaks out of the refrigerator 1 hour before cooking. Light the grill or preheat the broiler.

Bring a large pot of salted water to a boil. Cut the top $^1$/$_2$ inch off the heads of garlic so all the cloves are exposed. Add the garlic and onions to the water and boil the garlic for 15 minutes, using a slotted spoon to remove the onions after 5 minutes. Drain on paper towels, then lightly brush the onions and garlic with olive oil and season with salt and pepper to taste.

*On the Grill*   Take the steaks out of the marinade, season both sides with salt, and lay the steaks on the grill. Cook, turning once, until done to taste, about 4 to 5 minutes per side for rare. Let the meat rest for 10 minutes to reabsorb the juices before slicing. Meanwhile, place the onions and garlic on the grill and cook, turning once, until they are golden on both sides, about 10 to 15 minutes.

*In the Oven*    Take the steaks out of the marinade, season both sides with salt, and lay the steaks in a baking pan. Place the pan 4 inches from the heat source and broil, turning once, until done to taste, about 4 to 5 minutes per side for rare. Let the meat rest for 10 minutes to reabsorb the juices before slicing. Meanwhile, place the onions and garlic under the broiler and cook, turning once, until they are golden on both sides, about 8 to 10 minutes.

Slice the steaks $1/4$ inch thick and arrange in the center of a platter. When the garlic is cool enough to handle, squeeze the cloves from their skins. Arrange the garlic and onions around the steak and serve.

## Sautéed Spinach with Garlic

SERVES 4 TO 5

**1 1/2 tablespoons extra virgin olive oil**
**6 garlic cloves, thinly sliced**
**3/4 teaspoon coarse sea salt or kosher salt**
**1 1/2 pounds baby spinach, cleaned**

In a large wide saucepan over medium-high heat, warm the olive oil. Add the garlic and salt and cook, stirring, for 30 seconds. Add the spinach and sauté until wilted. Cover the pan and cook for another 30 to 60 seconds. Season with additional salt if desired.

# Filet Mignon with Baby Artichokes

This is a very refined steak recipe. Considered the queen of steaks, filet mignon is certainly the most tender, without the marbling and chewy, assertive flavor that you'll find in a sirloin or rib steak. Instead, filet mignon has a softer, almost melt-in-the-mouth texture and a mild sweetness that takes well to other flavors. Here the steaks are combined with earthy, caramelized baby artichokes for an impressive meal.

SERVES 4

I lemon, halved

8 baby artichokes

Coarse sea salt or kosher salt

Freshly ground black pepper

$^1/_2$ cup extra virgin olive oil

$^1/_4$ cup red wine vinegar

2 garlic cloves, minced

4 filets mignons (1$^1/_2$ inches thick)

$^1/_4$ cup snipped fresh chives

Light the grill or preheat the oven to 500°F. Fill a bowl with water, ice, and the juice from one lemon half. Trim the artichokes by first pulling off the tough outer leaves. Trim the bottoms and tops. Use kitchen shears or scissors to snip off any points remaining on the leaves. Halve the artichokes lengthwise. As you trim the artichokes, put the finished ones in the bowl of lemon water to keep them from turning brown.

Bring a large pot of salted water to a boil. Squeeze the other lemon half into the water and add the artichokes. Cook until the artichoke leaves begin to separate and the centers are tender enough to pierce with a knife, 6 to 8 minutes.

Meanwhile, in a large bowl, combine the olive oil, vinegar, and garlic and season with salt and pepper to taste. Drain the artichokes and add them to the bowl. Season the meat generously with salt and pepper.

**On the Grill**  Place the steaks and artichokes (reserve the marinade) on the grill and cook, covered, until the artichokes are browned around the edges and the meat is done to taste, 4 to 5 minutes per side for rare.

**In the Oven**  Place the steaks in a baking pan and surround them with the artichokes (reserve the marinade). Roast until the artichokes are browned around the edges and the meat is done to taste, about 4 to 5 minutes per side for rare.

Serve the steaks with the artichokes, drizzled with the reserved artichoke marinade, and garnish with the chives.

# Rib Steak with Citrus Rub

Prime rib is one of the most flavorful cuts of beef you can grill, especially when you cook it on the bone as I do here. Since it already has so much flavor, you really don't have to do too much to it—in fact, the less you do, the better. So in this recipe I keep it simple, seasoning the meat with salt, pepper, and a little bit of orange and lemon zest that I dry out first in the oven. The citrus adds a nice brightness to the meat, and extra citrus rub will keep for several weeks. Try it on other cuts of beef, on lamb or pork, or even as a seasoning salt for vegetables, baked potatoes, and popcorn.

Be sure to start this recipe the day before you want to serve it.

SERVES 4 TO 6

1 orange

1 lemon

2 tablespoons coarse sea salt or kosher salt

2 teaspoons freshly ground black pepper

2 double beef rib chops, each with 1 bone (about 2 pounds each)

Extra virgin olive oil for brushing

Preheat the oven to 200°F. Use a vegetable peeler to remove the zest from the orange and lemon. Spread the zest on a baking sheet in a single layer and bake until thoroughly dried, about 2 hours. Let cool before placing the zest in the bowl of a food processor. Process to a powder, then mix with the salt and pepper.

One day before cooking, season the meat all over with 2 tablespoons of the citrus rub and cover with plastic wrap. Refrigerate for 24 hours, turning the meat after 12.

Remove the meat from the refrigerator 2 hours before cooking. Light the grill or preheat the broiler. When the meat reaches room temperature, brush it with olive oil.

*On the Grill*  Place the meat on the grill and cook until it is done to taste, about 7 to 8 minutes per side for rare, 10 minutes for medium-rare, or 12 to 15 minutes for medium to well-done.

*In the Oven*  Position a broiler pan so that the top of the meat is 3 to 4 inches from the heat source. Broil the steaks for 7 minutes on each side for rare, then remove from the oven, taking great care with the pan since the fat will be extremely hot and will splatter. For medium to well-done meat, turn the oven to 500°F and roast for 5 to 10 minutes longer, until done to taste.

Let the meat rest on a carving board for 5 to 10 minutes to reabsorb the juices before slicing. Serve the meat sprinkled with additional citrus rub.

*A Better Grater* If you have one of those microplane graters (the ones inspired by the rasps used in carpentry), you can use it in this recipe and skip the step of grinding the mixture into a powder. Just grate the peel, dry it in the oven, and mix it with the salt and pepper. Don't try this with a regular box grater, though. The zest will clump together.

# Veal Chops with Green Peppercorns

Veal can easily dry out if you're not careful. Ideally, you want a veal chop to be charred lightly on the outside and pink and juicy all the way through. I like to brown the meat over high heat, directly over the hottest part of the grill, then move it to a cooler spot on the side to finish the cooking. In the oven it works best if you keep a little distance between the meat and the heat source, about 8 inches, depending on the size of your broiler.

In this simple but striking dish, the roasted red pepper sauce and fresh bell pepper salad add sweetness, while the vinegary, almost pickled flavor of green peppercorns really perks things up.

SERVES 4

¼ cup drained green peppercorns, 3 tablespoons of the liquid reserved

¼ cup thinly sliced shallot

6 tablespoons extra virgin olive oil, plus additional for brushing the peppers

4 veal rib or T-bone chops (1½ inches thick)

Coarse sea salt or kosher salt and freshly ground black pepper

3 red bell peppers

2 tablespoons chopped fresh flat-leaf parsley

Put the green peppercorns on a board and crush them well with the side of a large knife or the bottom of a heavy pan. Put them in a bowl with the shallot, ¼ cup of the olive oil, and 2 tablespoons of the reserved green peppercorn liquid. Season the chops on both sides with salt and pepper, then rub the peppercorn and shallot mixture all over. Wrap the meat well in plastic wrap and refrigerate for at least 2 hours and up to 12.

Light the grill or preheat the broiler. Stem and seed one of the bell peppers and slice it into thin strips. Put them in a bowl and toss with the parsley, 1 tablespoon of the remaining olive oil, and salt and pepper to taste. Set aside.

*On the Grill* Brush the remaining 2 bell peppers with oil and grill, turning frequently, until the skin is charred and blistered all over, about 10 to 15 minutes.

**In the Oven**  Halve the remaining 2 bell peppers lengthwise and discard the seeds and stems. Lay the peppers skin side up on a baking sheet, brush their skins lightly with olive oil, and place directly under the heat source. Broil until the skin is charred and blistered all over, about 3 minutes. (Do not turn the broiler off.)

When the peppers are done, immediately transfer them to a deep bowl and cover with a plate to steam. Let steam until cool, about 5 to 10 minutes.

**On the Grill**  Place the veal on the hottest part of the grill and cook until sear marks appear, about 5 to 6 minutes per side. Move the veal over to a cooler spot at the side of the grill and finish cooking until the meat is done to taste, about another 3 to 5 minutes per side for medium-rare.

**In the Oven**  Put the chops in a baking pan and place it 8 inches away from the heat source (or as far away as your broiler will allow). Broil until the chops are done to taste, about 6 to 7 minutes per side for medium-rare.

Meanwhile, rub the skin off the peppers using your hands or a metal spoon. Remove the seeds and stems if the peppers were grilled, and coarsely chop the peppers. Put them in a blender or food processor and add the remaining tablespoon of green peppercorn liquid, the remaining tablespoon of olive oil, and a generous pinch of salt and pepper. Puree until smooth. Taste and add more salt and pepper if necessary.

To serve, spoon some red pepper sauce onto the center of each plate. Top with a veal chop and then the red pepper–parsley salad.

---

**Green Peppercorns**  Immature black peppercorns are preserved in vinegar and sold in jars or cans. They are softer in texture and taste than black peppercorns.

# Veal Chops
## with Chanterelles & Chives

Veal and mushrooms make a classic combination. Here I use full-flavored chanterelles, set off with plenty of chives, for a vibrant, elegant veal dish that's hearty and robust at the same time. The techniques vary considerably in the recipe depending on whether you cook the veal on the grill or in the oven, but both versions are excellent—the roasted one is a little more refined, while the grilled one is more forthright.

If chanterelles are out of season or if you just can't find them, you can substitute cremini or shiitake mushrooms.

SERVES 4

**4 veal rib or T-bone chops (1 1/2 inches thick)**

**Coarse sea salt or kosher salt and freshly ground black pepper**

**1 1/2 cups roughly chopped chanterelles (about 1/4 pound)**

**1 tablespoon minced shallot**

**1 garlic clove, minced**

**1 tablespoon extra virgin olive oil**

**1/2 cup chicken broth (reduced-sodium if canned) if broiling**

**1/2 cup dry white wine if broiling; 2 tablespoons if grilling**

**1/4 cup snipped fresh chives for garnish**

*In the Oven*  Preheat the broiler. Season the chops on both sides with salt and pepper to taste. Lay the chops in a single layer in a flameproof baking pan and broil until they are browned, about 3 minutes on each side.

Meanwhile, in a bowl, combine the mushrooms with the shallot, garlic, olive oil, and a large pinch of salt and pepper. Remove the pan from the oven. Turn the chops over and pour the broth and wine into the pan.

Lower the oven to 425°F and spoon the mushroom mixture over and around the chops. Return the pan to the oven and roast for another 15 minutes or until done to taste. If the pan juices are too thin, remove the chops and mushrooms and place the pan on the stove over medium-high heat and let reduce for a couple of minutes. Serve garnished with chives.

*On the Grill*  Light the grill. Season the chops on both sides with salt and pepper.

In a bowl, combine the mushrooms with the shallot, garlic, olive oil, 2 tablespoons white wine, and a large pinch of salt and pepper. Use a double layer of heavy-duty aluminum foil to create a flat-bottomed pouch to contain the mushroom mixture. Fold the edges of the foil over and press tightly to seal well.

Place the foil pouch on the grill. Place the veal on the hottest part of the grill and cook until sear marks appear, about 5 to 6 minutes per side. Move the veal over to a cooler spot at the side of the grill and finish cooking until the meat is done to taste, about another 3 to 5 minutes per side for medium-rare. Meanwhile, listen to make sure the mushroom pouch does not make sizzling sounds, moving it to a cooler part of the grill if it begins to sputter or crackle.

Serve the chops topped with the mushroom mixture and garnished with chives.

# Lamb Chops
## with Mint & Garlic Relish

I prefer to keep my mint jelly for toast and to serve my lamb with a gutsy mix of mint, garlic, and pepper. Vinegar gives this bright, heady relish a slight pungency that accents the flavor of simple lamb chops. The recipe comes together so quickly you could make it after work, but because lamb chops are always special, it's also a great dish for entertaining.

SERVES 4 TO 6

**1 cup chopped fresh mint**

**3 tablespoons minced garlic**

**5 tablespoons extra virgin olive oil**

**Freshly ground black pepper**

**12 lamb rib chops (1$^1$/2 inches thick)**

**Coarse sea salt or kosher salt**

**$^1$/3 cup dry white wine**

**$^3$/4 cup diced red onion**

**$^3$/4 cup diced tomato**

**2 teaspoons freshly squeezed lemon juice**

In a bowl, combine $^1$/3 cup of the mint with 1 tablespoon of the garlic, 3 tablespoons of the olive oil, and a large pinch of black pepper. Season the chops generously on both sides with salt. Spread the mint-garlic mixture over both sides of the chops and wrap them tightly in plastic. Let marinate for 30 minutes at room temperature or refrigerate for at least 4 hours or overnight.

Light the grill or preheat the broiler. To make the relish, in a small saucepan over medium heat, combine the remaining 2 tablespoons of garlic and the remaining 2 tablespoons of olive oil with the white wine. Bring the mixture to a boil and simmer until almost dry, about 4 minutes. Let cool.

In a bowl, combine the cooled garlic mixture with the remaining mint, the red onion, tomato, lemon juice, and salt and pepper to taste.

*On the Grill*   Lay the chops on the grill and cook, turning once, until done to taste, about 3 to 5 minutes per side for medium-rare.

*In the Oven*   Lay the chops in a baking pan and place it as close to the heat source as possible. Broil, turning once, until the meat is done to taste, about 3 to 5 minutes per side for medium-rare.

Serve the chops immediately with the relish.

# Loin of Lamb with a Coriander Crust

In this unusual recipe I coat lamb loins with a flavorful crust of musky coriander seeds and their fresh counterpart, cilantro. For a sauce, I simmer apple cider with brandy and black pepper into a concentrated, spicy, and slightly sweet syrup. It's an intriguing combination that's stylish and compelling yet simple enough for weeknight entertaining.

Loin of lamb is an uncommon cut. Because it's so small, it grills or broils quickly and is very tender. If you can't get it, you can substitute pork tenderloin. Just be sure to cook it a little longer, until the internal temperature reaches 150°F.

SERVES 4 TO 6

$1/4$ cup coriander seeds

$1/4$ cup chopped fresh cilantro, plus additional sprigs for garnish

2 boneless lamb loins (about $3/4$ pound each)

Coarse sea salt or kosher salt

$1/4$ teaspoon freshly ground black pepper, plus additional to taste

2 cups apple cider

$1/4$ cup brandy

2 tablespoons apple cider vinegar

Extra virgin olive oil for brushing

In a skillet over medium-high heat, toast the coriander seeds, shaking constantly, until they are fragrant, about 3 minutes. Immediately transfer to a plate and let cool. In a spice mill, clean coffee grinder, or mortar and pestle, grind the toasted coriander seeds to a coarse powder. In a bowl, combine the powdered coriander with the fresh cilantro. Season the lamb with salt and pepper and pat the coriander mixture onto all sides. Wrap tightly in plastic wrap and refrigerate for at least 4 hours or overnight.

Preheat the broiler or light the grill. In a saucepan over medium heat, combine the apple cider and brandy with the $1/4$ teaspoon pepper and bring to a boil. Simmer until slightly syrupy and reduced by half, about 20 minutes. Stir in the cider vinegar and season with salt to taste.

*In the Oven*    Unwrap the lamb and brush it lightly with olive oil. Put it in a pan and place it about 5 inches from the heat source. Broil, turning once, for about 6 to 10 minutes for rare or 12 to 14 minutes for medium.

*On the Grill*    Unwrap the lamb and brush it lightly with olive oil. Grill the lamb with the grill cover on, for about 8 to 12 minutes for rare or up to 15 for medium. Turn the lamb every few minutes so it browns on all sides.

Transfer the lamb to a cutting board and let it rest for 5 minutes to reabsorb the juices. Meanwhile, gently warm the sauce over low heat. Slice the lamb $\frac{1}{4}$ inch thick and fan the slices in a circle on a platter. Spoon a little sauce over the meat, garnish with cilantro, and pass additional sauce at the table.

# Butterflied Leg of Lamb with Thyme & Honey

Impressive and delicious, this large cut of lamb is great for a party. The honey–soy sauce glaze contributes a glossy brown to the lamb without making it sweet, and the flavors of garlic and thyme really come through, eliminating the need for a sauce. I like lamb with a little lemon, so I use lemon thyme when I have it, and I serve lemon wedges on the side.

Since this is a pretty high-fat cut of meat, it is likely to catch fire on the grill. Simply cover the grill momentarily whenever you see a flare-up and keep a spray bottle of water nearby just in case. (You won't have this problem in the oven.)

Leftovers make the best lamb sandwiches ever.

SERVES 8

**1/2 cup soy sauce**

**1/4 cup extra virgin olive oil**

**1/4 cup thinly sliced garlic**

**2 tablespoons honey**

**2 tablespoons chopped fresh lemon thyme or regular thyme leaves, plus additional sprigs for garnish**

**1/2 teaspoon freshly ground black pepper**

**1 butterflied leg of lamb (about 4 pounds)**

**1/4 cup sliced scallions**

**Lemon wedges for garnish**

In a bowl, combine the soy sauce, olive oil, garlic, honey, thyme leaves, and pepper. In a large, deep dish rub the soy-honey-thyme mixture all over the lamb and cover with plastic wrap. Refrigerate for at least 4 hours or overnight, turning once or twice.

Preheat the oven to 500°F or light the grill.

*In the Oven*    Spread the lamb out flat on a rimmed baking sheet and roast until done to taste, about 40 minutes for rare, 50 minutes for medium.

*On the Grill*    Lay the lamb out flat on the grill and cook, turning and moving the lamb occasionally, until done to taste, about 40 to 60 minutes for rare and 10 minutes longer for medium.

Transfer the lamb to a carving board and let rest for 10 to 15 minutes to reabsorb the juices before carving. Thinly slice the lamb across the grain and serve it garnished with the scallions, thyme sprigs, and lemon wedges.

# Rack of Lamb (or Chops) with Black Olives & Lemon

Most of the recipes in this book will yield pretty similar results whether you make them on the grill or in the oven. This is an exception.

At Beacon I use the wood oven to roast racks of lamb with the very Moroccan-inflected flavors of olive and lemon. While roasting I add a mixture of chicken broth and wine, which reduces in the pan and turns into a sauce. You just can't do that on the grill since there is no roasting pan. Instead, I reserve some of the lemon and olive marinade to use as a bright and simple garnish. Both versions of this dish boast the briny, salty flavors of olives and the tart acidity of lemon. But while the roasted recipe, with its pan juices, is a little more refined, the grilled version, which takes on more of a char, is wonderfully rustic.

SERVES 4

**To Roast**
Four $^1/_2$-pound, 3-bone racks of lamb, frenched

Coarse sea salt or kosher salt and freshly ground black pepper

$^1/_3$ cup extra virgin olive oil

3 tablespoons pitted oil-cured black olives (about 15)

1 tablespoon drained capers

2 teaspoons chopped fresh flat-leaf parsley, plus extra for garnish

1 teaspoon minced garlic

1 teaspoon chopped shallot

$^1/_4$ teaspoon ground cumin

1 anchovy fillet (optional)

$^1/_4$ cup dry white wine

$^1/_4$ cup chicken broth (reduced-sodium if canned)

1 tablespoon freshly squeezed lemon juice

1 lemon, thinly sliced, pits removed and slices quartered

**To Grill**
8 lamb rib chops (about 1$^1/_2$ inches thick)

Coarse sea salt or kosher salt and freshly ground black pepper

$^1/_2$ cup extra virgin olive oil

$^1/_4$ cup pitted oil-cured black olives (about 20), coarsely chopped

1 tablespoon plus 1 teaspoon drained capers

2 tablespoons chopped fresh flat-leaf parsley, plus extra for garnish

1 1/2 teaspoons minced garlic

1 1/2 teaspoons chopped shallot

1/2 teaspoon ground cumin

1 anchovy fillet (optional)

2 tablespoons freshly squeezed lemon juice

1 lemon, thinly sliced crosswise, pits removed and slices cut into eighths

*In the Oven*   Season the lamb generously with salt and pepper. In a food processor, combine the olive oil, 1 tablespoon of the olives, the capers, parsley, garlic, shallot, cumin, anchovy, if using, and more pepper. Coat the lamb with this marinade and place it in a bowl. Cover and leave at room temperature for 30 to 45 minutes or refrigerate for at least 4 hours or overnight.

Preheat the oven to 500°F. Arrange the racks of lamb in a roasting pan large enough to hold them comfortably in one layer (or use 2 pans). Drizzle any marinade left in the bottom of the bowl over the lamb. Roast the lamb for 7 minutes.

Transfer the lamb to a plate. Skim off the fat from the roasting pan and add the wine, broth, and lemon juice. Return the lamb to the pan, browned side down. Sprinkle the lamb with the remaining 2 tablespoons olives and the lemon slices. Continue to roast the lamb for 7 to 9 minutes more for medium-rare or longer to taste. Serve the lamb with the pan juices and garnished with additional chopped parsley.

*On the Grill*   Season the lamb generously with salt and pepper. In a food processor, combine the olive oil, 1 1/2 tablespoons of the olives, the capers, parsley, garlic, shallot, cumin, anchovy, if using and more pepper. Place half of this mixture in a bowl (refrigerate the remaining marinade) and add the lamb chops, turning them and spooning the marinade over them to coat. Cover and marinate at room temperature for 30 to 45 minutes or refrigerate for at least 4 hours or overnight.

Light the grill. Lay the lamb chops on the grill and cook until seared, about 5 to 7 minutes. Turn the lamb over and grill until medium-rare, about another 5 minutes, or to taste.

*(continued)*

Meanwhile, combine the remaining marinade with the lemon juice and use it as a sauce. Garnish with the remaining 2$\frac{1}{2}$ tablespoons olives, the sliced lemons, and the parsley.

*Grilled or Roasted Lemons* One of my favorite ways to add a sharp lemony flavor to dishes is to add lemon slivers when grilling or roasting. I came up with this when I noticed the incredible things that high heat does to lemons. It mellows the bitterness of the pith, while the skin crisps and turns brown, becoming almost sweet. Whether roasted in thin wedges or grilled in round slices (so they don't fall through the grill), they are a dramatic, delicious touch that makes even the plainest grilled fish special. Just brush thin slices with oil, lay them on the grill or under the broiler, and watch until they brown (it happens quickly). You could even eat the slices by themselves, like very flavorful chips.

# Hot-Smoked, Slow-Cooked Barbecued Pork

Like the very best of southern barbecue, the pork shoulder in this recipe is cooked very slowly over a smoky fire and basted with a homemade, savory sauce. The prolonged cooking over indirect heat makes the meat so juicy and tender that it will fall apart at the touch of a fork. It reminds me of pulled pork but with a deep, complex flavor that comes from a dry rub of freshly ground spices.

This pork is excellent served with a side of the Yellow Pepper–Fennel Slaw (page 188). If you're in the mood for even more pork, try it with Roasted Fennel and Orange Salad with Onion-Bacon Vinaigrette (page 38). Or just pair it with your favorite recipe for coleslaw. No matter what you serve it with, be sure to offer plenty of extra barbecue sauce.

SERVES 8

**For the Pork**

2 tablespoons cumin seeds

1 tablespoon coriander seeds

1 tablespoon whole allspice

1 tablespoon black peppercorns

1 tablespoon mustard seeds

1 tablespoon celery seed

2 teaspoons hot red pepper flakes

2 1/2 to 3 pounds pork shoulder or loin, boned and tied (see sidebar, page 151)

Coarse sea salt or kosher salt

**For the Barbecue Sauce**

2 tablespoons extra virgin olive oil

1 cup minced onion

3 garlic cloves, minced

1 1/2 cups light molasses

One 6-ounce can tomato paste

3/4 cup white wine vinegar

1 teaspoon coarse sea salt or kosher salt

1/2 teaspoon Tabasco or other hot sauce

*(continued)*

To prepare the spice rub for the pork, in a heavy skillet over high heat toast the cumin, coriander, allspice, and black peppercorns for 2 minutes, shaking the pan frequently. Add the mustard seeds and celery seed to the pan and toast for 1 minute longer. Transfer the spices to a plate and let cool.

Using a spice mill, clean coffee grinder, or blender, grind the spices to a powder, then stir in the red pepper flakes.

Season the pork generously with salt, then rub 3 tablespoons of the spice mixture all over the meat. Wrap the pork in 2 layers of plastic wrap and chill for 4 hours or overnight.

If grilling over coals, light the grill using plenty of charcoal. If using firewood, add it now and let the wood and charcoal burn for about an hour or until most of the firewood is burned up; you'll be left with some ash and the charcoal. If using wood chips, soak them for at least 20 minutes, then add them to the coals after they are completely gray. Let the chips burn for 10 minutes. Move the charcoal and wood over to one side of the grill for indirect grilling. If using a gas grill, preheat the grill thoroughly, adding soaked wood chips according to the manufacturer's instructions. When the grill is hot and smoky, turn off the fire under half of the grill.

Meanwhile, prepare the barbecue sauce. In a saucepan over medium-high heat, warm the oil. Add the onion and garlic and cook, stirring, until the onion is soft and browned, about 10 to 12 minutes. Transfer to the bowl of a food processor or blender. Add the molasses, tomato paste, vinegar, salt, Tabasco, and 1 tablespoon of the spice rub and puree until smooth. Return the mixture to the saucepan and cook over medium-low heat, stirring occasionally, until the sauce has thickened slightly, about 15 minutes.

Place the pork on the grill over the side without the heat underneath. Cover the grill and let cook for 1 hour. Baste the meat with barbecue sauce, turn it over, baste the other side, and grill, covered, for another 45 minutes. Baste the meat with sauce 2 or 3 more times while it cooks and turn it once more. The pork is done when the meat is tender and cooked through (160°F) and the outside is a dark, glossy brown.

Transfer the pork to a carving board and let rest for 10 minutes to reabsorb the juices. Cut the meat into slices (they may fall apart, but don't worry; that's a good sign) and serve it with additional barbecue sauce.

NOTE   Extra spice rub can be stored in an airtight container. It's great rubbed onto chicken, fish, or seafood before grilling.

*Barbecued Pork Sandwiches* Leftover pork makes superb sandwiches. To make them, chop the pork and mix it with plenty of barbecue sauce. Pile it on a kaiser roll or white bread, with or without coleslaw, and serve with plenty of napkins.

# Roasted Pork Chops with Cabbage & Mustard

A fresh revision of pork and sauerkraut, this spunky dish is sure to change the mind of those who think they don't like cabbage. Combined with the pork drippings and cooked in a very hot oven, the cabbage becomes particularly savory, rich, and very tender, but without falling apart or turning into a soggy mush. A little bit of mustard sharpens the flavors and also complements the pork chops, which caramelize and crisp around the edges. It's a terrific combination that may well become a family classic, to be loved by adults and kids alike.

SERVES 6

$^1$/4 pound bacon, cut into $^1$/4-inch pieces

$^1$/2 head green cabbage (about 1 $^1$/2 pounds), cored and thinly sliced (about 10 cups)

Coarse sea salt or kosher salt and freshly ground black pepper

6 pork rib or loin chops (1 $^1$/4 inches thick), preferably brined (recipe follows)

$^1$/3 cup whole-grain mustard

Snipped fresh chives for garnish

Preheat the broiler. In a large skillet over medium-high heat, cook the bacon until it's browned and crisp, about 4 minutes. Use a slotted spoon to transfer the bacon to a paper towel–lined plate. Pour about half the bacon fat into a heatproof container and set aside.

Add half of the cabbage to the skillet and season with salt and pepper to taste. Cook the cabbage over medium-high heat, stirring, until wilted but still crisp, about 2 minutes. Transfer the cooked cabbage to a roasting pan or casserole large enough to hold the pork chops in a single layer. Add more bacon fat to the skillet if necessary and cook the remaining cabbage in the same way. Spread all the cabbage in the bottom of the roasting pan or casserole.

Season the pork chops with pepper (and salt if they are not brined), then coat them with the mustard on both sides. Lay the pork on top of the cabbage and broil until browned on both sides, about 5 minutes per side. Lower the oven to 400°F and roast the pork chops until cooked through, about 15 minutes longer, adding a little water to the pan if the cabbage seems dry. Serve the chops with the cabbage, garnished with the bacon and chives.

## *Brining Pork Chops*

Pork chops that have been brined are much juicier and more tender than their nonbrined counterparts. If you don't have time, you can skip this step, especially if you've gotten high-quality pork from a pig farm (see sidebar, page 151). But I really feel it's worth the time.

1 1/2 cups kosher salt
3/4 cup sugar
1 onion, sliced
1 teaspoon whole black peppercorns
1 clove

Pour 3 quarts water into a large pot and add the other ingredients. Bring to a boil over high heat, stirring until the sugar and salt have dissolved, and simmer for 15 minutes. Let cool completely.

Place the pork chops in a nonreactive bowl and pour the liquid over them to cover. Cover the bowl with plastic wrap and refrigerate for 1 to 3 hours.

Remove the pork from the brine and pat dry 30 minutes before using.

# Grilled Smoked Pork Chops with Pickled Vegetables

These taste nothing like purchased smoked pork chops, which are similar to ham. They are meaty, with a moist texture and a charred, smoky flavor, thanks to the wood on the grill and to a short brining. Brining keeps the meat from drying out, and the wood smoke thoroughly infuses the meat with flavor. I like to serve these pork chops with a colorful mix of homemade pickled vegetables. The vegetables retain their crunch and provide both a crisp texture and a zesty bite in contrast to the succulent, smoky meat. The vegetables do have to be made at least a day ahead but will then keep for almost a week, or even longer, in the refrigerator. Just keep in mind that they will soften as they sit.

SERVES 4

**I quart white wine vinegar**

**$^1$/2 cup sugar**

**3 tablespoons coarse sea salt or kosher salt, plus additional to taste**

**3 bay leaves**

**I tablespoon mustard seeds**

**I tablespoon black peppercorns**

**2 cups cauliflower florets**

**I cup sliced carrots in $^1$/4-inch-thick rounds**

**I small onion, peeled and sliced into $^1$/2-inch-thick rounds**

**I small red bell pepper, sliced into $^1$/2-inch-thick strips**

**4 pork rib or loin chops (I$^1$/2 inches thick), preferably brined (page 147)**

**Extra virgin olive oil for grilling**

**Freshly ground black pepper**

**Herb Oil (optional; recipe follows)**

**Chopped fresh flat-leaf parsley and/or snipped fresh chives for garnish**

At least 24 hours and up to 5 days before serving, combine the vinegar, sugar, salt, bay leaves, mustard seeds, black peppercorns, and I quart water in a saucepan. Bring to a boil over medium heat, stirring until the sugar and salt dissolve, and simmer for 5 minutes. Place the cauliflower, carrots, onion, and red pepper pieces in a large heatproof bowl and pour the liquid over them. Use a plate or cake pan to weigh the vegetables down so they stay submerged in the pickling liquid. Let cool, then refrigerate for at least 24 hours and up to 5 days.

If grilling over coals, light the grill using plenty of charcoal. If using firewood, add it now and let the wood and charcoal burn for about an hour or until most of the firewood is burned up; you'll be left with some ash and the charcoal. If using wood chips, soak them for at least 20 minutes, then add them to the coals after they are completely gray. Let the chips burn for 10 minutes. Move the charcoal and wood over to one side of the grill for indirect grilling. If using a gas grill, preheat the grill thoroughly, adding soaked wood chips according to the manufacturer's instructions. When the grill is hot and smoky, turn off the fire under half of the grill.

Lightly brush the pork chops with olive oil and season both sides with pepper (and salt if they are not brined). Place the chops over the part of the grill without the heat underneath and cover. Grill the chops for 10 minutes, then turn and cook for 10 to 15 minutes longer, until the chops are charred and cooked to an internal temperature of 150°F.

Serve the chops with the pickled vegetables, drizzled with the herb oil if desired. Garnish with chopped parsley and/or chives.

## Herb Oil

MAKES ABOUT 3/4 CUP

**1 cup extra virgin olive oil**
**1/2 small onion**
**1 tablespoon chopped fresh flat-leaf parsley**
**1 tablespoon snipped fresh chives**
**1/2 teaspoon coarse sea salt or kosher salt, plus additional to taste**

Combine all the ingredients in the bowl of a food processor or a blender and puree until very smooth. Taste and add more salt if desired. Transfer to a covered container and refrigerate for at least 4 hours and preferably overnight. Gently pour the flavored oil into a bowl and discard the sediment left in the container.

# Loin of Pork with Apples & Bitter Chocolate

What a difference a cooking method can make. When roasted, this dish offers complex, even elegant flavors. In the grilled version the pan juices are richer and more rustic with the taste of char and smoke. But in both versions you'll get the intriguing, haunting flavors of unsweetened cocoa and spices added to the classic combination of apples and pork. The cocoa rub is reminiscent of a Central American mole. It's applied 24 hours before cooking, penetrating the meat with a mysterious flavor that becomes warm and toasty tasting when cooked. Set off by the brandy and sweet apples, it makes a memorable party dish or Sunday supper for a crowd.

SERVES 10

1 jalapeño pepper

2 tablespoons coarse sea salt or kosher salt

2 tablespoons unsweetened cocoa powder

1 teaspoon dried thyme

1 teaspoon ground cinnamon

1 teaspoon freshly ground black pepper

1 boneless pork loin roast (about 4 pounds), trimmed and tied

1 1/2 cups chicken broth (reduced-sodium if canned)

1/2 cup brandy

3 Cortland apples, cored, peeled, and cut into 12 slices each

2 tablespoons unsalted butter, softened

Roast the jalapeño by placing it directly over the gas flame on your stovetop. Using kitchen tongs, turn the jalapeño until it is blistered and lightly charred all over. Or roast the jalapeño under the broiler as close to the heat source as possible. Put the pepper in a bowl and cover it with a plate. Let the pepper steam for at least 5 minutes or until cool. Wearing rubber gloves, use your hands or a spoon to peel the jalapeño, then mince it.

In a bowl, combine the jalapeño, salt, cocoa, thyme, cinnamon, and pepper. Rub this mixture thoroughly all over the pork, coating it evenly. Wrap the pork tightly in plastic wrap and refrigerate overnight or for up to 2 days, turning the meat every 12 hours or so.

*A Better Pig Is a Fatter Pig* These days pigs are bred to be lean and mean rather than plump and succulent, which makes the meat tough and bland, I think. Most of the pork you buy at the supermarket fits this bill. So to get the most fla-vorful, tender cuts of pork, your best bet is to go to a specialty butcher or to mail-order the meat directly from a pig farm that raises pigs the old-fashioned way (and as an added bonus may not use hormones and antibiotics). There are a lot of options here. One is Niman Ranch. They have an excellent online store at www.nimanranch.com, or call them at (510) 808–0340.

Preheat the oven to 500°F or light the grill. Remove the meat from the refrig-erator an hour before cooking.

*In the Oven*    Place the pork on a rack set in a roasting pan and cook for 30 minutes. Remove the pan from the oven and reduce the heat to 350°F. Lift the rack and meat out of the pan and add the chicken broth, brandy, and apples to the pan juices, scraping the bottom of the pan to loosen any caramelized, stuck-on bits. Set the rack and meat back over the apples in the pan and roast for another 35 to 45 minutes, basting with the pan juices occasionally, until the meat reaches an internal temperature of 150°F.

*On the Grill*    Place the pork on the grill and cook, turning, until the outside is browned and caramelized, about 20 to 30 minutes. Place the pork in a large flameproof pan and add the chicken broth, brandy, and apples. Push the coals to one side or turn off the gas on one side and place the pan over the side of the grill with-out the heat underneath. Cover the grill and cook until the meat reaches an in-ternal temperature of 150°F, about 40 to 50 minutes.

Transfer the pork and apples to a warm platter and let rest for 20 minutes (the meat will continue to cook as it sits). Skim the fat off the pan juices and place the pan over medium heat. Simmer the liquid to thicken it (about 5 to 10 min-utes), then whisk in the butter. Slice the meat and arrange it in the center of a large platter. Pour the pan juices over the top, arranging the apple slices around the meat, and serve.

# Sausage "Mixed Grill" with Green Apple & Potato Salad

I used to grill apples and sausages and serve them with potato salad. Then I noticed how well the textures of the potatoes and apples worked together, and I came up with this interesting salad. Grating green, crisp apples right into the potato salad gives it tart and sweet flavors that go perfectly with the rich, spicy taste of a sausage mixed grill. This recipe is best with a good mix of at least three or four kinds of sausages, including both mild and spicy types, but bear in mind that they will all cook differently, so you'll need to transfer each to a cooler part of the grill as it is ready. In addition to playing with the types of sausage you use, you can make this a more traditional mixed grill by also grilling lamb chops, sliced liver, or, my favorite, sweetbreads and kidneys.

SERVES 6

**2 pounds small red potatoes, quartered**

**Coarse sea salt or kosher salt**

**3 pounds mixed sausage, including chorizo, blood sausage, merguez, chipolata, Italian (sweet and/or hot), turkey, chicken, or other varieties**

**$^1/_4$ cup sherry vinegar**

**Freshly ground black pepper**

**2 tablespoons extra virgin olive oil, plus additional for drizzling**

**7 scallions, trimmed**

**2 green apples, grated with their skins**

Preheat the grill. Place the potatoes in a saucepan with enough water to cover them by 1$^1/_2$ inches. Salt the water well. Bring to a boil over high heat and cook, partially covered, until the potatoes are just tender throughout and can be pierced easily with a fork, about 4 to 6 minutes. Drain and transfer to a large bowl. Let cool slightly.

Lay the sausages on the grill and cook, turning, until cooked through, about 7 to 15 minutes, depending on their size.

Put the vinegar in a bowl and add a pinch of salt and pepper. Whisk in the olive oil, taste, and add more salt and pepper if necessary. Pour the vinaigrette over the potatoes and toss well. Thinly slice 5 of the scallions and add them to the potatoes along with the grated apples. Toss again, taste, and add more salt and pepper if necessary.

Slice the remaining 2 scallions lengthwise. Arrange the salad in a mound in the center of a large platter. Slice the sausages into 2-inch lengths. Surround the salad with the sausages and the scallions and drizzle the platter with olive oil. Serve warm or at room temperature.

# Venison Chops with Spicy Currant & Red Wine Sauce

Whether you shoot the deer yourself or know the hunter who did, or if you order it from a fancy catalog, you'll want a really nice recipe for the chops, since they're the most special part. Like lamb chops, venison chops should be cooked rare to medium-rare. Here I coat them in cracked black pepper and add a spicy currant and red wine sauce that's a perfect foil for the pleasantly gamy flavor of venison. Traditionally game is cooked in the fall or winter, but this recipe works wonderfully for the summer and is particularly great served with the Watercress Salad with Grilled or Roasted Red Onions and Aged Cheddar (page 40).

SERVES 4

8 venison chops, cut from a rack (about 2 pounds) (see Note)
2 tablespoons cracked black peppercorns or to taste
Coarse sea salt or kosher salt
$^3/_4$ cup dry red wine
2 tablespoons diced shallot
$^1/_2$ cup good-quality red or black currant jelly or preserves
Watercress sprigs for garnish

Rub the chops on both sides with 1 tablespoon of the peppercorns and salt to taste. Wrap in plastic wrap and let rest at room temperature for 30 minutes or refrigerate for at least 2 hours and up to 4.

Light the grill or preheat the broiler. In a saucepan over medium heat, combine the red wine, shallot, and the remaining tablespoon of peppercorns. Bring to a boil and simmer until syrupy and almost dry, about 12 minutes. Add the currant jelly, reduce the heat to low, and cook until the jelly has melted. Raise the heat and simmer for 3 minutes. Strain the sauce into a serving bowl.

*On the Grill*    Place the chops on the grill and cook for 2 to 3 minutes per side for rare.

*In the Oven*    Place the chops in a baking pan and broil directly under the heat source for 2 to 3 minutes per side for rare.

Serve the venison with the sauce, garnished with watercress sprigs.

NOTE    If you can't find venison chops or a rack near where you live, you can mail-order it from D'Artagnan, (800) 327–8246.

# Grilled Calves' Liver with Apple-Smoked Bacon & Vermouth

Liver seems to have been forgotten by many home cooks, but I think there are still people out there who love it as much as I do. Don't serve it to a five-year-old, but do encourage skeptical adults to give liver another chance. When good-quality calves' liver is seared quickly, not over-cooked, it's a wonderful thing. Here it's sliced fairly thin and cooked fast so that it stays juicy and moist. It has plenty of flavor, enhanced by the bacon and vermouth. Buy pale or rosy-colored liver (the darker brown it is, the older it is), and have it skinned and deveined if it is not already.

SERVES 4

**8 slices bacon, preferably applewood-smoked**
**$1/2$ cup sliced shallot**
**$1/4$ cup chicken broth (reduced-sodium if canned)**
**$1/4$ cup dry white vermouth**
**$1^1/2$ pounds calves' liver, sliced $1/2$ inch thick**
**2 tablespoons extra virgin olive oil**
**Coarse sea salt or kosher salt and freshly ground black pepper**
**Snipped fresh chives for garnish**

Light the grill. In a skillet over medium-high heat, cook the bacon until crisp, about 3 to 4 minutes. Transfer the bacon to a paper towel–lined plate. Pour the bacon fat into a heatproof measuring cup and return $1/4$ cup of the fat to the pan. Discard the remaining fat or reserve it for another use.

Heat the pan over medium heat and add the shallot. Cook, stirring, until lightly browned, about 2 minutes. Pour in the chicken broth and vermouth and simmer until slightly thickened, about 8 minutes. Keep warm.

Place the liver in a bowl and toss it with the olive oil and a pinch of salt and pepper. Lay the slices over a very hot grill and cook, turning once, until just pink at the center, about 2 minutes per side. Serve the liver with the bacon slices and shallot sauce. Garnish with snipped chives.

TUNA SALAD WITH POTATOES,
GREEN BEANS, OLIVES, &
HERB VINAIGRETTE

PEPPERED TUNA WITH RED WINE &
SHALLOTS

HERB-CRUSTED SALMON WITH
HORSERADISH BREAD SAUCE

HOT-SMOKED SALMON WITH
SPICY CUCUMBERS

SWEET ONION & THYME-GLAZED COD

STRIPED BASS WITH
OREGANO & VERJUICE

HALIBUT WITH QUICK LEMON
CONFIT & WHITE WINE

SWORDFISH STEAKS IN A
MUSTARD SEED CRUST

WOOD-GRILLED OR ROASTED TROUT
WITH CHERVIL VINAIGRETTE

WHOLE RED SNAPPER WITH
BABY FENNEL & NIÇOISE OLIVES

# 7 Fish & Seafood

SHRIMP WITH PARSLEY,
GARLIC, & LEMON BUTTER

SEA SCALLOPS ON ROSEMARY SKEWERS
WITH TOMATO-GINGER CHUTNEY

SEA SCALLOPS ON A POTATO DISK
WITH SPICY LEEK RELISH

GRILLED SOFT-SHELL CRAB
SANDWICHES ON ENGLISH MUFFINS
WITH TARRAGON MAYONNAISE

LOBSTER SALAD WITH RED ONION,
BASIL, & BIBB LETTUCE

LOBSTER WITH DILL & YELLOW
PEPPER—FENNEL SLAW

ROASTED SHELLFISH STEW WITH
MUSSELS, CLAMS, SHRIMP,
& LINGUIÇA SAUSAGE

SQUID WITH LEMON &
WHITE BEANS

# Tuna Salad with Potatoes, Green Beans, Olives, & Herb Vinaigrette

This is a play on the classic Niçoise salad, using fresh tuna in place of the traditional canned tuna. The tuna is coated in a briny mix of olives and capers, then charred and set on a substantial salad of green beans, boiled potatoes, and baby lettuces. I like to toss the green beans and potatoes in the dressing—a pungent, herby mix of basil and chives—while they are still warm. It really lets them soak up the flavors. You can do this in advance, but don't toss the lettuces until the last minute. An especially vibrant, summery dish, it's ideal as a light main course or as part of a buffet.

SERVES 4

1/4 cup chopped pitted Niçoise or Kalamata olives

I teaspoon minced drained capers

1/4 cup plus I teaspoon extra virgin olive oil, plus additional for cooking

1/2 teaspoon coarse sea salt or kosher salt, plus additional to taste

1/4 teaspoon freshly ground black pepper, plus additional to taste

One 3/4-pound piece tuna loin, preferably "grade A"

I 1/2 tablespoons white wine vinegar

I tablespoon chopped fresh flat-leaf parsley

I tablespoon chopped fresh mint

I tablespoon snipped fresh chives

I teaspoon minced shallot

1/2 teaspoon minced garlic

3/4 pound green beans, trimmed

8 small Red Bliss or fingerling potatoes, scrubbed and trimmed

2 cups baby salad greens, washed and spun dry

I hard-cooked egg, chopped, for garnish

Mince I tablespoon of the olives very finely and combine them in a bowl with the capers, I teaspoon of the olive oil, and the salt and pepper. Place the tuna in the bowl and turn it over a few times until it is well coated. Cover the bowl and refrigerate it for I hour.

Light the grill or preheat the broiler.

*On the Grill*   Lightly oil the grill or a grilling basket. Place the tuna on the grill (or use the basket) and cook for 2 to 3 minutes per side for rare or until done to taste.

*In the Oven*   Lightly oil a rimmed baking sheet and lay the tuna on it. Broil until the tuna is done to taste, about 2 to 4 minutes per side.

Let the tuna cool, then wrap it in plastic wrap and refrigerate it for at least 2 hours, or place it in the freezer for 15 to 30 minutes, until it is cold throughout.

To make the vinaigrette, in a bowl whisk together the vinegar, herbs, shallot, garlic, and salt and pepper to taste. Whisking constantly, drizzle in the $1/4$ cup of olive oil.

Fill a bowl with water and ice. Bring a large pot of salted water to a boil and add the green beans. Cook until crisp-tender, about 3 to 4 minutes, then use a slotted spoon, skimmer, or tongs to transfer the beans to the ice water (keep the cooking water at a boil). Drain the beans from the ice water after 3 seconds (this stops them from cooking any further). They should be still warm. Place them in a bowl and toss them with 2 tablespoons of the vinaigrette.

Place the potatoes in the pot of boiling water and cook until tender when pierced with a knife, about 15 to 20 minutes. Drain well. When cool enough to handle but still warm, quarter the potatoes. Put them in a bowl and toss with 2 tablespoons of the vinaigrette while they are still warm.

In another bowl, toss the baby greens with 2 tablespoons of vinaigrette. Mound the greens on a platter, lay the potatoes over them, and pile the green beans over the potatoes. Slice the tuna and fan it over the beans. Garnish with the remaining chopped olives and the hard-cooked egg and drizzle with the remaining dressing.

# Peppered Tuna
## with Red Wine & Shallots

This is the fish dish for the steak lover in the house. It's essentially steak au poivre, but the steaks are tuna. Like its beef counterpart, the fish is coated in a generous black pepper crust and seared until rare or medium-rare. Then I add a potent, syrupy red wine and port sauce that's chock-full of crunchy shallots. It all adds up to an easy, fast-cooking recipe with strong, satisfying flavors. Serve it with traditional steak accompaniments, like watercress salad and potatoes.

SERVES 4

**4 tuna steaks (1 1/4 inches thick), 6 ounces each**

**Coarse sea salt or kosher salt**

**2 teaspoons very coarsely ground black pepper**

**1 cup dry red wine**

**1/2 cup port**

**3 shallots, diced (about 3/4 cup)**

**1 cup cherry tomatoes, halved**

**2 teaspoons extra virgin olive oil**

**Basil sprigs for garnish (optional)**

Season the tuna steaks with salt on both sides, then pat the pepper all over them. Wrap in plastic wrap and refrigerate for 1 hour.

In a saucepan over medium heat, combine the wine, port, and shallots and bring to a boil. Simmer until syruplike and reduced, about 20 minutes. Keep warm.

Position a well-seasoned or lightly oiled cast-iron skillet 6 inches from the heat source and preheat the broiler for 10 minutes. You can also use an oiled heavy-duty baking pan. Or light the grill.

*In the Oven*   Carefully lay the tuna steaks in the preheated pan and broil until charred around the edges, about 2 minutes. Turn and cook for 2 minutes more for rare or until done to taste.

*On the Grill*  Lightly oil the grill or a grilling basket. Place the tuna on the grill (or use the basket) and cook for 2 to 3 minutes per side for rare or until done to taste.

In a bowl, toss the cherry tomatoes with the olive oil and season with salt and pepper to taste. Use a slotted spoon to spread the shallots on a platter, top with the tuna, and surround with the tomatoes. Drizzle with the red wine–port syrup and garnish with basil sprigs if desired.

# Herb-Crusted Salmon with Horseradish Bread Sauce

This is a very old-fashioned sauce based on the idea of using stale bread as an emulsifying agent to make what is essentially an eggless mayonnaise. It's a thrifty recipe designed to use up leftover bread and save on eggs. But it's also light and creamy, with the ability to incorporate other flavors beautifully. Here I add pungent horseradish, which is a natural with salmon, and plenty of herbs. Then I garnish the plate with a drizzle of herb oil for a colorful contrast. It's a great-looking, unique dish that's perfect to serve in the springtime.

SERVES 4

1/2 cup chopped fresh flat-leaf parsley

1/4 cup chopped fresh dill, plus additional sprigs for garnish

1 tablespoon chopped fresh tarragon

1 small shallot, minced

3 tablespoons freshly squeezed lemon juice or to taste

1/4 cup plus 1 tablespoon prepared horseradish

Coarse sea salt or kosher salt and freshly ground black pepper

1/3 cup plus 3 tablespoons extra virgin olive oil

4 skinless salmon fillets (1 1/2 inches thick), about 6 ounces each

1/2 cup fresh bread crumbs (see sidebar, page 19)

In the bowl of a food processor or blender, combine the parsley, dill, tarragon, shallot, 1 tablespoon of the lemon juice, 1 tablespoon of the horseradish, and a large pinch of salt and pepper. With the motor running, drizzle in 3 table-spoons of the olive oil to form a thin paste. Reserve 1/4 cup of this herb paste to use as garnish. Lay the salmon in a pan in a single layer and brush with the remaining herb paste, turning to coat both sides of the fish. Cover and refrigerate for at least 20 minutes and up to 2 hours.

Preheat the oven to 500°F or light the grill. Unwrap the salmon.

*In the Oven*    Place the salmon in a roasting pan and roast until done to taste, about 9 to 12 minutes.

*On the Grill*   Place the salmon on the grill (or use a grilling basket) and cook, turning once, until done to taste, about 4 to 6 minutes per side.

While the salmon is cooking, place the bread crumbs in the bowl of a food processor or blender with the remaining $1/4$ cup of horseradish, 1 tablespoon of the remaining lemon juice, and a pinch of salt and pepper. Blend to combine. With the motor running, drizzle in the remaining $1/3$ cup of olive oil and process until smooth.

Whisk the remaining tablespoon of lemon juice into the reserved herb paste, adding a little more olive oil if necessary to make it a pourable herb oil. To serve, place a pool of the bread sauce on each plate, top with a salmon fillet, then drizzle the fish and plate with the herb oil and garnish with fresh dill sprigs.

# Hot-Smoked Salmon with Spicy Cucumbers

In New York, smoked salmon means lox, which is cured with sugar, salt, and spices, then "cold smoked" at a very low temperature and cut into translucent slices. On the West Coast, in places like Oregon, fresh salmon is often hot smoked until the meat is opaque, as it is in this recipe. The salmon is smoked in a covered grill at a temperature high enough to cook the fish through yet low enough to give it time to absorb smoke in the process. The result is meatier and much less salty than cold-smoked salmon, with a great smoky flavor. I marinate the fish first in a honey glaze, and the glaze also absorbs the flavor of the smoke as it caramelizes into a lacquered, burnished color on the pink fish. This cooking technique can be used for any of the fattier fishes, such as trout, bluefish, or mackerel. A refreshing salad of cucumbers, herbs, vinegar, and spice cuts through the sweet smoky flavors, making a very refreshing accompaniment.

SERVES 4

**For the Salmon**

1/2 cup white wine vinegar or rice vinegar

1/4 cup honey

1 tablespoon minced jalapeño pepper

1 tablespoon minced fresh cilantro

2 teaspoons soy sauce

Freshly ground black pepper

4 salmon fillets, skin on (about 6 ounces each)

Extra virgin olive oil for brushing

**For the Cucumber Salad**

3 large cucumbers, peeled and halved lengthwise

1/3 cup extra virgin olive oil

1/4 cup chopped fresh mint

1/4 cup white wine vinegar or rice vinegar

2 small jalapeño peppers, seeded and minced

2 tablespoons chopped fresh cilantro

1/2 teaspoon hot red pepper flakes

In a food processor or blender, puree the vinegar, honey, jalapeño, cilantro, soy sauce, and pepper to taste until smooth. Lay the fillets in a deep dish that can accommodate them snugly in a single layer and pour the marinade over them.

Cover tightly with plastic wrap and refrigerate for at least 1 hour and up to 12 hours.

To make the cucumber salad, use a spoon to scrape the seeds from the cucumbers, then thinly slice them. Place the cucumbers in a bowl with the olive oil, mint, vinegar, jalapeños, cilantro, and red pepper flakes and toss to combine. Chill the salad until ready to serve (up to 4 hours).

If grilling over coals, light the grill using plenty of charcoal. If using firewood, add it now and let the wood and charcoal burn for about an hour or until most of the firewood is burned up; you'll be left with some ash and the charcoal. If using wood chips, soak them for at least 20 minutes, then add them to the coals after they are completely gray. Let the chips burn for 10 minutes. Move the charcoal and wood over to one side of the grill for indirect grilling. If using a gas grill, preheat the grill thoroughly, adding soaked wood chips according to the manufacturer's instructions. When the grill is hot and smoky, turn off the fire under half of the grill.

Brush the half of the grill without the heat underneath it with oil or oil a grilling basket. Place the salmon, skin side down, on the oiled side of the grill (or in the grilling basket placed over the side of the grill without the heat underneath). Cover the grill. Start checking for doneness after 7 minutes. It's done when the flesh is opaque on the top but still pink in the center. If it's not done, keep checking it every few minutes. Use a spatula to pry the fish from the grill or grilling basket (don't worry if the skin sticks, just leave it there; note that it will scrub off easiest while still warm).

Serve the fish accompanied by the cucumber salad.

# Sweet Onion & Thyme-Glazed Cod

A honeyed glaze; soft, caramelized onions; and the herbal fragrance of fresh thyme bring out the inherent sweetness in this moist, delicate fish. Although caramelizing the onions is time consuming, the payoff in flavor is big, and they can be made several days ahead. Then assembling and cooking the cod is quick, making this good for a dinner party, since most of the work can be done in advance. Serve it with a salad of bitter greens such as arugula as a bracing contrast.

SERVES 4

**¹/₂ cup honey**

**3 tablespoons white wine vinegar**

**Grated zest of ¹/₂ lemon**

**I tablespoon fresh thyme leaves, plus additional sprigs**

**4 cod fillets (I inch thick)**

**I¹/₂ tablespoons unsalted butter**

**2 Spanish onions, thinly diced**

**Coarse sea salt or kosher salt and freshly ground black pepper**

**I tablespoon freshly squeezed lemon juice or to taste**

In a small bowl, whisk together the honey, vinegar, lemon zest, and thyme leaves. Lay the cod fillets in a container that holds them snugly in a single layer and pour the glaze over them to cover. Cover the container in plastic wrap and refrigerate for at least I hour and up to overnight.

Melt the butter in a large saucepan over medium heat. When the foam subsides, add the onions, a couple of thyme sprigs, and a large pinch of salt and pepper. Cook over medium-low heat, stirring occasionally, until golden brown and caramelized, about 45 minutes. Stir in the lemon juice and season with additional salt and pepper if necessary.

Preheat the broiler or light the grill.

*In the Oven*   Lay the cod in a roasting pan lined with aluminum foil, season with salt and pepper, and brush the tops with more of the honey glaze. Broil 5 inches from the heat source until the cod is cooked through and the glaze is caramelized, about 5 to 7 minutes.

*On the Grill*    Season the cod with salt and pepper, lay it on the grill (or use a grilling basket), and brush the tops with more of the honey glaze. Cook, turning once, until the cod is done to taste and the glaze is caramelized, about 5 to 7 minutes.

To serve, lay a bed of caramelized onions on each plate and place the cod over the onions. Garnish with thyme sprigs.

# Striped Bass
## with Oregano & Verjus

Verjus is the juice from wine grapes before it is fermented to become wine. It is slightly more acidic than wine but milder than vinegar, with a sweet fresh taste that makes it a great complement to an oily fish such as striped bass. Here, verjus is combined with fresh oregano and cherry tomatoes to make a light, brothy sauce with a subtle earthy note that enhances the fish. You can substitute red snapper for the striped bass if you'd prefer.

Asparagus with Herbs and Cheese Crisps (page 198) or a simple sauté of spinach (page 125) would make a great side dish with the fish.

SERVES 4

**1 cup verjus (see Note)**

**1 cup vegetable broth (reduced-sodium if canned)**

**2 tablespoons extra virgin olive oil if roasting, ¹/₄ cup if grilling**

**4 wild striped bass fillets, skin on (6 to 7 ounces each)**

**4 teaspoons unsalted butter if roasting**

**Coarse sea salt or kosher salt and freshly ground black pepper**

**¹/₂ cup halved cherry tomatoes**

**¹/₄ cup fresh oregano leaves, plus additional sprigs for garnish**

*In the Oven*

Preheat the oven to 450°F. In a bowl, whisk together the verjus, vegetable broth, and olive oil.

Place the fish in a baking dish just large enough to accommodate the fillets in a single layer. Dot each fillet with 1 teaspoon butter and season them with salt and pepper. Pour the verjus mixture over the fish and scatter the tomatoes and oregano leaves over all.

Roast the fish for 15 to 20 minutes, until opaque throughout. Serve in shallow bowls with the tomatoes and broth from the pan spooned over the fish. Garnish with oregano sprigs.

*On the Grill*

Light the grill. In a saucepan over medium heat, combine the verjus, vegetable broth, 2 tablespoons of the olive oil, and a pinch of salt and pepper and bring to a boil. Simmer the mixture until it is reduced by a third, about 10 to 15 minutes. Add the tomatoes and cook for 2 minutes more.

In a small bowl, whisk together the remaining 2 tablespoons olive oil, the oregano leaves, and a pinch of salt and pepper. Rub both sides of the fillets with this mixture and place them on the grill (or use a grilling basket). Cook the fish, turning once, until charred around the edges and opaque throughout, about 10 minutes.

Serve the fillets in shallow bowls, spooning some of the verjus and tomato mixture over the top. Garnish with oregano sprigs.

NOTE    You can find verjus in some large supermarkets and specialty food markets. You can also mail-order it from Navarro Vineyards, by phone at (800) 537–WINE, or online at www.navarrowines.com. Or, you could substitute white wine in this recipe, which will give you a slightly mellower dish.

# Halibut with Quick Lemon Confit & White Wine

This simple dish gets its bright flavor from a simmered, jammy lemon confit that's both tart and slightly sweet. Halibut fillets are coated with the mixture, then roasted or grilled, which allows the confit's flavor to permeate the mild fish, while the lemons caramelize and crisp. Leftover lemon confit can be used in myriad ways—try it on broiled scallops or use it as a marinade for grilled shrimp.

SERVES 4

**3 lemons**

**I cup dry white wine**

**3 tablespoons sugar**

**I teaspoon fresh thyme leaves, plus additional sprigs**

**I teaspoon freshly ground black pepper, plus additional to taste**

**1/4 teaspoon coarse sea salt or kosher salt, plus additional to taste**

**4 halibut fillets, skin on (I inch thick, 6 ounces each)**

**Extra virgin olive oil**

**Watercress sprigs for garnish**

Slice 2 of the lemons in half lengthwise, then thinly slice into half-moons. Slice the remaining lemon into thin rounds. Reserve the rounds.

Place the half-moons of lemons, wine, sugar, thyme leaves, pepper, and salt in a saucepan and bring to a boil over medium heat. Cover and simmer until the lemons are soft, about 10 minutes. Uncover and cook slowly until the liquid has a syrupy consistency, 25 to 30 minutes more. Let cool.

Preheat the oven to 450°F or light the grill. Transfer the lemons and their liquid to the bowl of a food processor and pulse until finely chopped (do not let them become a puree). You can also finely chop the lemons by hand.

Brush the skin sides of the halibut fillets with olive oil and place, skin side down, on a rimmed baking sheet. Season the fillets with salt and pepper, then spread the tops and sides of each fillet with the lemon confit. Scatter the thyme sprigs over the fillets and top with the reserved lemon rounds.

*In the Oven*  Place the pan in the oven and roast until the fish is opaque throughout, about 10 minutes.

*On the Grill*  Using a wide spatula, transfer the fillets to the grill. Cook with the grill cover on until the fillets are opaque throughout, about 10 minutes (do not turn).

Serve the fillets drizzled with olive oil and garnished with watercress sprigs.

# Swordfish Steaks in a Mustard Seed Crust

A combination of whole-grain and Dijon mustards makes a sharp, tangy crust for swordfish, keeping it moist and juicy in the center and caramelizing around the edges. This is an incredibly fast, easy recipe with a lot of flavor for the effort. I like to serve the fish with braised celery (recipe follows) or simple boiled potatoes tossed with parsley or dill.

If your swordfish steaks are thinner than the fat medallions I call for, reduce the cooking time by a few minutes. The old rule of thumb, 10 minutes per inch, works well here. You could also substitute mahimahi or shark.

SERVES 4

**¹/2 cup Dijon mustard**

**¹/2 cup whole-grain mustard**

**¹/4 cup extra virgin olive oil**

**3 tablespoons freshly squeezed lemon juice**

**¹/4 teaspoon freshly ground black pepper**

**4 skinless swordfish medallions (1¹/2 to 2 inches thick), 6 ounces each**

**Chopped fresh dill for garnish (optional)**

In a bowl, whisk together the mustards, olive oil, lemon juice, and pepper. Lay the swordfish in a pan in a single layer. Pour all of the mustard mixture over the fish, turning to coat both sides. Cover and refrigerate for at least 20 minutes and up to 2 hours.

Preheat the broiler or light the grill.

*In the Oven*   Place the swordfish in a roasting pan, leaving behind any of the mustard mixture not clinging to it. Broil the fish 5 inches away from the heat source, turning and brushing with some of the remaining mustard mixture every 5 minutes, until the fish is no longer pink in the middle, about 15 to 20 minutes.

*On the Grill*   Lay the fish on the grill, leaving behind any of the mustard mixture not clinging to it, and cook for 5 minutes. Turn the fish, brush the tops with some of the remaining mustard mixture, and cook for 10 minutes. Turn once again, brush the tops with more mustard mixture, and cook until no longer pink in the middle, about 5 minutes more.

Garnish the swordfish with dill if desired.

## Braised Celery

SERVES 4

**2 teaspoons extra virgin olive oil**
**I bunch celery, outer stalks discarded, inner stalks sliced into 4-inch lengths**
**$^1/_2$ cup chicken or vegetable broth (reduced-sodium if canned) or water**
**2 tablespoons drained capers**
**Coarse sea salt or kosher salt and freshly ground black pepper**
**Chopped fresh parsley or dill for garnish**

Warm the oil in a saucepan with a tightly fitting lid over medium heat. Add the celery and cook, stirring, until lightly browned, about 5 minutes. Pour the broth and capers over the celery and season with salt and pepper to taste.

Cover the pan and simmer, reducing the heat if necessary, until the celery is tender, about 7 to 8 minutes. Garnish with parsley or dill.

# Wood-Grilled or Roasted Trout with Chervil Vinaigrette

When I first started experimenting with high-heat cooking, I found that it works extremely well with fish—especially trout. The high temperature crisps up the skin, which gives the soft fish a little bit of crunch. Grilling the trout over a wood fire gives it a terrific smoky flavor, but roasting it keeps the taste nice and subtle.

Whichever way you cook it, the sauce for the fish (also its marinade) is as simple as tossing herbs and oil in the blender. A chervil vinaigrette, seasoned with shallots and Champagne vinegar, lends a subtle herbal-onion flavor to the trout. If you can't find chervil (a leafy, anise-flavored herb that looks a little like cilantro), substitute chives.

SERVES 4

**I cup chopped fresh chervil or chives**

**³/4 cup chopped fresh flat-leaf parsley**

**3 tablespoons roughly chopped shallot**

**3 tablespoons freshly squeezed lemon juice**

**2 tablespoons Champagne vinegar or white wine vinegar**

**I cup extra virgin olive oil**

**I teaspoon coarse sea salt or kosher salt, plus additional to taste**

**Freshly ground black pepper**

**4 skin-on boned trout (10 to 14 ounces), heads removed**

To prepare the vinaigrette, in a blender, puree the chervil, parsley, shallot, lemon juice, and vinegar with ¹/2 cup of the olive oil. Transfer the mixture to a small bowl and stir in the remaining oil, the salt, and pepper to taste.

If grilling over coals, light the grill using plenty of charcoal. If using firewood, add it now and let the wood and charcoal burn for about an hour or until most of the firewood is burned up; you'll be left with some ash and the charcoal. If using wood chips, soak them for at least 20 minutes, then add them to the coals after they are completely gray. Let the chips burn for 10 minutes. Move the charcoal and wood over to one side of the grill for indirect grilling. If using a gas grill, preheat the grill thoroughly, adding soaked wood chips according to the manufacturer's instructions. When the grill is hot and smoky, turn off the fire under half of the grill. If roasting, preheat the oven to 500°F.

Meanwhile, sprinkle the inside of the trout with salt and pepper to taste. Spoon about half of the vinaigrette over the trout, both inside and out. Rub the vinaigrette into the fish. Cover the trout and refrigerate for 15 to 30 minutes.

*On the Grill*  Spray one side of a 15-inch piece of aluminum foil with cooking spray. Use it to cover the side of the grill without the heat underneath (sprayed side facing up). Place the fish on top of the foil and cover the grill. Check the fish after 10 minutes. It's done when the flesh is opaque and the skin is crisp. If it's not done, keep checking it every few minutes.

*In the Oven*  Lay the fish on a rack in a roasting pan and roast for 15 to 25 minutes, depending on the size of the trout, until the flesh is opaque.

Serve immediately, with the remaining vinaigrette as the sauce.

# Whole Red Snapper with Baby Fennel & Niçoise Olives

This is not a spur-of-the-moment recipe. The snapper needs to be ordered from your fishmonger a few days in advance, then marinated overnight. But it's worth planning ahead for this spectacular, dramatic dish. Cooked on the bone, the snapper's flesh remains succulent, permeated with the anise flavor of fennel and sparked by lemon, garlic, and salty, meaty olives, all of which counterbalance the sweetness of the fish. If you can't get one large fish, or don't want to bother, you can use two smaller ones, about 3 1/2 pounds each. Just be sure to reduce the cooking time.

SERVES 6

**1 small fennel bulb**

**2 1/2 lemons, plus additional lemon wedges for serving**

**1/2 cup chopped pitted Niçoise olives**

**1/2 cup chopped fresh flat-leaf parsley**

**1/2 cup extra virgin olive oil, plus additional for drizzling**

**1/4 cup minced garlic**

**1/2 teaspoon coarse sea salt or kosher salt**

**1/2 teaspoon freshly ground black pepper**

**1 very fresh whole 6-pound red snapper, scaled and cleaned**

Trim the fennel and finely chop it, including the feathery fronds. Put them in a large bowl. Squeeze the juice of 2 of the lemons over the bowl with the fennel fronds. Stir in the olives, parsley, olive oil, garlic, and salt and pepper. Stuff as much of this filling into the cavity of the fish as will fit, then rub the remaining mixture over the fish. Wrap the fish tightly in 2 layers of plastic wrap. Refrigerate overnight.

If grilling over coals, light a fire of wood and coals 2 hours before serving. Remove the fish from the refrigerator 1 hour before serving. If gas grilling or roasting, light the grill or preheat the oven to 500°F.

*On the Grill*  Let the fire burn down until only hot coals remain, then rake them to one side. Alternately, turn off the gas under one side of the grill. Tie the fish with butcher's twine at 3-inch intervals and place over the side of the grill without the heat underneath, using a fish rack if desired. Cook in a covered grill until done to taste, about 40 to 45 minutes, turning once.

*In the Oven*    Lay the fish on a rimmed baking sheet and roast for 20 minutes. Reduce the oven temperature to 400°F and roast for another 30 minutes. If the fish is still too rare (check by looking at the flesh near the spine), turn the oven off and leave the fish in the cooling oven until it is done to taste.

To serve, lay the fish on a platter, removing the twine if necessary, and drizzle with more olive oil and lemon juice from the remaining lemon half. Fillet and serve with the filling, garnished with additional lemon wedges.

# Shrimp with Parsley, Garlic, & Lemon Butter

This is my high-heat, deconstructed shrimp scampi. The flavors are clean: garlic, butter, parsley, chile, and lemon wedges that all get tossed with the shrimp at the last minute. All you really need is some crusty sourdough for sopping up the juices, but you could serve this with boiled potatoes, rice, or pasta, passing the shrimp in a big bowl for a large group or serving it on individual plates as an elegant appetizer. The dish takes on different characteristics when roasted or grilled but is always garlicky, buttery, and fresh. I like to use jumbo shrimp, which are called U-15s (indicating that there are under 15 shrimp in a pound).

SERVES 4 TO 6

**2 lemons**

**1 cup (2 sticks) unsalted butter**

**$1/4$ cup minced garlic**

**1 dried red chile pepper, halved crosswise, seeds removed (wear gloves)**

**$1/2$ cup chopped fresh flat-leaf parsley**

**Coarse sea salt or kosher salt and freshly ground black pepper**

**2 pounds extra-large shrimp (15 to 20 per pound), peeled and deveined, tails left on**

**1 tablespoon extra virgin olive oil for grilling**

**2 to 3 tablespoons dried unseasoned bread crumbs**

Preheat the oven to 500°F or light the grill. Juice one of the lemons.

Melt the butter in a skillet over medium heat. Add the garlic and chile and cook until the garlic is fragrant, about 3 to 4 minutes. Remove the chile.

*In the Oven*  Add the lemon juice and half of the parsley to the butter sauce and season with salt and pepper. Lay the shrimp in one layer in a gratin dish. Slice the remaining lemon lengthwise in half, then slice each half into 3 wedges. Cut the wedges crosswise into thin wedges and scatter them over the shrimp. Pour the butter sauce over the top and sprinkle with the bread crumbs. Roast until the shrimp are just pink, about 5 to 6 minutes. Garnish with the remaining parsley and serve.

*On the Grill*  Slice the remaining lemon crosswise into thin rounds. In a bowl, toss the shrimp with the lemon slices and olive oil and season with salt and pepper. Place the shrimp and lemon in a grilling basket and grill until the shrimp are pink and slightly charred, about 3 minutes per side. Transfer the lemon slices to a board and roughly chop them. Add the chopped lemon and the bread crumbs to the butter sauce in the pan. Season with salt and pepper and bring to a simmer over medium heat. Cook the sauce for 2 to 3 minutes, then add the lemon juice and half of the parsley. Serve the shrimp with the sauce, garnished with the remaining parsley.

# Sea Scallops on Rosemary Skewers with Tomato-Ginger Chutney

Using rosemary branches to skewer scallops makes for a whimsical presentation and also imparts a little of rosemary's slightly piney flavor. Keep in mind that the high heat will probably cause the rosemary leaves to brown or fall off when they're cooked, so don't expect them to look the way they do when assembled. Or if you really love their fresh green leaves, individually wrap the ends of the sprigs in aluminum foil before cooking. In either case, you can also garnish the plates with fresh rosemary sprigs.

Great for hors d'oeuvres or the main course, these scallops taste as good as they look. Their mellow caramelized flavor is offset by a bold chutney made spicy with chile peppers, coriander, and cardamom and a little sweet with candied ginger. The chutney can be prepared a few days in advance and kept in the refrigerator.

SERVES 4

**16 small rosemary branches**

**16 large sea scallops (see sidebar)**

**6 tablespoons extra virgin olive oil**

**Coarse sea salt or kosher salt and freshly ground black pepper**

**$^1/_2$ cup finely chopped onion**

**2 garlic cloves, minced**

**2 jalapeño peppers, seeded and diced**

**2 teaspoons ground coriander**

**1 teaspoon dry mustard**

**$^1/_2$ teaspoon ground cardamom**

**$^1/_2$ cup dry white wine**

**5 large ripe tomatoes, cored, seeded, and diced**

**1 cup finely chopped candied ginger**

**Juice of $^1/_2$ lemon**

Strip enough leaves off each rosemary branch to make room for 1 scallop and coarsely chop the rosemary leaves. Thread the scallops horizontally onto the branches and lay them on a plate. Drizzle 3 tablespoons of the olive oil and the chopped rosemary leaves evenly over the scallops and season with salt and pepper to taste. Turn gently to coat and let them sit at room temperature for 30 minutes.

Preheat the oven to 500°F or light the grill.

Meanwhile, prepare the tomato chutney. Warm the remaining 3 tablespoons of olive oil in a medium saucepan over medium heat. Add the onion and cook, stirring, until translucent, 3 to 4 minutes. Add the garlic, jalapeños, coriander, dry mustard, and cardamom and cook for another minute. Add the wine and simmer for 2 minutes. Stir in the tomatoes and candied ginger and simmer until thick and jammy, about 20 to 30 minutes. Season with salt and pepper to taste and cover to keep warm.

*In the Oven*  Lay the scallops on a rimmed baking sheet and roast until they are opaque throughout, about 5 minutes.

*On the Grill*  Place the scallops on the grill (or use a grilling basket) and cook, turning once, until they are opaque throughout, about 5 minutes.

To serve, spread the tomato chutney in a serving dish. Arrange the scallops on top, then sprinkle the lemon juice over all.

---

*Buying Sea Scallops*  Unless you can find live sea scallops in the shell, "dry" (frozen) scallops are preferable to "wet" scallops. Since scallop boats go out for over a week at a time, fast-frozen sea scallops may actually taste fresher than fresh scallops that have been soaked in brine and preservatives to keep them from spoiling. These brined scallops are referred to as "wet"; they inevitably lose their liquid to the pan as soon as they are heated, which slows their cooking and prevents them from developing a golden brown, caramelized outer crust. Live sea scallops are sometimes available at specialty markets and are worth the price. The shells should close up when you squeeze down on them, and they should smell fresh, not fishy. To shuck a live scallop, slide the blade of a sharp knife along the top shell to detach the scallop without cutting into it. Use the knife to detach the scallop from the bottom shell, then pull away and discard the membrane and viscera that surround the scallop.

# Sea Scallops on a Potato Disk with Spicy Leek Relish

This is a fun recipe in which the main protein and side dish are prepared at the same time—a kind of elegant all-in-one meal. I came up with it because cooked scallops give off delicious juices as they sit, so I wanted to create a raft that would absorb them. Potatoes work perfectly. For a sauce I add a smoky, spicy ancho chile and leek jam that combines beautifully with the sweet scallops and crisp potatoes. It makes for an out-of-the-ordinary scallop dish with quite a kick.

SERVES 4

2 ancho chiles

7 tablespoons extra virgin olive oil, plus additional for brushing

4 large leeks (white and light green parts only), chopped

2 celery stalks, finely chopped

2 garlic cloves, finely chopped

1 teaspoon coarse sea salt or kosher salt, plus additional to taste

$3/4$ cup dry white wine

$3/4$ cup chicken or vegetable broth (reduced-sodium if canned)

1 lemon

3 Idaho potatoes, scrubbed and cut crosswise into $1/2$-inch-thick slices

Freshly ground black pepper

16 large sea scallops (see sidebar, page 181)

2 tablespoons chopped fresh flat-leaf parsley

2 teaspoons snipped fresh chives

To make the leek jam, pour enough boiling water over the ancho chiles to cover them and let soak, turning once, until softened, about 15 minutes. Drain the chiles and, wearing gloves, remove the stems, veins, and seeds and discard. Chop the chiles.

In a saucepan over medium-low heat, warm 3 tablespoons of the olive oil and add the chiles, leeks, celery, garlic, and salt. Cook gently, stirring, for 5 minutes. Do not let the vegetables brown. Add the wine and broth and bring to a simmer. Simmer, covered, for 30 minutes. Uncover the pan and simmer until the mixture is slightly caramelized and jammy, about 15 minutes more.

Preheat the oven to 500°F or light the grill. Slice the lemon lengthwise into quarters and remove the seeds. Thinly slice the quarters into small wedges. Brush the potatoes with olive oil and season them with salt and pepper to taste on both sides.

In a bowl, toss the scallops with the remaining $\frac{1}{4}$ cup olive oil, the lemon wedges, parsley, and a pinch of salt and pepper.

*In the Oven*    Lay the potatoes in a single layer on a rimmed baking sheet. Lay the scallops on another baking sheet. Roast the potatoes for 5 minutes, then flip them over. Place the baking sheet with the scallops in the oven, roasting the scallops and potatoes for another 5 minutes.

*On the Grill*    Lay the potatoes on the grill and cook until charred around the edges on one side, about 5 minutes. Place the scallops in a large grill basket. Flip the potatoes and lay the scallops on the grill. Cook the potatoes and scallops for another 5 minutes, turning the scallops once.

To serve, place 4 potato disks on each plate and top each disk with a scallop. Spoon the leek jam over the scallops and potatoes and serve, sprinkled with the chives and garnished with extra potatoes if desired.

# Grilled Soft-Shell Crab Sandwiches on English Muffins with Tarragon Mayonnaise

At my restaurants I serve soft-shell crabs in pretty fancy guises. But behind the scenes, my line cooks and I love to make soft-shell crab sandwiches. For our purposes they are ideal—fast-cooking, delicious, and easy to eat while standing up. Well, the word got out about these sandwiches, and soon the waitstaff and managers were asking for them too. Eventually we decided to share our secret with the customers and put the sandwiches on the menu. They were an instant success. You'll see why: the combination of charred, juicy crabs, crunchy English muffins, and a piquant herbal mayonnaise is a winner.

Make sure you toast the English muffins until they are dark and very crisp all over. This ensures that all those nooks and crannies will soak up the sweet juice from the crabs and hold a layer of the mayonnaise without turning to mush. I like to serve the sandwiches with lettuce, tomato, onions, and even a pickle, but they are also terrific plain. Don't make these ahead; they need to be assembled and eaten immediately.

Buy cleaned soft-shell crabs the day you will use them, or at most a day in advance, and refrigerate them. Or buy them live and clean them right before cooking (see sidebar). If you are wary of the raw egg in the mayonnaise, blend fresh tarragon, mustard, and a little tomato paste with purchased mayonnaise for a passable if not quite as luscious approximation. Leftover mayonnaise, by the way, is good on everything.

SERVES 4

I egg yolk

I tablespoon freshly squeezed lemon juice

I tablespoon tarragon vinegar or white wine vinegar

2 teaspoons tomato paste

1 1/2 teaspoons Dijon mustard

1/8 teaspoon coarse sea salt or kosher salt, plus additional to taste

Freshly ground black pepper

2/3 cup grapeseed oil or canola oil

1/3 cup extra virgin olive oil, plus additional for brushing

2 tablespoons chopped fresh tarragon leaves

4 soft-shell crabs, cleaned

*How to Clean Soft-Shell Crabs*  Crabs should be cleaned immediately before cooking. Place a crab on a cutting board and use a sharp knife to cut straight across the front of the crab, removing less than a $1/2$-inch strip, which will include the eyes and mouth. To remove the gills, pull up on half of the top shell to expose the gills and pull them away. Repeat on the other side. Turn the crab belly up and pull off the tail flap.

**4 English muffins**
**Unsalted butter for the muffins**
**Lettuce, sliced tomatoes, sliced red onion, and pickles for serving (optional)**

Preheat the broiler or light the grill.

To make the tarragon mayonnaise, in a blender or food processor, blend the egg yolk with the lemon juice, vinegar, tomato paste, mustard, salt, and pepper to taste. With the motor running, slowly drizzle in the oils in a very thin stream and process until the mixture is emulsified. (Don't rush the oils; it will take a few minutes to fully incorporate them, but adding them too fast will cause the mayonnaise to break.) Transfer to a bowl and fold in the tarragon.

Brush the crabs with olive oil and season them with salt and pepper.

*In the Oven*  Place the crabs on a rimmed baking sheet and broil them directly under the heat source until charred, about 2 to 3 minutes per side.

*On the Grill*  Place the crabs on the grill (or use a grilling basket) and cook, turning once, until they are charred all over, about 2 to 3 minutes per side.

*(continued)*

Toast the English muffins until they are deeply golden all over and spread them with butter while still warm. Layer on the mayonnaise, crabs, and accompaniments if desired and serve immediately.

*Fixing a Broken Mayonnaise*   If your mayonnaise curdles and separates, place a spoonful of this broken mayonnaise in a clean stainless-steel bowl and whisk in a teaspoon of very cold water, until smooth. Gradually whisk in the rest of the broken mayonnaise. If the mayonnaise does not completely come together, start over with another egg yolk, drizzling in the broken mayonnaise in place of the oil.

# Lobster Salad with Red Onion, Basil, & Bibb Lettuce

This zesty salad, filled with herbs and sweet red onions, takes on a slightly smoky flavor from using grilled or broiled lobster meat. It's a terrific dish for a buffet or a light summer main course, or serve it as an elegant appetizer at your fanciest dinner party. If you really want to go all out, you can add other types of seafood to the dressing, including lump crabmeat and shrimp. But either way, don't count on any leftovers.

SERVES 4

2 cooked lobsters (about 1 1/4 pounds each), meat removed from the shell

2 tablespoons unsalted butter, melted

Coarse sea salt or kosher salt and freshly ground black pepper

1/4 cup mayonnaise

2 tablespoons Dijon mustard

2 tablespoons freshly squeezed lemon juice

1 tablespoon extra virgin olive oil

3/4 cup thinly sliced red onion

1/2 cup chopped fresh basil

1 large or 2 small heads Bibb or Boston lettuce for serving

Preheat the broiler or light the grill. In a bowl, toss the lobster meat with the butter and a pinch of salt and pepper.

*In the Oven*  Lay the lobster meat in a single layer on a rimmed baking sheet and place it directly under the heat source. Broil until it's charred around the edges, about 5 minutes.

*On the Grill*  Place the lobster meat in a grill basket and grill until charred, turning once, about 5 minutes.

Let the lobster cool.

In a large bowl, whisk together the mayonnaise, mustard, lemon juice, and olive oil and season with salt and pepper to taste. Add the lobster, onion, and basil to the bowl and toss to coat them with the dressing. Serve the salad over a bed of lettuce.

# Lobster with Dill & Yellow Pepper–Fennel Slaw

Boiled lobster is a wonderful thing, but grilled or broiled lobster is even better. The meat takes on a slightly caramelized flavor, getting even sweeter, if you can imagine that. In this recipe I brush split boiled or steamed lobsters with a dill butter, char them, then serve them with a tangy slaw made from crunchy fennel and yellow bell pepper instead of the usual cabbage. It's a gorgeous dish with the complementary flavors of dill and licorice from the fennel brought together by the succulent lobster. The slaw, by the way, is also excellent with a pork sandwich (page 145).

You can usually buy lobsters already boiled or steamed (and split in half if you like), but if you want to buy live ones and cook them yourself, the recipe follows.

SERVES 4

**For the Slaw**
1/4 cup extra virgin olive oil

2 tablespoons dry white wine

1 teaspoon white wine vinegar

2 fennel bulbs, cored, trimmed, and thinly sliced, fronds reserved

1 yellow bell pepper, thinly sliced

2 tablespoons chopped fennel fronds

Coarse sea salt or kosher salt and freshly ground black pepper

**For the Lobster**
1/2 cup (1 stick) unsalted butter, melted

2 tablespoons chopped fresh dill

1/2 teaspoon coarse sea salt or kosher salt

Freshly ground black pepper

4 cooked lobsters (about 1 1/4 pounds each), split in half lengthwise, claws removed and cracked

To prepare the slaw, in a large bowl, whisk together the olive oil, white wine, and vinegar. Add the fennel, yellow pepper, and fennel fronds and toss to coat them in the dressing. Season with salt and pepper to taste and let sit for 1 hour, until the vegetables have wilted.

Light the grill or preheat the broiler. In a bowl, combine the melted butter, dill, salt, and a large pinch of black pepper.

*On the Grill*  Place the lobsters in a grilling basket. Grill, basting with half of the dill butter, until the lobsters are charred, about 5 minutes.

*In the Oven*  Lay the lobsters on a baking sheet and brush them with half of the dill butter. Broil until charred, about 5 minutes.

Place the remaining dill butter in small bowls to dip the lobster in, and serve with the slaw.

## How to Boil a Lobster

**4 lobsters (about 1 $\frac{1}{4}$ pounds each)**
**2 lemons, sliced**
**2 tablespoons hot red pepper flakes**
**1 tablespoon coarse sea salt or kosher salt**

Fill an 8-quart pot three-quarters full of water. Bring the water to a boil. Add the lobsters, lemons, red pepper flakes, and salt and boil, covered, for 10 minutes. Remove the lobsters from the water with tongs and let drain for a few minutes.

# Roasted Shellfish Stew with Mussels, Clams, Shrimp, & Linguiça Sausage

This exuberant seafood stew has the same spectacular impact as its Mediterranean relatives bouillabaisse and paella, but it's also much easier to prepare since everything goes in the pot at once. Thinly sliced Idaho potatoes cook in the soup, and their starch thickens the broth, while linguiça sausage adds spice and richness. (If you can't find linguiça substitute chorizo sausage.) I like to use shell-on shrimp since it's meant to be a rustic, roll-up-your-sleeves kind of dish, and it's easy to pull the shrimp from their shells just as you're doing with the mussels and clams. Of course, shelled shrimp are fine to use, but the shells give the broth nice flavor and color, too. For relaxed, festive entertaining, serve the soup outdoors with plenty of cold beer or a big pitcher of sangria and grilled or toasted sourdough bread for mopping up all that tasty broth.

SERVES 4 TO 6

16 cherrystone or topneck clams

32 mussels, scrubbed in cold water and debearded

2 tablespoons extra virgin olive oil

16 jumbo shrimp, deveined, shells left on

1 pound linguiça sausage, cut into 16 chunks

1/2 Spanish onion, chopped (about 1 cup)

3 garlic cloves, chopped

6 small Red Bliss or fingerling potatoes, halved and thinly sliced

2 large ripe tomatoes, diced

1/2 teaspoon hot red pepper flakes

1/2 cup dry white wine

2 cups chicken or vegetable broth (reduced-sodium if canned)

3 tablespoons chopped fresh flat-leaf parsley for garnish

Preheat the oven to 500°F. Wash the clams and mussels in a bowl of cold water, changing the water several times. Discard any shellfish that don't close when tapped.

In a flameproof, ovenproof casserole or very large skillet over high heat, warm 1 tablespoon of the olive oil. Add the shrimp and cook, stirring, until the shells are slightly browned, about 2 minutes. Transfer to a plate and set aside.

Add the remaining tablespoon of oil to the pan. Add the sausage and cook, stirring occasionally, until well browned on all sides, about 2 to 3 minutes. Add the onion and cook, stirring, until translucent, about 3 minutes. Add the garlic and cook for 1 minute longer. Stir in the potatoes, tomatoes, and red pepper flakes. Pour in the wine and bring to a simmer. Cook for 30 seconds. Add the broth and stir in the shrimp, clams, and mussels.

Place the casserole in the oven and roast until the clams and mussels have opened, about 15 to 20 minutes. Serve garnished with the parsley.

# Squid with Lemon & White Beans

The nutty earthiness of gigante beans, the saline flavor of squid, fresh baby spinach, and plenty of lemon combine in this unusual warm salad. You can use another kind of dried bean here, like cannellini, but if you haven't tasted gigantes, I encourage you to try them—often used in Greek cuisine, I think they're one of the best-flavored dried beans. Their cooking time varies depending on the freshness of the beans, but you want to be sure to cook them through so that they are creamy on the inside yet not mushy.

Buy cleaned baby squid and cook them quickly over a very hot fire (or under a very hot broiler). The idea is to char them well while the flesh remains white and opaque. They will curl as soon as they're done, and it's important not to overcook them, or they will become tough and rubbery. This recipe makes a lot, so it's great party food.

SERVES 8 AS A MAIN COURSE, 16 AS AN APPETIZER

1 pound dried gigante beans, sorted

1 whole clove

1 medium onion, peeled

1 bay leaf

2 slices bacon (optional)

$1/2$ teaspoon freshly ground black pepper, plus additional to taste

5 lemons

2 pounds cleaned baby squid, tentacles removed and bodies halved lengthwise

$1/4$ cup extra virgin olive oil

Coarse sea salt or kosher salt

1 small red onion, very thinly sliced

2 cups baby spinach

$1/2$ cup chopped fresh flat-leaf parsley or basil or a combination

2 tablespoons snipped fresh chives

Place the beans in a large pot and add enough cold water to cover them by 2 inches. Bring to a boil, then turn off the heat and let cool completely. Alternately, place the beans in a large bowl, cover with cold water, and refrigerate overnight.

Drain the beans and return them to the pot. Add enough water to cover the beans by 2 inches. Stick the clove into the onion and add it to the pot along with the bay leaf, bacon if desired, and pepper. Bring to a simmer and cook, covered loosely, frequently skimming the foam that accumulates, until the beans are tender, about 45 to 60 minutes.

Juice 2 of the lemons and reserve the juice. Slice one of the lemons lengthwise into quarters and slice each quarter into thin wedges. In a large bowl, toss the squid with 2 tablespoons of the olive oil, the lemon wedges, and a pinch of salt and pepper and let sit for 30 minutes.

Light the grill or preheat the broiler.

*On the Grill*  Lay the squid out on the grill (or use a grilling basket) and cook, turning once, until they are curled and opaque (their ends will be singed), about 2 minutes per side.

*In the Oven*  Spread the squid out on a rimmed baking sheet and roast until they are curled and opaque (their ends will be singed), about 3 to 5 minutes.

When the beans are done, reserve I cup of the cooking liquid and drain. Discard the onion, bacon, and bay leaf and transfer the beans to a salad bowl. While the beans are warm, toss them with the remaining 2 tablespoons olive oil, the reserved lemon juice, red onion, and salt and pepper to taste. Fold in the baby spinach and herbs, moistening with some of the reserved cooking liquid from the beans if the mixture seems dry. Cut the remaining lemons into wedges. Serve the squid over the beans, with the lemon wedges.

# 8  *Vegetables*

# Asparagus & Portobello Mushroom Bundles with Mozzarella

These pretty bundles—made up of portobello mushroom caps topped with asparagus, cheese, and onion—have a nice compact presentation and a great combination of flavors. The meatiness of the mushrooms and the toasty browned cheese get a lift from the fresh green flavor of asparagus. For a lighter, less substantial side dish, leave off the cheese. Serve this hot or at room temperature.

SERVES 4

**1 bunch jumbo asparagus (about 1 pound), bottoms trimmed, lower stalks peeled**

**3 tablespoons extra virgin olive oil, plus additional for drizzling**

**3/4 teaspoon coarse sea salt or kosher salt**

**4 large portobello mushroom caps**

**2/3 cup grated fresh mozzarella cheese**

**4 thin slices red onion, separated into rings**

**Freshly ground black pepper**

Preheat the oven to 500°F or light the grill. In a large bowl, toss the asparagus with 1 tablespoon of the olive oil and 1/2 teaspoon of the salt. Brush the mushrooms with 2 tablespoons of the remaining olive oil and sprinkle them with the remaining 1/4 teaspoon salt.

*In the Oven*  Spread the asparagus in a single layer on a rimmed baking sheet. Lay the mushrooms on another rimmed baking sheet. Place the pans in the oven and roast, shaking the pans every 5 minutes, until the vegetables are browned and tender, about 15 to 20 minutes.

*On the Grill*  Lay the asparagus and mushrooms on the grill (or use a grilling basket) and cook, turning, until charred and tender, about 15 to 20 minutes.

When ready to serve, preheat the broiler. Lay the mushroom caps, gill side up, on a baking sheet and top with the asparagus. Sprinkle with the mozzarella. Place the baking sheet directly under the heat source and broil until the cheese melts and is golden around the edges, about 1 to 2 minutes. Watch carefully so the cheese doesn't burn. Serve garnished with red onion rings, a drizzle of olive oil, and plenty of freshly ground pepper.

*Jumbo Asparagus* I prefer to use jumbo asparagus that are as thick as my thumb whenever I can get them. They're amazingly sweet and flavorful, and they look especially impressive. The stalks do need to be peeled all the way up to 2 inches from the top, but this is well worth the trouble and not nearly as time consuming as it sounds.

# Asparagus with Herbs & Cheese Crisps

This dish looks exciting, tastes phenomenal, and has the added bonus of demonstrating the simple yet impressive skill of making crisp, wafer-thin Parmesan crackers (called *fricos* in Italy). For the *fricos*, grated Parmesan is spread thinly on a nonstick pan, heated, and within minutes the cheese has formed a golden, pliable wafer. Then I like to form the wafers as you would tuiles—that is, by draping them over a bottle or rolling pin to lend a nice curve (the French name *tuile* comes from their resemblance to the curved roofing tiles used on the Mediterranean). When the *frico* cools, it becomes a deliciously crisp, savory cracker. I lay the dressed asparagus in the curve of the *frico*, but you can also crumble the cracker over the asparagus. Extra broken crackers are a great snack or garnish for salads. In this case I consider genuine Parmigiano-Reggiano a must, because you're cooking it.

SERVES 4

1/2 cup grated Parmigiano-Reggiano cheese (about 2 ounces)

1 bunch jumbo asparagus (about 1 pound), bottoms trimmed, lower stalks peeled

6 tablespoons extra virgin olive oil

3/4 teaspoon coarse sea salt or kosher salt

2 tablespoons chopped fresh mint

2 tablespoons snipped fresh chives

1 1/2 tablespoons freshly squeezed lemon juice

1/4 teaspoon freshly ground black pepper

Pear, grape, or cherry tomatoes, halved, for garnish (optional)

Warm a nonstick pan over medium heat. Use a spatula to spread 2 tablespoons of cheese into a thin round in the pan and cook until lightly browned, about 3 minutes. Lay the round across a rolling pin or bottle to form it into a curve and let cool. Repeat with the remaining cheese. Reserve until serving time (these can be made up to 2 days in advance and stored carefully in an airtight container).

Preheat the oven to 500°F or light the grill. In a large bowl, toss the asparagus with 2 tablespoons of the olive oil and 1/4 teaspoon of salt.

*In the Oven*    Spread the asparagus in a single layer on a rimmed baking sheet and roast, shaking the pan to toss them every 5 minutes, until the asparagus are browned and tender with crisp tops, about 15 to 18 minutes.

*On the Grill*    Lay the asparagus on the grill (or use a grilling basket) and grill, turning, until browned and tender, about 15 to 18 minutes.

Mix the mint and chives together and set aside. In a bowl, whisk the lemon juice with the remaining $1/2$ teaspoon salt and the pepper. Whisking constantly, drizzle in the remaining $1/4$ cup of olive oil.

To serve, arrange a *frico* on each plate and lay the asparagus spears in the curve. Top with the herbs and drizzle with some of the dressing. Garnish with tomatoes if desired.

---

*Asparagus Gratin* This recipe can also be made into a gratin by omitting the cheese crisps. Simply layer the roasted or grilled asparagus in a small gratin dish, sprinkle with the herbs and dressing, and top with the cheese. Bake at 500°F until the cheese is browned and bubbling, about 8 to 10 minutes.

---

# Grilled or Roasted Summer Vegetables

Take advantage of the height of summer produce with this simple, straightforward recipe that highlights all the vegetables you can carry home from a farmer's market or roadside stand or bring in from your garden. Feel free to improvise, using any combination of summer squash, tomatoes, zucchini, and eggplant (I find that Asian eggplant is the sweetest and cooks the fastest). The veggies get a quick roast or grill, then a toss with lemon vinaigrette that enhances their summery freshness. This is a compatible side dish for just about every summer meal. Any leftovers can be stuffed between pieces of crusty bread for a fabulous sandwich.

SERVES 4 TO 6

**2 tablespoons freshly squeezed lemon juice**

**I tablespoon minced garlic**

**$^1/_2$ teaspoon coarse sea salt or kosher salt, plus additional to taste**

**Freshly ground black pepper**

**6 tablespoons extra virgin olive oil**

**2 small zucchini, sliced $^1/_4$ inch thick on a diagonal**

**2 small yellow summer squash, sliced $^1/_4$ inch thick on a diagonal**

**I Asian eggplant or 2 small Italian eggplants, sliced $^1/_4$ inch thick on a diagonal**

**I large tomato, halved and seeded**

**I medium red onion, peeled and sliced $^1/_4$ inch thick**

**I large portobello mushroom cap, sliced into 4 strips**

**Chopped fresh basil for garnish**

Light the grill or preheat the oven to 500°F.

In a bowl, whisk together the lemon juice, garlic, salt, and pepper. Whisking constantly, drizzle in the olive oil and continue to whisk until smooth. Set aside half of this dressing.

Place the zucchini, yellow squash, and eggplant slices in a large bowl and place the tomato, onion, and mushroom slices in 3 separate bowls. Drizzle enough of the remaining dressing into each bowl to coat the vegetables and toss well.

*On the Grill*  Lay the vegetables on the grill (or use a grill basket) and grill, turning occasionally, for 15 to 20 minutes, removing each vegetable when it is soft and browned.

*In the Oven*  Lay the vegetables in a single layer on rimmed baking sheets and roast, tossing occasionally, for 15 to 20 minutes, removing each vegetable when it is soft and browned.

Serve the vegetables on a platter, seasoned with salt and pepper to taste, drizzled with the reserved dressing, and garnished with basil.

---

*Asian Eggplant*  Asian eggplants are slender and long like zucchini, ranging in color from dark purple to lilac to white or light green. They tend to have thinner skins and fewer seeds than large American eggplants, making them sweeter, more delicate, and faster cooking. Italian eggplants can also be used in this recipe, but they are essentially a miniature version of an American eggplant and will not be as sweet or cook as quickly.

---

# Smoky Corn Succotash

Corn can be roasted or grilled either shucked or unshucked, depending on the flavor and texture result you prefer. When cooked in the husk, the kernels steam and end up tasting a lot like sweet boiled corn, though with a smokier edge. Here I grill or roast shucked ears, so the kernels develop a concentrated, toasted corn flavor and take on some char. Then, to complete the dish, the kernels are sliced from the cobs and served with simmered fresh shell beans, basil-flecked tomatoes, and savory red onions and scallions. You can serve this dish by mixing all of the vegetables together in a bowl, but I like to pass them in separate bowls, letting everyone build their own succotash as they please.

If you can't find cranberry beans, feel free to use any other shell bean, be it favas, lima beans, or even fresh shell peas—as long as they are fresh. This dish is all about summer, and canned or dried beans just won't be the same.

SERVES 6

**2 cups fresh shelled cranberry beans (from 1 1/2 pounds)**

**6 ears of corn, shucked**

**3 medium tomatoes, cubed**

**2 tablespoons extra virgin olive oil**

**1 tablespoon chopped fresh basil**

**Coarse sea salt or kosher salt and freshly ground black pepper**

**2 cups diced red onions**

**3/4 cup chopped scallions**

**4 tablespoons unsalted butter**

Place the beans in a large pot. Add enough water to cover them by 1 inch and bring to a boil. Turn down the heat, partially cover the pot, and simmer for about an hour. The beans should be soft and creamy but still separate and intact. Watch carefully to make sure that they do not burn, adding more water if necessary as the beans cook. There should be at least 1 cup of juice remaining in the pot when the beans are cooked. The beans can be made a few hours in advance and reheated gently in their juice.

Light the grill or preheat the oven to 500°F.

*On the Grill*  Place the ears on the grill and cook, turning occasionally, until they just start to turn brown around the edges, about 10 minutes.

*In the Oven*    Place the corn on a rimmed baking sheet and roast, turning occasionally, until it just starts to turn brown, about 15 minutes.

Let the corn cool. Holding the corn in a large bowl, slide a sharp knife along the cobs to cut away all the kernels, then run the back of the knife along the cobs to scrape the liquid into the bowl. Set aside.

In a bowl, mix together the tomatoes, olive oil, basil, and salt and pepper to taste. Place the diced onions and chopped scallions in separate serving bowls.

When ready to serve, put the beans, 1 cup of the reserved cooking liquid, and 2 tablespoons of the butter in a small saucepan. Cook over medium heat until the butter melts. Season to taste with salt and pepper. Transfer the beans to a serving bowl.

Place the corn and remaining 2 tablespoons butter in a small saucepan and heat until the butter melts and the corn is heated through. Season with salt and pepper to taste. Transfer to a serving bowl.

Serve the bowls of vegetables while the beans and corn are still warm. Let people assemble their own plates of succotash to taste.

# Mediterranean Stuffed Zucchini with Cilantro-Yogurt Sauce

This dish definitely takes its inspiration from the Mediterranean. I remember how my Lebanese grandmother would serve a bowl of yogurt with garlic and mint at almost every meal when I was a child. She also used to stuff summer squash with meat, rice, vegetables, or tomatoes, and the yogurt was a great accompaniment, turning into a creamy sauce with a garlicky kick.

SERVES 6

**3 garlic cloves**

**3 medium zucchini, trimmed**

**3 tablespoons extra virgin olive oil**

**I small onion, chopped**

**2 tablespoons chopped fresh cilantro**

**2 tablespoons chopped fresh mint**

**$1/8$ teaspoon ground cumin**

**I teaspoon coarse sea salt or kosher salt, plus additional to taste**

**$1/4$ teaspoon freshly ground black pepper, plus additional to taste**

**3 tablespoons dried unseasoned bread crumbs**

**I cup plain yogurt**

**2 tablespoons cream or milk**

**Lemon wedges for serving (optional)**

Preheat the oven to 500°F or light the grill.

Finely chop 2 of the garlic cloves. Cut off one quarter of each zucchini at the stem end, chop this finely, and set aside. Halve the zucchini lengthwise and scoop out the seeded flesh to form zucchini boats with $1/4$-inch-thick walls. Chop the scooped-out zucchini and add it to the reserved chopped zucchini.

In a pan, warm I tablespoon of the oil over medium heat. Add the onion and chopped garlic and cook, stirring, until the onion is translucent, about 10 minutes. Add the chopped zucchini, I tablespoon each of the cilantro and mint, and the cumin. Season with $3/4$ teaspoon of the salt and the pepper and cook, stirring, for another 3 minutes. Transfer to a bowl and let cool slightly. Stuff the zucchini boats with this mixture.

*In the Oven*   Place the stuffed zucchini in a baking dish just large enough to hold them. Sprinkle the bread crumbs over them, drizzle with the remaining 2 tablespoons olive oil, and season with salt and pepper to taste. Roast until the bread crumb topping is browned, about 12 minutes.

*On the Grill*   Sprinkle the zucchini with the bread crumbs, drizzle them with the remaining 2 tablespoons oil, and season with salt and pepper. Place the stuffed zucchini in a grill basket or directly on the grill and cook, covered, until tender, about 10 minutes.

Meanwhile, place the yogurt in a bowl and stir it with a whisk to loosen it. Whisk in the cream or milk. Add the remaining tablespoon each of cilantro and mint. Using the side of a chef's knife or a mortar and pestle, mash the remaining garlic clove with the remaining $1/4$ teaspoon salt to form a paste. Whisk the garlic puree into the yogurt. Serve the zucchini hot, drizzled with the sauce and a squeeze of lemon if desired.

# Baby Eggplant with Harissa & Mint

Spicy and aromatic, this recipe will surprise eggplant-phobes. Eggplant absorbs flavors so well that just brushing it with harissa (a pungent Middle Eastern chili-garlic paste) and mint creates a complex sauce that makes the dish. Served hot or at room temperature, this is a great addition to a summer barbecue. Or take it a simple step further, pureeing the eggplant to make a wonderful dip.

SERVES 4

4 small Japanese eggplants, halved lengthwise

1/4 cup extra virgin olive oil, plus additional for drizzling

3 tablespoons chopped fresh mint, plus additional for garnish

4 teaspoons harissa or other hot sauce (see Note)

I tablespoon freshly squeezed lemon juice

1/2 teaspoon coarse sea salt or kosher salt, plus additional to taste

Freshly ground black pepper

Lemon wedges for serving

Score the cut sides of the eggplants lightly into a crosshatch pattern. In a bowl, whisk together the olive oil, mint, harissa, lemon juice, salt, and pepper to taste. Lay the eggplants on a platter, cut sides up, and brush them with the harissa mixture. Let sit at room temperature for 30 minutes to I hour.

Preheat the broiler or light the grill.

*In the Oven*   Lay the eggplant, cut sides up, on a baking sheet and place 4 inches from the heat source. Broil, turning when the tops are well browned, until the eggplants are completely tender, about 10 to 12 minutes.

*On the Grill*   Lay the eggplants cut sides down on the grill and cook, turning when the cut sides are well browned, until completely tender, about 12 to 15 minutes.

Drizzle the eggplants with a little olive oil, season with salt and pepper to taste, and sprinkle with chopped mint. Serve with lemon wedges.

NOTE   Harissa is available at specialty and Middle Eastern food markets.

## Spicy Eggplant Dip

This lively dip is a nod to the baba ghanoush of my Lebanese heritage. Serve it with Grilled Herb and Olive Oil Flatbread (page 228), toasted pita wedges, or cut-up raw vegetables.

MAKES ABOUT 1¹/₂ CUPS

> 1 garlic clove, coarsely chopped
>
> 1 tablespoon chopped fresh mint
>
> Scooped-out flesh from 1 recipe Baby Eggplant with Harissa and Mint (opposite page)
>
> 2 tablespoons tahini
>
> 4 teaspoons freshly squeezed lemon juice or more to taste
>
> 1 tablespoon extra virgin olive oil
>
> ¹/₄ teaspoon coarse sea salt or kosher salt or more to taste

In the bowl of a food processor, pulse together the garlic and mint. Add the remaining ingredients and process until smooth. Taste and add more salt or lemon juice if desired.

# Crispy Stuffed Onions with Herbs

Onions are usually relegated to a supporting role, but here they're the star of a stunning side dish. The soft, sweet onions, imbued with herbs and topped with crisp bread crumbs, are an excellent foil for roast beef or grilled steak.

SERVES 4

**2 Spanish onions, peeled and halved crosswise**

**2 tablespoons extra virgin olive oil**

**2 garlic cloves, minced**

**$1/4$ cup chopped fresh flat-leaf parsley**

**I tablespoon chopped fresh mint**

**2 teaspoons chopped fresh oregano**

**I tablespoon freshly squeezed lemon juice**

**Coarse sea salt or kosher salt and freshly ground black pepper**

**4 teaspoons fresh bread crumbs (see sidebar, page 19)**

**I to 2 cups chicken or vegetable broth (reduced-sodium if canned) or water**

**I tablespoon unsalted butter, melted**

Preheat the oven to 500°F. Remove the inner core from the onion halves to form $1/2$-inch-thick cups. Set the onion cups aside.

Using a knife or a food processor, chop the onion cores. Heat the olive oil in a skillet over medium-high heat. Add the chopped onion and garlic and cook, stirring, until softened, about 5 minutes. Stir in the parsley, mint, oregano, lemon juice, and salt and pepper to taste.

Stuff the onion halves with this mixture and sprinkle with the bread crumbs. Place the stuffed onions in a gratin dish that holds them snugly and add enough broth or water to cover the bottom of the dish by I inch. Drizzle the onions with the melted butter and cover the pan with aluminum foil.

Roast the onions for 20 minutes, then uncover and cook until the bread crumbs are crisp and browned and the onions are tender when pierced with a knife, about 15 to 20 minutes more.

Rib Steak with Citrus Rub,
page 128

Rack of Lamb with Black
Olives & Lemon, page 140

Hot-Smoked Salmon
with Spicy Cucumbers,
page 164

Sea Scallops on Rosemary Skewers
with Tomato-Ginger Chutney, page 180

Roasted Shellfish Stew with Mussels, Clams, Shrimp, & Linguica Sausage, page 190

Smoky Corn Succotash, page 202

Thin-Crust Pizza with
Charred Lobster & Tomatoes, page 244

Roasted Peach & Blueberry Cake with Pan Juices, page 250

Apple Cheddar Pie, page 260

Grilled Pineapple with Gin, Juniper, & Lime, page 268

Chocolate Angel Food Cake with Roasted Brandied Strawberries & Chocolate Sauce, page 271

# Caramelized Onion & Roquefort Gratin

Appealing and unusual, this gratin combines the strong sharpness of Roquefort with the soft, round sweetness of onion and the milkiness of ricotta cheese, set off by a sprinkle of crunchy nuts. It's terrific as a side dish with roasted or grilled poultry or meats or could even be a light lunch if you serve it with a salad. Though the gratin needs to finish in the oven, if your grill is set up and you want to give the onion slices that extra char, go ahead and grill them. And if you're lucky enough to have leftovers of this gratin, tossing them with hot pasta creates an excellent sauce.

SERVES 8 TO 10

5 large Spanish onions

4 tablespoons unsalted butter, plus additional for gratin dish

Coarse sea salt or kosher salt and freshly ground black pepper

2 tablespoons extra virgin olive oil

1 $^1$/2 cups ricotta cheese

1 cup Roquefort cheese or other blue cheese, crumbled (about $^1$/4 pound)

$^1$/2 cup chopped walnuts

Thinly slice 3 of the onions. Melt the butter in a large pan over medium-low heat. Add the sliced onions and season with salt and pepper to taste. Toss well and cook gently, stirring occasionally, until the onions are meltingly soft and caramelized, about 45 to 60 minutes.

Meanwhile, preheat the broiler or grill. Cut the remaining onions into $^1$/2-inch slices and brush them lightly with the oil. Season them with salt and pepper.

*In the Oven*   Lay the onion slices on a baking sheet and broil, as close to the heat as possible, until browned, about 3 to 5 minutes. Carefully turn the onions over, keeping the slices intact, and broil until browned on the other side, about 3 more minutes.

*On the Grill*   Lay the onion slices on the grill and grill until they are seared on the bottom. Carefully turn the onions over, keeping the slices intact, and grill until seared on the other side, about 5 to 8 minutes total.

*(continued)*

Preheat the oven to 350°F. In a bowl, stir the cheeses together and season with pepper to taste.

Butter a casserole dish and spread a thin layer of caramelized onions on the bottom. Spoon dollops of the cheese mixture onto the onions, then lay half of the broiled or grilled onion slices over the cheese. Repeat this process, ending with the caramelized onions, topped with a little more of the cheese. Bake, uncovered, until bubbling and lightly browned, about 40 to 45 minutes, sprinkling on the walnuts after 30 minutes.

# Toasted Brussels Sprouts with Bacon

As I like to point out, bacon is great on everything. In this case it has a good shot at converting people who say they hate Brussels sprouts. Roasting the sprouts endows them with sweet, soft centers and crisp outer leaves, and tossing them with crunchy bits of bacon makes them a great savory side dish for fall or winter meals. Serve this at Thanksgiving or with roast chicken. If you can find Brussels sprouts on the stalk, it will ensure that you have fresh, sweet-tasting sprouts.

SERVES 4 TO 6

**1 1/2 pounds Brussels sprouts (about 5 cups)**
**Coarse sea salt or kosher salt**
**4 slices bacon**
**Freshly ground black pepper**

Preheat the oven to 500°F or light the grill. Trim the Brussels sprouts and score the bottoms with an X.

Bring a large pot of salted water to a boil. Add the Brussels sprouts and cook until crisp-tender, about 3 minutes. Drain.

In a skillet, cook the bacon until crisp, then transfer it to a paper towel–lined plate. Reserve half of the bacon fat.

*In the Oven*    Transfer the Brussels sprouts to a large casserole and roast for 5 minutes. Pour the reserved bacon fat over the Brussels sprouts, season with salt and pepper to taste, and add 2 tablespoons water. Toss well and roast until tender, about another 15 minutes.

*On the Grill*    When the Brussels sprouts are cool enough to handle, halve them and place them in a large bowl. Add the reserved bacon fat, season with salt and pepper to taste, and toss well. Transfer to a large grill basket and grill, turning once, until tender and lightly browned, about 10 minutes.

Transfer the Brussels sprouts to a bowl. Dice the bacon, sprinkle it over the Brussels sprouts, and serve.

# Roasted Carrots with Honey & Black Pepper

This recipe turns the commonplace, humble carrot into a unique, full-flavored side dish. A generous amount of black pepper gives it spark and vibrancy, while the honey becomes a lacquered glaze that accentuates the sweetness of the carrots. If you're pressed for time, use packaged baby carrots and you'll be able to make the dish at lightning speed.

SERVES 6

1 large bunch carrots (about 2 pounds), peeled and cut into $^3/_4$-inch slices on a diagonal

3 tablespoons unsalted butter, melted

$^1/_4$ teaspoon coarse sea salt or kosher salt, plus additional to taste

$^1/_4$ teaspoon coarsely ground black pepper, plus additional to taste

$^1/_2$ cup honey

Grated zest and juice of 1 orange

Preheat the oven to 475°F. In a large bowl, toss the carrots with 2 tablespoons of the butter and season with the $^1/_4$ teaspoon salt and liberal coarse grindings of pepper. Lay the carrots out in a single layer on rimmed baking sheets and roast until they are browned and almost tender, about 30 minutes.

Meanwhile, in a saucepan over medium heat, combine the remaining tablespoon of butter with the honey, orange zest and juice, and the $^1/_4$ teaspoon pepper. Bring to a simmer and cook for 1 minute. Season with salt to taste.

Transfer the carrots to a casserole or gratin dish and pour the honey mixture over them. Return the carrots to the oven and roast, uncovered, stirring once, until brown and caramelized, about 8 minutes.

# Roasted Winter Squash with Maple & Cayenne Glaze

This may become the only way you want to eat winter squash. The squash is cut into crescents and coated in a sweet, spicy sauce, then roasted until the glaze caramelizes, practically candying the soft squash. The glaze is extremely quick to mix up in a saucepan. The squash wedges keep their shape, and the glaze gives them a dark gloss, making this a lovely, elegant presentation of traditional flavors spiked with chile. It makes an ideal Thanksgiving side dish.

SERVES 4

1 tablespoon extra virgin olive oil

1 large or 2 small acorn squash, cut into 1 1/2-inch wedges, seeds discarded

Coarse sea salt or kosher salt and freshly ground black pepper

2 tablespoons unsalted butter

1/2 cup maple syrup

1/4 teaspoon cayenne pepper or to taste

Pinch of hot red pepper flakes

Preheat the oven to 500°F. Brush a rimmed baking sheet with some of the oil. Brush the squash wedges with the remaining oil and season with salt and pepper to taste. Lay the wedges flat on the baking sheet so they look like crescents. Roast until slightly softened, about 10 minutes.

Meanwhile, in a saucepan over medium heat, melt the butter and stir in the maple syrup, cayenne, red pepper flakes, and salt and pepper to taste. Brush the squash with some of this glaze and continue to roast until the glaze is thick and caramelized, about 10 minutes. Use tongs to turn the wedges over, then brush them with more glaze. Continue to roast until the glaze is thick and the squash is soft, another 5 to 10 minutes. Drizzle the squash with more of the remaining glaze before serving.

# Roasted Winter Root Vegetables with Balsamic Vinegar

This cozy dish is for those cold months when it's a pleasure to turn on your oven. The root vegetables of the season become concentrated at high heat, their starch converting to sugar and forming a caramelized crust—a far cry from the effect that boiling has on the same ingredients (think turnips). Feel free to make substitutions here, using more of your favorite vegetables or adding any other roots that you find in the market. This dish goes particularly well with roast poultry or pork. It's a forgiving recipe; if you need to cook meat at a different temperature, go ahead and roast the vegetables simultaneously, keeping them in the oven a little more or less as needed.

SERVES 6

**Coarse sea salt or kosher salt**

**2 parsnips, peeled**

**4 carrots, peeled**

**I large celery root, trimmed**

**I medium rutabaga, peeled**

**2 turnips, peeled**

**2 beets, peeled**

**2 sweet potatoes, peeled**

**3 tablespoons extra virgin olive oil, plus additional for brushing the pan and drizzling the vegetables**

**Freshly ground black pepper**

**I $^1$/2 cups chicken or vegetable broth (reduced-sodium if canned)**

**$^1$/4 cup balsamic vinegar, plus additional for drizzling**

**Fresh flat-leaf parsley, chopped, for garnish**

Preheat the oven to 400°F. Bring a large pot of salted water to a boil. Add the vegetables and boil until they are a bit less than halfway cooked, about 10 minutes. Drain and slice the vegetables $^1$/2 inch thick, slicing the carrots and parsnips on a diagonal. Transfer to a bowl and toss with the olive oil and salt and pepper to taste.

Brush a large roasting pan or casserole with a little olive oil. Transfer the vegetables to the pan and spread them in a single layer. Roast for about 30 minutes, tossing well after about 15 minutes. Pour the broth and vinegar over the vegetables and cover with foil. Continue to roast for another 45 minutes, turning them occasionally, until the vegetables are soft. Uncover the pan and roast for another 15 to 20 minutes, until the liquid cooks off and the vegetables are browned around the edges.

Transfer the vegetables to a platter and drizzle with olive oil and vinegar. Garnish with parsley.

# Scalloped Potatoes with Two Cheeses

Grilling the potatoes adds a welcome smokiness to this decadent side dish, making it a perfect partner for grilled meats or poultry. Known as Beacon Potatoes at my restaurants, these have become a customer favorite as well as my family's favorite at home!

SERVES 6

**4 Idaho potatoes, peeled and quartered lengthwise**

**Extra virgin olive oil for brushing**

**1 teaspoon coarse sea salt or kosher salt, plus additional to taste**

**$^1/_4$ teaspoon freshly ground black pepper, plus additional to taste**

**6 unpeeled garlic cloves**

**1 tablespoon unsalted butter, softened**

**1 cup milk**

**1 cup heavy cream**

**1 teaspoon fresh thyme leaves**

**$^1/_8$ teaspoon freshly grated nutmeg**

**2 cups grated Gruyère cheese (about $^1/_2$ pound)**

**$^3/_4$ cup grated Parmesan cheese (about 3 ounces)**

Light the grill. Brush the potatoes with olive oil and season them with salt and pepper.

Lay the potatoes on the grill (or in a grilling basket) and grill, turning once, until charred on both sides, about 8 to 10 minutes. Let the potatoes cool slightly, then cut into $^1/_4$-inch slices.

Preheat the oven to 325°F. Slice one of the garlic cloves in half. Rub the cut sides all over the inside of a shallow 1$^1/_2$-quart gratin or casserole dish. Brush the inside of the dish with the softened butter.

Smash the remaining 5 garlic cloves with the side of a knife and put them in a large saucepan. Add the milk, cream, thyme, and nutmeg. Bring the mixture to a boil, then reduce the heat and simmer for 5 minutes. Strain the mixture into a bowl, discarding the garlic and herbs. Stir in 1 teaspoon salt and $^1/_4$ teaspoon pepper.

Mix the cheeses together in a small bowl.

Cover the bottom of the gratin dish with an overlapping layer of one quarter of the potato slices. Pour a quarter of the cream mixture over the potatoes. Sprinkle with a quarter of the grated cheese mixture. Continue layering the casserole in this manner until all the ingredients are used up. Using a spatula, press down hard on top of the gratin to compact it.

Bake the gratin for 50 to 60 minutes, until the top is crusty and golden brown and a knife easily cuts through the potatoes. Transfer the gratin to a rack and cool for at least 10 minutes before serving.

# Crispy Potato Wedges with Mustard & Thyme

This is a great, easy alternative to French fries that will appeal to both kids and adults with its flavorful crust of mustard and herbs.

The potatoes need to be cooked partially before the final crisping in the oven or on the grill. If you're roasting them, it's easy enough to turn on the oven and bake the potatoes while you prepare the rest of the meal. But if you're grilling and would rather not turn the oven on, the microwave works just fine (and is much quicker).

SERVES 4

**2 large Idaho potatoes**

**$1/2$ cup Dijon mustard**

**2 tablespoons extra virgin olive oil**

**1 tablespoon chopped fresh thyme or 1 teaspoon dried**

**$1/2$ teaspoon coarse sea salt or kosher salt**

**$1/4$ teaspoon freshly ground black pepper**

Preheat the oven to 400°F or light the grill. Pierce the potatoes with a fork and bake them until almost cooked, about 30 to 40 minutes. (Or microwave them on high for 6 minutes, turning them after 3 minutes.)

In a large bowl, stir together the mustard, olive oil, thyme, salt, and pepper. When cool enough to handle, cut the partially cooked potatoes lengthwise into 4 wedges each. Toss the wedges in the mustard mixture until thoroughly coated.

*In the Oven*    Raise the oven temperature to 500°F. Lay the potato wedges with one of their cut sides down on a rimmed baking sheet and roast for 20 minutes, turning them onto the other cut side after 10 minutes.

*On the Grill*    Lay the potato wedges on the grill over medium heat. Cover the grill and cook until the potatoes are tender in the center and crisp on the outside, 10 to 15 minutes.

*Potato Variations* Once you've tried this recipe, feel free to experiment with other flavorings, making them spicy with red pepper flakes, substituting another fresh herb like oregano for the thyme, or even using dry herbs in a pinch. You can also play around with the mustard you use, trying horseradish mustard or whole-grain mustard. Or skip the mustard entirely and use plenty of Parmesan cheese instead.

# Charred Fennel
## with Sweet Red Pepper

This gorgeous, surprising combination is ideal in autumn, when red peppers are still abundant and fennel is just starting up again as the cool weather sets in. The pale greens and golden browns of roasted or grilled fennel are set off by a bright-colored topping of sliced red pepper. Balsamic vinegar highlights the sweetness of the vegetables and simultaneously balances it with acid. Since the vegetables are great hot or at room temperature, feel free to make this ahead.

SERVES 4

I red bell pepper

$^1/_4$ cup extra virgin olive oil, plus additional for brushing the pepper

2 tablespoons plus I teaspoon balsamic vinegar

$^1/_2$ teaspoon coarse sea salt or kosher salt, plus additional to taste

Freshly ground black pepper

2 fennel bulbs, trimmed and thinly sliced lengthwise

Chopped fennel fronds for garnish

Preheat the broiler or light the grill.

*In the Oven*  Halve the pepper lengthwise and discard the seeds and stem. Lay the pepper skin side up on a baking sheet, brush it lightly with olive oil, and place directly under the heat source. Broil until the skin is charred and blistered all over, about 3 minutes.

*On the Grill*  Brush the pepper with oil and grill it, turning frequently, until the skin is charred and blistered all over, about 15 minutes.

Immediately transfer the pepper to a deep bowl and cover with a plate to trap the steam. Let steam until cool, about 5 minutes, then rub the skin off the pepper using your hands or a metal spoon. Remove the seeds and stem if necessary and thinly slice the pepper into strips. Place the pepper strips in a bowl and toss with 3 tablespoons of the olive oil, the balsamic vinegar, the $^1/_2$ teaspoon salt, and a good amount of pepper.

Preheat the oven to 500°F or add more charcoal to the grill if necessary. In a bowl, toss the fennel with the remaining tablespoon of olive oil and a generous pinch of salt and pepper.

*In the Oven* Spread the fennel in a single layer on 1 or 2 rimmed baking sheets and roast, tossing once, until tender and browned, about 8 to 10 minutes.

*On the Grill* Place the fennel in a grill basket and grill, turning once, until tender and browned, about 8 to 10 minutes.

Spread the fennel on a platter. Scatter the red pepper slices on top, then drizzle with some of the balsamic vinaigrette remaining in the bowl and garnish with chopped fennel fronds. Serve warm or at room temperature.

# Globe Artichokes Stuffed with Pine Nuts, Herbs, & Garlic

These artichokes are filled with a mix of eastern Mediterranean flavors that is simultaneously savory, sweet, bright, and crunchy. A stuffing of bread crumbs, olives, lemon zest, onions, garlic, pine nuts, raisins, herbs, and anchovies is packed between the leaves, and the whole thing is roasted until the bread crumbs and outer leaves are crisp while the inner leaves stay soft. Eat this substantial side dish with your hands, pulling off the leaves and scraping them between your teeth to capture the artichoke and filling. You can also serve these big artichokes as a starter course, and as a bonus, after eating an artichoke, other foods taste sweeter (this is caused by a substance in artichokes called *cynarine,* which also makes it difficult to pair artichokes with wine; but you could try a dry Riesling).

SERVES 4

I lemon

4 globe artichokes

Coarse sea salt or kosher salt

$^1/_2$ cup golden raisins

$^1/_3$ cup dry white wine

7 tablespoons extra virgin olive oil

2 tablespoons unsalted butter

$^1/_4$ cup pine nuts

$^1/_4$ cup finely chopped onion

$^1/_4$ cup finely chopped red bell pepper

4 anchovy fillets, minced

2 garlic cloves, minced

I cup fresh bread crumbs

2 tablespoons minced Kalamata olives

I tablespoon chopped fresh mint

I tablespoon chopped fresh flat-leaf parsley

Freshly ground black pepper

Grate the zest from the lemon and set aside.

Fill a bowl with water, ice, and the juice from half the lemon. Trim the artichokes by first pulling off the tough outer leaves. Trim off the bottoms so the artichokes can stand upright, and then the tops. Use kitchen shears or scissors to snip off any points remaining on the leaves. As you trim the artichokes, put the finished ones in the bowl of lemon water to keep them from turning brown.

Bring a large pot of salted water to a boil. Place the artichokes in the water and cover them with a heatproof plate or a round of parchment or wax paper just smaller than the pot to keep them submerged. Cook until tender, about 25 minutes. When cool enough to handle, use a thin sharp knife to cut the center leaves, and a spoon to scoop out the hairy choke from each artichoke.

Meanwhile, in a small pot over medium heat, combine the raisins and wine and bring to a simmer. Turn off the heat, letting the raisins cool in the wine.

Preheat the oven to 450°F. To prepare the filling, in a skillet over medium heat combine 6 tablespoons of the olive oil with the butter and heat until the butter is melted. Add the pine nuts and cook, tossing, for 1 minute. Add the onion and bell pepper and cook for 2 minutes longer. Add the anchovies and garlic and cook for another 30 seconds. Remove from the heat and stir in the raisins and wine.

Place the bread crumbs in a large bowl. Add the raisin mixture and the olives and toss well. Toss in the mint, parsley, and reserved lemon zest and season generously with salt and pepper.

Place the artichokes in a pan just large enough to hold them upright. Put filling in their cavities and in between their leaves. Drizzle them with the remaining tablespoon of olive oil. Pour 2 tablespoons water into the bottom of the pan and roast until the filling is browned and crisp, about 20 minutes. Serve hot or warm.

# Roasted Baby Artichokes with Lemon & Garlic

With their mild, meaty flavor, baby artichokes don't need a lot of seasonings. But, like most foods, they can still benefit from judicious additions of lemon and garlic. When roasted, the artichokes become very tender on the inside, while the outer leaves crisp up. Sprinkle them with salt and pepper and serve hot or at room temperature.

The choke of a baby artichoke is undeveloped, so you can pop the whole small bulb in your mouth after trimming and removing a few tough outer leaves. It makes cleaning them fast and easy.

SERVES 4

**1 lemon, halved crosswise**

**16 baby artichokes**

**1/4 cup extra virgin olive oil**

**3 large garlic cloves, chopped**

**2 teaspoons chopped fresh rosemary leaves**

**1/2 teaspoon coarse sea salt or kosher salt, plus additional to taste**

**Freshly ground black pepper**

Preheat the oven to 500°F. Fill a bowl with water, ice, and the juice from half the lemon. Trim the artichokes by first pulling off the tough outer leaves. Trim the bottoms and tops. Use kitchen shears or scissors to snip off any points remaining on the leaves. Halve the artichokes lengthwise. As you trim the artichokes, put the finished ones in the bowl of lemon water.

Slice the remaining lemon half in half again, then very thinly slice. You should end up with half-moons of lemon. Drain the artichokes and pat dry.

In a large bowl, toss together the artichokes, olive oil, garlic, rosemary, salt, and pepper to taste. Mound the lemon slices in your hands and gently squeeze them over the bowl to release some of the juice, then toss the slices with the artichokes. Transfer the contents of the bowl to a gratin dish and sprinkle with 2 tablespoons water.

Roast until the artichokes are tender, about 20 to 25 minutes. Sprinkle with more salt and pepper to taste and serve hot, warm, or at room temperature.

# 9 *Flatbreads & Pizzas*

# Grilled Bruschetta with Toppings

Possibly the original pizza, bruschetta (bru-sketta) is nothing more than grilled bread drizzled with olive oil and sprinkled with salt. Toppings for bruschetta can be as simple or innovative as you like. The classic—a mix of ripe summer tomatoes with basil, garlic, and olive oil—is sublime in summer when you can get ripe tomatoes, but I also like to make other, seasonal toppings for a change of pace. Here I've included the original tomato version, a crab and fennel variation, and one with figs and prosciutto. But don't limit yourself to these; you can use the bruschetta as a tasty base for almost anything. And you can even play with the bread. Try olive, herb, cheese, or nut breads. Bruschetta is great for entertaining. The topping can be made in advance, then piled on the toast at the last minute. Pass around trays of baguette bruschetta as finger food or serve big slices of rustic bread as a knife-and-fork appetizer.

SERVES 8 AS AN APPETIZER, UP TO 12 AS AN HORS D'OEUVRE

4 large slices sourdough bread or I small baguette, sliced crosswise
  $^1$/4 inch thick
Extra virgin olive oil for brushing
Coarse sea salt or kosher salt and freshly ground black pepper
Toppings of choice (opposite page)

Light the grill or preheat the broiler. Brush both sides of the bread slices with olive oil and season them with salt and pepper.

*On the Grill*   Lay the bread slices directly onto the grill or use a grilling basket. Grill until charred on one side, about I to 2 minutes, then turn and grill until browned, about I minute longer.

*In the Oven*   Lay the bread slices on a baking sheet and place it as close to the heat source as possible. Broil the bread until golden brown on one side, about I to 2 minutes. Turn the slices over and broil for another 30 seconds to I minute, until browned.

Mound toppings onto the bread and serve at once (so the toast doesn't turn soggy).

# BRUSCHETTA TOPPINGS

## Tomato & Basil

**2 ripe tomatoes, diced**

**2 tablespoons chopped fresh basil or mint**

**1 tablespoon extra virgin olive oil**

**1 garlic clove, minced (optional)**

**Pinch of hot red pepper flakes**

**Pinch of coarse sea salt or kosher salt**

Combine all the ingredients in a bowl.

## Crabmeat with Fennel

**$1/2$ pound lump crabmeat, picked over to remove any bits of shell**

**$1/4$ cup chopped fennel bulb**

**$1 1/2$ tablespoons chopped fennel fronds**

**$1/2$ tablespoon chopped fresh basil**

**1 tablespoon extra virgin olive oil**

**1 tablespoon freshly squeezed lemon juice**

**1 teaspoon white wine or Champagne vinegar**

**$1/4$ teaspoon coarse sea salt or kosher salt and freshly ground black
pepper**

Combine all the ingredients in a bowl.

## Prosciutto & Fig

**$1/4$ pound sliced prosciutto**

**1 pint fresh figs, sliced**

**Coarse sea salt or kosher salt and freshly ground black pepper**

**Extra virgin olive oil for drizzling**

**Fresh thyme sprigs for garnish (optional)**

Lay the prosciutto on the bread slices, cutting it if necessary to fit. Top with the figs
and sprinkle with salt and pepper to taste. Drizzle with olive oil and garnish with
thyme if desired.

# Grilled Herb & Olive Oil Flatbread with Spreads & Dips

Basically pizza without the toppings, flatbread is a staple in my restaurants. It's a great garnish for salads, soup, or steak tartare or to hold spreads and dips. Try the salmon tartare, white bean, deviled egg, and tomato and avocado salsa spreads on pages 232–233, then let your imagination take over. Just be sure to use sushi-quality salmon for the salmon tartare.

SERVES 8 TO 12 AS AN HORS D'OEUVRE OR GARNISH

I teaspoon active dry yeast

Pinch of sugar

1$^3$/$_4$ cups plus 2 tablespoons bread flour

5$^1$/$_2$ tablespoons extra virgin olive oil

1$^1$/$_2$ teaspoons fine sea salt or kosher salt, plus additional for sprinkling

$^1$/$_2$ cup mixed chopped fresh herbs such as chives, parsley, basil, oregano, mint, thyme, rosemary, etc.

Warm $^1$/$_4$ cup water to 110–115°F (it should feel warm to the touch). In the bowl of an electric mixer fitted with a dough hook, mix the yeast with the warm water and sugar. Let sit for 15 minutes. If the yeast is not foaming, discard it and begin again with fresh yeast.

Add the flour, 1$^1$/$_2$ tablespoons of the olive oil, salt, and an additional $^1$/$_2$ cup water to the foaming yeast and mix on medium speed until the dough is smooth and elastic and springs back when pinched, about 15 minutes. Cover the bowl and let rise in a warm place until doubled in bulk, about 1$^1$/$_2$ to 2 hours. (Or let rise in the refrigerator overnight, then bring to room temperature before proceeding.)

About 30 minutes before you want to bake the flatbreads, place a pizza stone or an inverted baking sheet in the middle of the oven and preheat to 500°F or light the grill.

Press the risen dough down and turn it onto a flat, lightly floured surface. Lightly knead the dough a few times. Divide the dough into 2 equal balls. Roll out each round on a piece of parchment paper to $\frac{1}{4}$-inch thickness (they will be about 10 inches in diameter). Scatter the herbs over the dough and use a rolling pin to press them in. Brush each flatbread with 2 tablespoons of the remaining olive oil and sprinkle with salt. Slide the rounds, on the paper, onto cookie sheets or upside-down rimmed baking sheets.

*In the Oven*  Trim the parchment paper, leaving a narrow border around the dough. Slide the flatbreads on the paper onto the preheated pizza stone or baking sheet one at a time and cook until the bottom is browned and crisp, about 8 to 10 minutes.

*On the Grill*  Chill the flatbreads in the refrigerator until they are firm enough to slide from a baking sheet or board onto the grill, about 30 minutes to an hour. Slide the flatbreads off the paper onto the grill, herbed side up. Cover the grill and cook for 5 minutes. Flip the flatbreads over and continue to grill, covered, until crisp and browned, about another 5 minutes.

Cut the flatbreads into wedges and serve with dips if desired (pages 232–233).

# Grilled Whole Wheat Flatbread with Fennel Seeds

Made with whole wheat flour and toasted fennel seeds, these Moroccan-inspired flatbreads have a rustic, earthy taste that really stands on its own but is also excellent with dips. Try them as an accompaniment to soup or salad, as a snack with drinks, or whenever a crispy bread is called for. If you want to vary the flavor, try using other seeds, such as celery, cumin, caraway, or coriander, in place of the fennel.

SERVES 8 TO 12 AS AN HORS D'OEUVRE OR GARNISH

**I teaspoon active dry yeast**

**Pinch of sugar**

**I $^1$/4 cups plus 2 tablespoons bread flour**

**$^1$/2 cup whole wheat flour**

**5 $^1$/2 tablespoons extra virgin olive oil**

**I $^1$/2 teaspoons fine sea salt or kosher salt, plus additional for sprinkling**

**2 teaspoons fennel seeds**

Warm $^1$/4 cup water to 110–115°F (it should feel warm to the touch). In the bowl of an electric mixer fitted with a dough hook, mix the yeast with the warm water and sugar. Let sit for 15 minutes. If the yeast is not foaming, discard it and begin again with fresh yeast.

Add the flours, I $^1$/2 tablespoons of the olive oil, the salt, and an additional $^1$/2 cup water to the foaming yeast and mix on medium speed until the dough is smooth and elastic and springs back when pinched, about 15 minutes. Cover the bowl and let rise in a warm place until doubled in bulk, about I $^1$/2 to 2 hours. (Or let rise in the refrigerator overnight, then bring to room temperature before proceeding.)

About 30 minutes before you want to bake the flatbreads, place a pizza stone or an inverted baking sheet in the middle of the oven and preheat to 500°F or light the grill.

Press the risen dough down and turn it onto a flat, lightly floured surface.

Lightly knead the dough a few times. Divide the dough into 2 equal balls. Roll out each round on a piece of parchment paper to $1/4$-inch thickness (they will be about 10 inches in diameter). Scatter the fennel seeds over the dough and use a rolling pin to press them in. Brush each flatbread with 2 tablespoons of the remaining olive oil and sprinkle with salt. Slide the rounds, on the paper, onto cookie sheets or upside-down rimmed baking sheets.

*In the Oven*  Trim the parchment paper, leaving a narrow border around the dough. Slide the flatbreads and parchment paper onto the preheated pizza stone or baking sheet one at a time and cook until the bottom is browned and crisp, about 8 to 10 minutes.

*On the Grill*  Chill the flatbreads in the refrigerator until they are firm enough to slide from a baking sheet or board onto the grill, about 30 minutes to an hour. Slide the flatbreads off the paper onto the grill, seeded side up. Cover the grill and cook for 5 minutes. Flip the flatbreads over and continue to grill, covered, until crisp and browned, about another 5 minutes.

Cut the flatbreads into wedges and serve with dips if desired (see sidebar, pages 232–233).

# DIPS FOR FLATBREADS

## Salmon Tartare

**¹/₂ pound sushi-quality skinless salmon fillets**

**I teaspoon mustard seeds**

**I tablespoon chopped fresh dill**

**I tablespoon freshly squeezed lemon juice**

**I teaspoon extra virgin olive oil**

**¹/₄ teaspoon coarse sea salt or kosher salt**

**Freshly ground black pepper to taste**

Use a large knife to roughly chop the salmon fillets (don't overdo this; you want rough pieces, not a paste). Put the salmon in a bowl.

Using an electric spice mill or a mortar and pestle, coarsely crush the mustard seeds. Add to the bowl with the salmon and mix in the remaining ingredients. Serve immediately or chill for up to I day.

## Puree of White Beans

**2 tablespoons chopped fresh flat-leaf parsley**

**I garlic clove, minced**

**I 15-ounce can white beans, drained (about I ¹/₂ cups)**

**2 tablespoons extra virgin olive oil**

**2 teaspoons Champagne or white wine vinegar**

**¹/₄ teaspoon coarse sea salt or kosher salt**

**Freshly ground black pepper to taste**

In the bowl of a food processor, pulse together the parsley and garlic. Add the remaining ingredients and puree until smooth. Add more salt and/or pepper if desired.

## Deviled Egg Spread

You can dress this up by garnishing the spread with caviar or smoked salmon if you like.

- **3 tablespoons sour cream**
- **1 tablespoon snipped fresh chives**
- **1 teaspoon Dijon mustard**
- **1 teaspoon prepared horseradish**
- **1/4 teaspoon coarse sea salt or kosher salt**
- **Freshly ground black pepper**
- **3 hard-cooked eggs, chopped**

In a bowl, stir together the sour cream, chives, mustard, horseradish, and a pinch of salt and pepper. Fold in the chopped eggs and add more salt and/or pepper to taste.

## Roasted Tomato & Avocado Salsa

- **1 jalapeño**
- **1 tablespoon extra virgin olive oil, plus additional for brushing the pepper**
- **3 medium tomatoes, cut into sixths**
- **1 1/2 teaspoons coarse sea salt or kosher salt**
- **Freshly ground black pepper**
- **1 avocado, pitted and coarsely chopped**
- **2 tablespoons chopped fresh cilantro**
- **1 tablespoon finely chopped red onion**
- **1 tablespoon freshly squeezed lime juice**

Preheat the broiler. Brush the jalapeño with olive oil. Broil the pepper as close to the heat source as possible, turning, until well charred, 3 to 5 minutes. Immediately transfer the jalapeño to a small bowl and cover with a plate. Let steam for 5 minutes. Turn the broiler off and preheat the oven to 450°F.

In a bowl, toss the tomatoes with the tablespoon of olive oil, 1 teaspoon of the salt, and pepper to taste. Spread them in a single layer on a rimmed baking sheet and roast until their juices begin to caramelize, 18 to 20 minutes. Let cool.

Remove the skin from the jalapeño using a metal spoon or your fingers. (Make sure to wear gloves while working with chiles.) Seed, stem, and chop the jalapeño.

Chop the tomatoes and place them in a large bowl. Add the jalapeño, avocado, cilantro, onion, lime juice, and the remaining ½ teaspoon salt. Gently toss to combine and add more salt and/or pepper if desired.

# Thin-Crust Pizza Dough

$3/4$ teaspoon active dry yeast

Pinch of sugar

$1^3/4$ cups plus 2 tablespoons bread flour

$1^1/2$ tablespoons extra virgin olive oil, plus additional for the bowl

$1^1/2$ teaspoons fine sea salt or kosher salt

Warm $1/4$ cup of water to 110–115°F (it should feel warm to the touch). In the bowl of an electric mixer fitted with a dough hook, mix the yeast with the warm water and sugar. Let sit for 15 minutes. If the yeast is not foaming, discard it and begin again with fresh yeast.

Add the flour, oil, salt, and an additional $1/2$ cup water to the foaming yeast and mix on medium speed until the dough is smooth and elastic and springs back when pinched, about 15 minutes.

Gather the dough into a ball and place it in a lightly oiled bowl, turning the dough to coat it with oil. Cover the bowl with plastic wrap and let the dough rise in a warm place until doubled in bulk, about $1^1/2$ to 2 hours. (Or let it rise in the refrigerator overnight, then bring to room temperature before proceeding.)

Bake or grill according to the individual recipe.

## Basic Tomato Sauce

This spicy tomato sauce could hardly be simpler. It's also great on pasta.

MAKES 2¹/₂ CUPS, ENOUGH FOR FIVE 10-INCH PIZZAS

3 tablespoons extra virgin olive oil

¹/₂ cup chopped onion

3 garlic cloves, thinly sliced

¹/₄ teaspoon hot red pepper flakes or to taste

I teaspoon coarse sea salt or kosher salt

I 28-ounce can whole Italian plum tomatoes

Stems from I bunch basil (reserve leaves for another purpose)

¹/₄ teaspoon freshly ground black pepper

Warm the olive oil in a large skillet over medium heat. Add the onion, garlic, red pepper flakes, and salt and cook, stirring, until the onion is limp and translucent, about 10 minutes.

Add the tomatoes and their juice, the basil stems, and the pepper. Bring to a boil over medium heat, breaking up the tomatoes with a spoon. Simmer, uncovered, for 20 minutes, stirring occasionally. Turn off the heat and let cool slightly.

Remove the basil stems. Puree the sauce in the bowl of a food processor or blender. Press the sauce through a coarse strainer set over a large bowl and discard the solids. (Alternately, use a food mill with a coarse setting.) Let cool before using. Refrigerate for up to I week or freeze for up to 6 months.

# Thin-Crust Pizza with Three Cheeses & Basil

This is the Margherita pizza of my repertoire. I combine three cheeses for a flavor that no one cheese can provide. The Parmesan contributes a sharp bite; Asiago has a sweet nuttiness; and the Bel Paese rounds out the cheese flavor with its smooth, full-flavored creaminess. Together I find them more interesting on pizza than plain mozzarella.

Grilling the pizzas gives them a wonderful smokiness. While it may seem intimidating to slide pizzas onto the grill, once you've tried it you'll realize it's not as hard as it seems, especially when the dough is well chilled.

MAKES TWO 10-INCH PIZZAS, SERVING 4 TO 6

**1 recipe Thin-Crust Pizza Dough (page 234)**

**Unsalted butter, softened, for brushing**

**Extra virgin olive oil for brushing**

**Coarse sea salt or kosher salt and freshly ground black pepper**

**1 cup Basic Tomato Sauce (page 235)**

**$^2/_3$ cup ($2^1/_2$ ounces) grated Bel Paese cheese**

**$^2/_3$ cup (2 ounces) grated Asiago cheese**

**$^2/_3$ cup (3 ounces) grated Parmesan cheese**

**$1^1/_2$ cups fresh basil leaves, cut into thin strips**

Place a pizza stone or an inverted baking sheet in the middle of the oven and preheat the oven to 500°F or light the grill.

Press the risen pizza dough down and turn it onto a flat surface. Lightly knead the dough a few times. Divide the dough into 2 equal balls. Roll out each round on a piece of parchment paper to $^1/_4$-inch thickness (they will be about 10 inches in diameter). Slide the rounds, on the paper, onto cookie sheets or upside-down rimmed baking sheets.

Brush the pizza dough with softened butter and olive oil and sprinkle with salt and pepper to taste. Spread a thin layer of sauce over the crust. Sprinkle the cheeses over the sauce.

*In the Oven*   Trim the parchment paper, leaving a narrow border around the pizzas. Slide the pizzas and parchment paper, one at a time, onto the preheated pizza stone or baking sheet. Cook until the crust is crisp and the cheese is bubbling, about 7 minutes.

*On the Grill*   Chill the pizzas in the refrigerator until they are firm enough to slide from a baking sheet or board onto the grill, about 30 minutes to an hour. Slide the pizzas off the paper onto the grill and cook, with the grill covered, until the edges are crisp and the dough is cooked through, about 6 to 8 minutes.

Scatter the basil over the pizzas, slice, and serve.

# Thin-Crust Pizza with Asparagus & Prosciutto

Charred asparagus and salty, meaty prosciutto make an excellent topping for pizza. The thin pizza cooks so quickly that the prosciutto warms up and gets a little crisp around the edges but doesn't have time to dry out, while the soft asparagus almost melts into the cheese. A little more interesting than your ordinary tomato-and-mozzarella combination, it's a fun appetizer to serve at a dinner party.

MAKES TWO 10-INCH PIZZAS, SERVING 4 TO 6 AS A MAIN COURSE, 8 TO 12 AS AN APPETIZER

I large bunch asparagus (about 1 1/4 pounds), trimmed

2 tablespoons extra virgin olive oil, plus additional for brushing

Coarse sea salt or kosher salt and freshly ground black pepper

I recipe Thin-Crust Pizza Dough (page 234)

Unsalted butter, softened, for brushing

I cup Basic Tomato Sauce (page 235)

1 1/3 cups (6 ounces) grated mozzarella cheese, preferably fresh

2/3 cup (about 3 ounces) grated Parmesan cheese

6 to 8 slices prosciutto (3 to 4 ounces), cut into thin strips

Place a pizza stone or an inverted baking sheet in the middle of the oven and preheat the oven to 500°F or light the grill.

In a large bowl, drizzle the asparagus with the 2 tablespoons olive oil and sprinkle with salt and pepper to taste. Toss well.

*In the Oven*  Spread the asparagus on a rimmed baking sheet and roast, tossing every 5 minutes, until browned and tender, about 12 minutes.

*On the Grill*  Lay the asparagus on the grill and cook, turning every 5 minutes, until browned and tender, about 12 minutes.

Transfer the asparagus to a cutting board and slice them into 1-inch lengths. Set aside.

Press the risen pizza dough down and turn it onto a flat surface. Lightly knead the dough a few times. Divide the dough into 2 equal balls. Roll out each round on a piece of parchment paper to $\frac{1}{4}$-inch thickness (they will be about 10 inches in diameter). Slide the rounds, on the paper, onto cookie sheets or upside-down rimmed baking sheets.

Brush the pizza dough with softened butter and olive oil and sprinkle with salt and pepper to taste. Spread a thin layer of sauce over the crust. Sprinkle the cheeses over the sauce, then scatter the asparagus pieces and the prosciutto over all.

*In the Oven*  Trim the parchment paper, leaving a narrow border around the pizza. Slide the pizzas and parchment paper, one at a time, onto the preheated pizza stone or baking sheet. Cook until the crust is crisp and the cheese is bubbling, about 7 minutes.

*On the Grill*  Chill the pizzas in the refrigerator until they are firm enough to slide from a baking sheet or board onto the grill, about 30 minutes to an hour. Slide the pizzas off the paper onto the grill and cook, with the grill covered, until the edges are crisp and the dough is cooked through, about 6 to 8 minutes.

# Thin-Crust Pizza with White Truffle Oil & Mushrooms

This is deluxe mushroom pizza taken to a new level, with wild mushrooms and a drizzle of truffle oil. Always use truffle oil very sparingly, since it can overpower almost anything and go from luxuriously fragrant to just plain overwhelming with more than a few drops. I sometimes leave off the tomato sauce and make this a white pizza. You can make it either way.

MAKES TWO 10-INCH PIZZAS, SERVING 4 TO 6

1/4 cup extra virgin olive oil, plus additional for brushing

1/2 cup chopped shallot

2 garlic cloves, chopped

1/2 cup dry white wine

7 cups sliced mushrooms, a mixture of white and wild or exotic mushrooms such as cremini, oyster, shiitake, etc.

I teaspoon coarse sea salt or kosher salt

1/4 teaspoon freshly ground black pepper

I teaspoon fresh thyme leaves

I recipe Thin-Crust Pizza Dough (page 234)

Unsalted butter, softened, for brushing

I cup Basic Tomato Sauce (optional; page 235)

1 1/3 cups (6 ounces) grated mozzarella cheese, preferably fresh

1/3 cup (about 1 1/2 ounces) grated Parmesan cheese

White truffle oil for drizzling

Place a pizza stone or an inverted baking sheet in the middle of the oven and preheat the oven to 500°F or light the grill.

To prepare the mushroom topping, warm the olive oil in a large skillet over medium heat. Add the shallot and cook, stirring, for I to 2 minutes. Add the garlic and cook for another 30 seconds, then pour in the white wine. Bring to a simmer and cook until most of the liquid is gone and the mixture has a thick, syrupy consistency, about 3 minutes. Add the mushrooms, salt, and pepper and continue to cook, stirring, for 5 minutes. Stir in the thyme leaves and cook until the mushrooms are very tender, about 5 minutes longer. Let cool.

Press the risen pizza dough down and turn it onto a flat surface. Lightly knead the dough a few times. Divide the dough into 2 equal balls. Roll out each round on a piece of parchment paper to $^{1}/_{4}$-inch thickness (they will be about 10 inches in diameter). Slide the rounds, on the paper, onto cookie sheets or upside-down rimmed baking sheets.

Brush the pizza dough with softened butter and olive oil and sprinkle with salt and pepper to taste. Spread a thin layer of sauce over the crust if desired. Sprinkle the cheeses over the sauce, then scatter the mushroom mixture over all.

*In the Oven*  Trim the parchment paper, leaving a narrow border around the pizza. Slide the pizzas and parchment paper, one at a time, onto the preheated pizza stone or baking sheet. Cook until the crust is crisp and the cheese is bubbling, about 7 minutes.

*On the Grill*  Chill the pizzas in the refrigerator until they are firm enough to slide from a baking sheet or board onto the grill, about 30 minutes to an hour. Slide the pizzas off the paper onto the grill and cook, with the grill covered, until the edges are crisp and the dough is cooked through, about 6 to 8 minutes.

Drizzle a very small amount of truffle oil over the pizzas (too much will overpower the mushrooms) before serving.

# Thin-Crust White Pizza with Caramelized Onions & Clams

You'll have a hard time ordering in a white clam pizza once you've been blown away by the caramelized onions and clams on this homemade version. This sauceless white pizza has an unusual flavor, thanks to lush, milky ricotta, which unites the saltiness of the clams with the sweet onions, unencumbered by other strong flavors. If you can find fresh ricotta, use it here.

MAKES TWO 10-INCH PIZZAS, SERVING 4 TO 6

4 tablespoons unsalted butter, plus softened butter for brushing

2 large Spanish onions, thinly sliced

Coarse sea salt or kosher salt and freshly ground black pepper

$^1/_2$ cup dry white wine

24 littleneck clams, scrubbed in cold water

1 recipe Thin-Crust Pizza Dough (page 234)

2 tablespoons extra virgin olive oil, plus additional for brushing

1$^1/_3$ cups (11 ounces) fresh ricotta cheese

$^1/_4$ cup (1 ounce) grated Parmesan cheese

Chopped fresh oregano or flat-leaf parsley for garnish (optional)

Place a pizza stone or an inverted baking sheet in the middle of the oven and preheat the oven to 500°F or light the grill.

To prepare the caramelized onions, melt 3 tablespoons of the butter in a large skillet over medium-low heat. Add the sliced onions and season with a large pinch of salt and pepper. Toss well and cook gently, stirring occasionally, until the onions are meltingly soft and caramelized, about 45 to 60 minutes. Let cool.

Meanwhile, prepare the clams. In a large pot with a tight-fitting lid, combine the white wine with the remaining tablespoon of butter and cook over medium heat until the butter is melted. Add the clams, cover, and steam until they have opened, about 5 minutes (discard any clams that have not opened). Using a slotted spoon, transfer the clams to a plate to cool and reserve the cooking liquid.

Bring the cooking liquid to a boil over medium heat and simmer until it is reduced to half its volume and has a syrupy consistency, about 2 minutes. Strain through a very fine strainer (or use a strainer lined with cheesecloth or a coffee filter) and season with salt and pepper to taste. Remove the clams from their shells and roughly chop them. Place the chopped clams in a bowl and mix in enough of the strained cooking liquid to moisten them.

Press the risen pizza dough down and turn it onto a flat surface. Lightly knead the dough a few times. Divide the dough into 2 equal balls. Roll out each round on a piece of parchment paper to $1/4$-inch thickness (they will be about 10 inches in diameter). Slide the rounds, on the paper, onto cookie sheets or upside-down rimmed baking sheets.

Brush the pizza dough with softened butter and olive oil and sprinkle with salt and pepper to taste. Spread a thin layer of ricotta over the crust, then spread the onions on top. Sprinkle the clams over the onions and dust the Parmesan cheese over all. Drizzle each pizza with 1 tablespoon olive oil.

*In the Oven*  Trim the parchment paper, leaving a narrow border around the pizza. Slide the pizzas and parchment paper, one at a time, onto the preheated pizza stone or baking sheet. Cook until the crust is crisp and the cheese is bubbling, about 7 minutes.

*On the Grill*  Chill the pizzas in the refrigerator until they are firm enough to slide from a baking sheet or board onto the grill, about 30 minutes to an hour. Slide the pizzas off the paper onto the grill and cook, with the grill covered, until the edges are crisp and the dough is cooked through, about 6 to 8 minutes.

Garnish with the oregano or parsley if desired before serving.

# Thin-Crust Pizza with Charred Lobster & Tomatoes

Everyone loves lobster, and everyone loves pizza, and here they are combined for a dish that could be called Waldy's Sicilian version of a New England lobster roll. It's a fun, summery, easy-to-eat way to dress up pizza and dress down lobster. Everyone will love it.

MAKES FOUR 5-INCH PIZZAS, SERVING 4

> 1 recipe Thin-Crust Pizza Dough (page 234)
> Unsalted butter, softened, for brushing
> Extra virgin olive oil for brushing
> Coarse sea salt or kosher salt and freshly ground black pepper
> 1 cup Basic Tomato Sauce (page 235)
> 1 small red onion, thinly sliced and separated into rings
> 2 ripe yet firm large tomatoes, thinly sliced
> 1 cup (4$\frac{1}{2}$ ounces) grated mozzarella cheese, preferably fresh
> 2 cooked lobsters (about 1$\frac{1}{2}$ pounds each), tail and claw meat
>     removed from the shell and cut into 1-inch pieces
> Fresh basil leaves, sliced into ribbons, for garnish

Place a pizza stone or an inverted baking sheet in the middle of the oven and preheat the oven to 500°F or light the grill.

Press the risen pizza dough down and turn it onto a flat surface. Lightly knead the dough a few times. Divide the dough into 4 equal balls. Roll out each round on a piece of parchment paper to $\frac{1}{4}$-inch thickness (they will be about 5 inches in diameter). Slide the rounds, on the paper, onto cookie sheets or upside-down rimmed baking sheets.

Brush the pizza dough with softened butter and olive oil and sprinkle with salt and pepper to taste. Spread a thin layer of sauce over each crust and top it with the onion rings and then the tomato slices. Sprinkle the mozzarella on top and arrange the lobster meat on top of the cheese.

*In the Oven*   Trim the parchment paper, leaving a narrow border around the pizza. Slide the pizzas and parchment paper, one or two at a time, onto the preheated pizza stone or baking sheet. Cook until the crust is crisp and the cheese is bubbling, about 7 minutes.

*On the Grill*   Chill the pizzas in the refrigerator until they are firm enough to slide from a baking sheet or board onto the grill, about 30 minutes to an hour. Slide the pizzas off the paper onto the grill and cook, with the grill covered, until the edges are crisp and the dough is cooked through, about 6 to 8 minutes.

Garnish with the basil before serving.

ROASTED SUMMER BERRY SHORTCAKES

ROASTED PEACH & BLUEBERRY
CAKE WITH PAN JUICES

PEACHES WITH BALSAMIC VINEGAR
& ROQUEFORT

ALMOND RICOTTA CAKE WITH
MOSCATO ROASTED APRICOTS

NECTARINE & ALMOND CROSTATA

# 10 *Desserts*

FIGS WITH MADEIRA & ORANGE ZEST

APPLE CHEDDAR PIE

CARAMELIZED APPLE
BREAD PUDDING

GINGERBREAD CAKE WITH
BALSAMIC ROASTED PEARS

CARAMELIZED BANANAS WITH
BLOOD ORANGES, RUM & SPICES

GRILLED PINEAPPLE WITH GIN,
JUNIPER, & LIME

TOASTED FARMER'S CHEESE WITH
HONEY & DRIED FRUIT COMPOTE

CHOCOLATE ANGEL FOOD CAKE
WITH ROASTED BRANDIED
STRAWBERRIES & CHOCOLATE SAUCE

CHOCOLATE PIZZAS WITH
FRUIT VARIATIONS

# Roasted Summer Berry Shortcakes

Usually berry shortcakes call for fresh berries that have been macerated in sugar, making the topping somewhat akin to a fruit salad. In my version the berries are roasted, which intensifies their flavors and reduces their juices to a jammy syrup. This makes for a robust shortcake with a deep, rich berry flavor. Trust me; it's worth turning your oven on in the summer for this.

SERVES 6

**For the Shortcakes**

$^1$/2 cup (1 stick) cold unsalted butter

1 $^1$/4 cups all-purpose flour

3 tablespoons sugar, plus additional for sprinkling

1 tablespoon baking powder

$^1$/2 teaspoon fine sea salt or kosher salt

$^3$/4 cup heavy cream

Fresh mint sprigs, for garnish

**For the Berries**

$^3$/4 cup sugar

1 vanilla bean

Grated zest of 1 lemon

2 pints raspberries

2 pints strawberries, hulled and halved

1 pint blueberries or currants

**For the Cream**

1 $^1$/2 cups cold heavy cream

1 tablespoon superfine sugar

Preheat the oven to 375°F. In a small saucepan (or in a bowl in the microwave), gently melt 2 tablespoons of the butter.

To prepare the shortcakes, combine the flour, sugar, baking powder, and salt in the bowl of a food processor. Cut the remaining 6 tablespoons of butter into pieces and add them to the flour mixture. Pulse the mixture until the ingredients are combined and have the consistency of coarse meal. (Alternately, mix the dry ingredients by hand with a whisk, then cut in the butter using 2 knives.) Pour in the cream and pulse or mix until just combined. Turn the dough out on a floured board and pat it into a rectangle about $^3$/4 inch thick.

Butter a baking sheet. Brush the top of the dough with the melted butter and sprinkle with sugar. Cut the dough into 6 equal squares and lay them on the baking sheet.

Bake the shortcakes until they are firm to the touch and golden, about 15 minutes. Let cool on a wire rack.

To roast the berries, preheat the oven to 450°F. Place the sugar in a large bowl. Split the vanilla bean lengthwise and use the tip of a paring knife to scrape the vanilla seeds into the bowl with the sugar. Add the lemon zest and rub the sugar between your fingers to distribute the vanilla and zest evenly. Add the berries and toss to coat them with the sugar.

Spread the berries in a single layer on a rimmed baking sheet and roast, tossing once, until the juices are thick and bubbling, about 10 minutes.

To serve, lightly whip the cream with the superfine sugar until soft peaks form. Split the shortcakes crosswise and place one on each plate. Layer the bottom half with some of the berries and their juices and a dollop of whipped cream, then replace the top. Surround the shortcakes with the remaining berries and cream, drizzle with the rest of the berry juices, and garnish with fresh mint.

# Roasted Peach & Blueberry Cake with Pan Juices

This is the ideal cake to take on picnics since it is made in advance and served right out of the pan. Summer fruit is roasted until it's just this side of preserves, then layered over a tender, homemade vanilla cake and refrigerated until the cake has absorbed the fruit juices. The result is a tender, fruity sponge, each slice streaked with the bright sunset shades of purple, pink, and yellow and tasting of summer. You can substitute apricots or nectarines for the peaches and raspberries or blackberries for the blueberries if you like. Any which way, a scoop of ice cream is the perfect accompaniment.

SERVES 10 TO 12

**9 large ripe peaches, pitted and sliced**

**9 cups blueberries**

**2$\frac{1}{2}$ cups sugar**

**Juice of 1$\frac{1}{2}$ lemons**

**$\frac{1}{3}$ vanilla bean**

**14 tablespoons (1$\frac{3}{4}$ sticks) unsalted butter, 1 stick softened**

**4 large eggs**

**2 teaspoons vanilla extract**

**2 cups all-purpose flour**

**1 tablespoon baking powder**

**1 teaspoon salt**

**1 cup milk**

**Whipped cream for serving**

Preheat the oven to 500°F. In a bowl, toss together the peaches, blueberries, 1$\frac{1}{2}$ cups of the sugar, and the lemon juice. Pour all but 3 cups of the fruit into a 9 × 13-inch baking pan. Cover the reserved 3 cups of fruit and refrigerate until serving time. Split the vanilla bean lengthwise and scrape out and reserve the seeds. Bury the pod in the fruit in the baking pan and dot the top with 6 tablespoons of the butter. Bake for 30 minutes, stirring the mixture halfway through. Let the mixture cool on a rack. Retrieve and discard the vanilla pod.

Lower the oven temperature to 350°F. Grease and flour a 9-inch round cake pan. In the bowl of an electric mixer fitted with the paddle attachment, cream the remaining 1 cup sugar and 1 stick butter until very smooth and fluffy. Beat in the eggs, vanilla extract, and vanilla seeds. In a small bowl, combine the flour, baking powder, and salt. On low speed, add the flour mixture to the batter in 3 additions, alternating with the milk in 2 additions. Pour the batter into the prepared pan and bake for 40 minutes, until a tester inserted into the middle of the cake comes out clean. Let cool, then unmold the cake from the pan.

With a long serrated knife, slice the cake horizontally into 3 layers. Line a clean 9-inch round cake pan with plastic wrap, leaving plenty of overhang. Place the bottom layer of cake in the pan, cut side up. Using a slotted spoon, layer half of the fruit over the cake. Top with the middle layer of cake and spoon on the remaining fruit (reserve the remaining fruit "pan juices" to garnish the cake). Cover with the top cake layer, cut side down. Press down gently on the cake and cover with the overhanging plastic wrap. Chill the cake for at least 8 hours and preferably overnight.

When ready to serve, unmold the cake and garnish each slice with a generous drizzle of the reserved pan juices, the reserved raw fruit, and a dollop of cream.

# Peaches with Balsamic Vinegar & Roquefort

Roquefort cheese and vinegar may sound like odd ingredients for a dessert, but they are actually a winning combination when anchored by sweet summer peaches. The idea came to me when I was served a cheese platter on which there were peaches and Roquefort, which struck me as really interesting and delicious. Cooking concentrates the peaches, and a little balsamic vinegar heightens their fruitiness, while the creaminess and bite of the cheese adds richness and takes this dessert off the beaten track. Serve this alone or with a crisp cookie—but not with ice cream—and it will surprise and delight. Or treat this as a fruit and cheese course and serve it before a light dessert.

SERVES 4

**1 cup sugar**

**$^{1}/_{2}$ vanilla bean, split lengthwise**

**4 large ripe peaches, halved and pitted**

**$^{1}/_{3}$ cup balsamic vinegar**

**$^{3}/_{4}$ cup sliced almonds**

**3 tablespoons ($^{3}/_{4}$ ounce) crumbled Roquefort or other blue cheese**

Preheat the oven to 500°F or light the grill.

In a saucepan, combine the sugar with $^{2}/_{3}$ cup water and the vanilla bean and bring to a boil, stirring occasionally until the sugar dissolves. Simmer for 2 minutes, then set aside.

Score the peach halves with an X on their skin sides. Put them in a large bowl and add the sugar syrup, vanilla bean, and balsamic vinegar. Toss to coat. Place the almonds in a small pan with a heatproof handle.

*In the Oven*　Arrange the peaches skin side down in a single layer in a 9- × 13-inch roasting pan. Pour the balsamic syrup over the peaches and roast, basting once or twice, for 8 minutes. Turn the peaches over and roast for another 5 to 10 minutes, until the peaches are soft and their skins look caramelized. Meanwhile, place the pan of almonds in the oven and toast, tossing them frequently, until they are golden and fragrant, about 3 to 5 minutes.

*On the Grill*  Let the peaches sit in the syrup for 15 minutes. Use tongs to pull the peaches from the syrup and place them on the grill, cut sides down. Grill for 2 to 4 minutes, basting with the balsamic syrup. Turn the peaches over and baste, filling their cavities with syrup. Grill for another 2 to 4 minutes, until the peaches are soft and the syrup has begun to caramelize. Place the pan of almonds on the grill and toast, shaking, until golden and fragrant, 2 to 4 minutes.

To serve, place 2 peaches, skin side down, on each plate. Sprinkle with blue cheese, drizzle with more of the balsamic syrup, and garnish with the toasted almonds.

# Almond Ricotta Cake with Moscato Roasted Apricots

Almond flavors always work well with stone fruits, in this case apricots. This country-style almond cake has a light, delicate texture and a moist creaminess that comes from the addition of ricotta cheese. Moscato, a perfumed sweet wine, reduces and combines with the juice of roasted apricots, giving the dessert intense fragrance and elegance. Leftover apricots are also excellent served over ice cream or yogurt.

SERVES 12

**For the Cake**

3/4 cup (1 1/2 sticks) unsalted butter, melted and cooled

1/2 cup ricotta cheese

1 cup sugar

1 teaspoon almond extract

Pinch of fine sea salt or kosher salt

4 large eggs

1/2 cup cake flour

1/2 cup almond flour (see note)

1 teaspoon baking powder

Whipped cream or ice cream for serving

**For the Apricots**

1 2/3 cups Moscato or other white dessert wine (1 375-milliliter bottle)

1/2 cup plus 2 tablespoons sugar

1 teaspoon freshly squeezed lemon juice

1 pound ripe apricots (about 6 to 8), quartered and pitted

2 tablespoons unsalted butter, cut into pieces

Preheat the oven to 350°F. To prepare the cake, butter and flour a 10-inch cake pan and line it with parchment or wax paper. In the bowl of an electric mixer fitted with the whisk attachment, combine the butter, ricotta cheese, sugar, almond extract, and salt. Beat at medium speed for 5 minutes. Add the eggs, one at a time, beating until fully incorporated after each addition. In a small bowl, whisk together the flours and baking powder, then fold them into the batter.

Scrape the batter into the prepared pan and bake for 30 to 35 minutes, until a tester inserted into the center of the cake comes out clean. Let cool thoroughly before removing from the pan.

To prepare the apricots, in a saucepan over medium heat, combine the Moscato, $1/2$ cup of the sugar, and the lemon juice and bring to a simmer, stirring until the sugar is dissolved. Simmer until the liquid is reduced and syrupy, about 12 to 15 minutes.

Meanwhile, to roast the apricots, preheat the oven to 500°F. Spread the apricot halves in a single layer on a rimmed baking sheet, dot them with the butter, and sprinkle with the remaining 2 tablespoons sugar. Roast until they begin to brown, about 8 to 10 minutes. Pour the Moscato syrup over the apricots and return them to the oven for 10 minutes, until they are tender.

To serve, cut wedges of the cake and garnish with apricots, a drizzle of Moscato syrup, and whipped cream or ice cream.

NOTE You can order almond flour from the King Arthur Flour Baker's Catalogue, (800) 827–6836. Or, to make your own almond flour, place $1/2$ cup plus 1 tablespoon blanched sliced almonds in the bowl of a food processor with 3 tablespoons of flour from the recipe and process until the almonds are the consistency of coarse meal. Stir well, being sure to get into the corners, and continue to process until finely ground (do not overprocess or the mixture will become pasty and unusable).

# Nectarine & Almond Crostata

A crostata is a rustic, free-form tart. Here I make it with purchased puff pastry, which is a fast and wonderfully flaky base for slices of roasted or grilled nectarines. High heat browns the nectarines and reduces their juices, so when they are baked on the pastry they don't give off a lot of liquid that could make the crust soggy. Underneath the nectarines lies a thin layer of frangipane, a custardy almond pastry cream, which complements the fruit, while a topping of demerara sugar adds a sweet crunch.

SERVES 6

**For the Nectarines**
**6 ripe nectarines (about 1 3/4 pounds), halved and pitted**
**2 tablespoons sugar**

**For the Frangipane**
**1/2 cup sliced blanched almonds**
**1/3 cup sugar**
**2 tablespoons unsalted butter, softened**
**1 large egg yolk**
**1 teaspoon grated lemon zest**
**1/2 teaspoon vanilla extract**
**1/8 teaspoon almond extract**
**Pinch of fine sea salt or kosher salt**

**For the Crostata**
**1 sheet puff pastry (about 8 ounces), thawed if frozen**
**2 tablespoons sliced almonds**
**1 tablespoon demerara sugar**

Preheat the broiler or light the grill. In a large bowl, toss the nectarines in the sugar.

*In the Oven*   Lay the nectarines skin side down on a rimmed baking sheet and place it about 3 inches from the heat source. Broil until the nectarines are browned, about 6 to 8 minutes.

*On the Grill*   Lay the nectarines cut side down on the grill and cook, turning once, until lightly seared, about 8 minutes.

Let the nectarines cool slightly, then slice each half into 4 wedges.

Preheat the oven to 400°F. To make the frangipane, pulse the almonds in a food processor or blender until they are the consistency of sand. Add the other ingredients and pulse until just combined.

If the puff pastry isn't already rolled into a sheet $^1/8$ inch thick (most commercial brands are), do this on a floured board. Place the puff pastry on a baking sheet and cut it into an 11-inch circle (reserve the scraps for another use). Pour the frangipane onto the middle of the pastry and spread it thinly, leaving a 1$^1/2$-inch border. Arrange the nectarine slices in an overlapping pattern on the frangipane. Sprinkle the fruit with the almonds and sugar and fold the border of puff pastry in over the fruit.

Bake until the pastry is deep golden brown, about 25 to 30 minutes. Serve slightly warm or at room temperature.

# Figs with Madeira & Orange Zest

If you've never had a grilled or roasted fig, you should try this recipe. In the Mediterranean, where outdoor cooking is prevalent and figs are abundant, they are often cooked at high heat to soften their texture and heighten their sweetness. Here I add Madeira, a fortified wine, and orange zest, which accents both the flavor of figs and the smoky flavors of roasting or grilling. The Madeira reduces into a syrup that mixes with the red, portlike juices of the figs and fresh orange segments in this simple yet intense dessert. Serve this when figs are in season, with crisp cookies.

SERVES 6

**2 oranges**

**1 cup sugar**

**$^1/_2$ cup Madeira**

**1 pint fresh figs**

**1 tablespoon extra virgin olive oil, hazelnut oil, or walnut oil**

Light the grill or preheat the oven to 500°F. Using a vegetable peeler, remove the zest from half of one of the oranges.

In a small saucepan, combine the sugar, Madeira, and orange zest with $^1/_2$ cup water and bring to a boil, stirring occasionally. Simmer for 2 minutes, then turn off the heat and set aside.

Trim the stems from the figs and cut an X into their skins where the stems were. Place the figs in a dish or baking pan (if roasting) large enough to hold them snugly in one layer and pour the syrup over them.

*On the Grill*  Let the figs macerate in the Madeira syrup for 15 minutes, then place them on the grill and cook, basting with the syrup and turning every minute or two, until soft throughout, about 5 to 10 minutes.

*In the Oven*  Place the baking pan with the figs in the oven and roast, basting occasionally, for 5 to 10 minutes. Turn the figs and roast until they are soft and the syrup has begun to thicken, another 3 to 5 minutes.

Cut the top and bottom off the oranges and stand them up on a cutting board on one of the flat sides. Using a small knife, cut away the peel and white pith, following the curve of the fruit, until the flesh is exposed. Cut the segments of fruit away from the membranes that connect them. Dice the segments, then place them in a bowl. Add the oil to the fruit and toss to combine.

To serve, spoon some of the oranges onto each dessert plate and arrange 2 or 3 figs beside them. Drizzle the oranges and figs with the Madeira syrup.

# Apple Cheddar Pie

My dad, Waldense Malouf, Sr., had a famous line: "Apple pie without cheese is like a kiss without a squeeze." But while my dad would just sprinkle cheese over his slice of pie, I now make pie with grated cheese in both the crust and filling. The crust is incredibly savory with a great crunch—a little like Cheddar goldfish snacks. (You can freeze it for up to 2 months if you want to have it on hand during apple season.) I like to serve sliced Cheddar with the pie so that it really feels like an after-dinner fruit and cheese course, but you can always serve it with ice cream on top.

Whether or not you're convinced about the cheese, grilling or roasting the apples is a great solution to the problems of a soggy bottom crust and the gap between the fruit and the top crust inherent in most apple pies. The caramelized apples condense and shrink so they are not as moist, and when you put them in the pie they stay put, making this a more compact, flavorful pie. I think it's the best apple pie in the world, and I know my dad would agree.

MAKES ONE 9-INCH PIE, SERVING 6

$1^3/4$ cups plus 2 tablespoons all-purpose flour

$3/4$ teaspoon fine sea salt or kosher salt

$3/4$ cup ($1^1/2$ sticks) cold unsalted butter, cut into pieces

$1^3/4$ cups grated extra-sharp good-quality Cheddar cheese
   (about 7 ounces), plus additional slices for serving if desired

1 large egg, lightly beaten

2 pounds Granny Smith apples (5 or 6 large), peeled and cored

$1/4$ cup granulated sugar

$1/2$ cup packed dark brown sugar

Juice of $1/2$ lemon

$1/2$ vanilla bean, split lengthwise, seeds scraped with a knife

In the bowl of a food processor, pulse $1^3/4$ cups of the flour with $1/2$ teaspoon of the salt. Add the butter and pulse 3 or 4 times, until the mixture has the consistency of oatmeal. Add 1 cup of the cheese and pulse to distribute. Do not overprocess; it should not be smooth. Transfer to a bowl. Make a well in the flour mixture and add the egg. Use a fork to stir the egg into the flour mixture, then sprinkle the dough with up to 3 tablespoons of water (add them one at a time), using as little as needed to form the dough into a mass. Divide the dough in half and pat each half into a disk. Place one disk in a pie plate and use your fingers to pat it to line the pan. Place the other disk between 2 sheets of wax paper and use a rolling pin to roll the dough into a 10-inch circle. Refrigerate the dough for at least 1 hour, well wrapped. Remove the pie dough from the refrigerator 15 minutes before baking.

Preheat the broiler or light the grill.

*In the Oven*  Slice each apple into 8 wedges and place them in a bowl. Sprinkle the granulated sugar over them and toss to coat. Spread the apples in a single layer on a rimmed baking sheet and broil for 5 to 7 minutes, turning once. The apples should be caramelized and golden brown.

*On the Grill*  Halve the apples and place them in a bowl. Sprinkle the granulated sugar over the apples and toss to coat. Grill until caramelized around the edges, about 15 minutes, turning once. Cool and then slice.

Preheat the oven to 375°F. Place the apples in a bowl with the brown sugar, lemon juice, seeds from the vanilla bean, remaining $1/4$ teaspoon salt, remaining 2 tablespoons flour, and remaining $3/4$ cup cheese and toss. Fill the bottom crust with the apples and brush the rim with water. Cover with the top crust, trim to create an even border, then roll to form a crust and crimp the edges together. Cut 4 slits into the top crust to allow steam to escape and place the pie on a baking sheet on the bottom shelf of the oven. Bake for 45 minutes to 1 hour, until the juices are bubbling and the fruit is tender. (You can gauge the firmness of the fruit by sliding a thin knife through the opening in the crust and piercing the fruit.) If the crust browns before the apples are cooked, loosely cover the pie with aluminum foil. Let sit for at least 30 minutes before serving warm, with extra cheese if desired.

---

*Extra-Sharp Cheddar Cheese*  Even if you don't like extra-sharp Cheddar on your cheeseburger or in sandwiches, try it in this pie. The sharpness is tempered by the apples but has enough flavor to shine through and add complexity.

---

# Caramelized Apple Bread Pudding

This unusual bread pudding is comforting, indulgent, and fun to make. The difference comes from grilling or roasting the apples, which caramelizes and condenses their juices. The cooked apples are layered with buttered slices of bread, a tangy sour cream–infused custard, and dried cranberries or cherries. The pudding emerges from the oven soft and sweet in the center and a little crunchy around the edges from a topping of nearly burned sugar. Whipped cream or a scoop of ice cream is gilding the lily—in the best possible way.

SERVES 8

**5 tablespoons unsalted butter, softened**

**4 large Granny Smith apples, peeled and cored**

**1 1/4 cups sugar**

**12 slices homemade-style white sandwich bread**

**1/2 cup dried cranberries or dried sour cherries**

**2 1/2 cups milk**

**Pinch of fine sea salt or kosher salt**

**6 large egg yolks, lightly beaten**

**1 cup sour cream at room temperature**

**1 teaspoon vanilla extract**

**1 teaspoon ground cinnamon**

**1/4 teaspoon ground mace**

**Whipped cream or ice cream for serving**

Preheat the broiler or light the grill. Brush the inside of a 9-inch square pan with 1 tablespoon of the butter.

*In the Oven*    Slice each apple into 8 wedges and place them in a bowl. Sprinkle 1/4 cup of the sugar over them and toss to coat. Spread the apples in a single layer on a rimmed baking sheet and place it directly under the heat source. Broil for 5 minutes, turning once.

*On the Grill*    Halve the apples and place them in a bowl. Sprinkle 1/4 cup of the sugar over them and toss to coat. Place them on the grill and cook for 15 minutes, turning once. Cool and then slice.

Preheat the oven to 350°F. Spread both sides of the bread with the remaining butter and cut the slices diagonally into triangles.

Place the dried fruit in a bowl and pour in enough very hot water to cover them. Let sit until plump, about 5 to 10 minutes, then drain.

In a saucepan over medium heat, combine the milk with $3/4$ cup of the remaining sugar and the salt and bring to a simmer, stirring until the sugar is dissolved. Meanwhile, place the egg yolks in a large heatproof bowl and whisk them a few times. When the milk is simmering, pour a little into the egg yolks, whisking constantly, to warm them. Whisking continuously, gradually pour the rest of the milk into the yolks. Add the sour cream, vanilla, cinnamon, and mace, whisking until smooth.

Arrange a third of the bread triangles in a single overlapping layer in the bottom of the prepared pan. Spread half the sliced apples evenly over the bread, then scatter half the plumped and drained dried fruit over that. Make another layer of overlapping bread triangles, then apples, then dried fruit, finishing with the rest of the bread. Slowly pour the custard over the bread, being sure to soak the top. Press gently on the bread with the back of a spatula to ensure that it becomes saturated with custard.

Sprinkle the remaining $1/4$ cup sugar all over the top of the custard and place the baking pan in a larger roasting pan. Place the roasting pan on a rack in the center of the oven and carefully pour very hot water into the roasting pan to come halfway up the sides of the pudding. Bake until a tester inserted into the center of the pudding comes out clean and the custard is set, about 1 hour. Run the pudding under the broiler for about 2 minutes to brown the top. Serve warm, with whipped cream or ice cream.

# Gingerbread Cake
## with Balsamic Roasted Pears

In this recipe I serve moist, soft gingerbread cake with pears that have been roasted in a balsamic vinegar syrup. The balsamic syrup balances the sweetness of the pears, heightening their flavor and adding richness and depth. Since pears are at their peak in the fall and into winter, just when everyone is in the mood for gingerbread, they make ideal partners.

SERVES 6 TO 8

**For the Cake**

**2 cups all-purpose flour**

**1 tablespoon ground ginger**

**2 teaspoons baking soda**

**1 teaspoon ground cinnamon**

**1 teaspoon fine sea salt or kosher salt**

**2/3 cup sugar**

**5 tablespoons unsalted butter, softened**

**1 large egg**

**3/4 cup light molasses**

**1 cup whole milk**

**Whipped cream or ice cream for serving**

**For the Pears**

**2/3 cup balsamic vinegar**

**1 cup sugar**

**1/2 vanilla bean, split lengthwise**

**6 ripe Bosc pears, peeled, cored, and cut into 6 wedges each**

Preheat the oven to 350°F. To prepare the cake, grease and flour a 10-inch cake pan. In a large bowl, whisk together the flour, ginger, baking soda, cinnamon, and salt and set aside.

In the bowl of an electric mixer fitted with the whisk attachment, combine the sugar, butter, and egg and beat at medium speed for 3 minutes. With the motor running, drizzle in the molasses and beat until it is incorporated. Turn the mixer to low and add the dry ingredients alternately with the milk in 3 additions, mixing until incorporated after each addition. Pour the batter into the prepared pan.

Bake until a tester inserted into the center of the cake comes out clean and the top of the cake springs back when pressed, about 1 hour and 15 minutes. Let cool on a wire rack.

To roast the pears, preheat the oven to 500°F. In a small saucepan over medium heat, bring the balsamic vinegar, sugar, and vanilla bean to a simmer; cook for 3 to 5 minutes, until syrupy. Arrange the pear wedges in a single layer in a shallow baking dish and pour the balsamic syrup over them. Roast, basting occasionally, for 10 to 15 minutes or until tender. Keep warm.

To serve, cut pieces of the cake and garnish with the pears, a drizzle of balsamic syrup, and whipped cream or ice cream.

# Caramelized Bananas with Blood Oranges, Rum, & Spices

In this luscious dessert, roasted bananas are caramelized with brown sugar and rum, in the same vein as the Bananas Foster I used to make as an apprentice in Florida. But here spices and blood oranges add another dimension to what can otherwise be an overly round, sweet flavor. Use ripe, speckled bananas—the solid yellow ones are not ripe enough. Serve this as is with plenty of sour cream, or use it as a topping for cake, ice cream, or both.

SERVES 6

**3 small blood oranges**

**$1/4$ cup dark rum**

**1 teaspoon whole allspice**

**2 whole cloves**

**$1/2$ cup packed dark brown sugar**

**2 tablespoons unsalted butter**

**1 tablespoon freshly squeezed lemon juice**

**$1/4$ teaspoon freshly ground black pepper**

**$1/4$ teaspoon ground cinnamon**

**$1/8$ teaspoon freshly grated nutmeg**

**4 ripe bananas, peeled, halved lengthwise, then cut crosswise into quarters**

**Sour cream for serving**

Preheat the broiler and position a rack 6 inches from the heat source. Squeeze 2 of the blood oranges and strain the juice (you should have $1/4$ cup).

In a saucepan over medium heat, combine the orange juice, rum, allspice, and cloves and bring to a boil. Simmer for 5 minutes, then add the sugar and continue to simmer, stirring until the sugar dissolves, until the mixture is syrupy, about 5 minutes. Stir in the butter, lemon juice, black pepper, cinnamon, and nutmeg.

Cut the top and bottom off the third orange and stand it up on a cutting board on one of its flat sides. Using a small knife, cut away the peel and white pith, following the curve of the fruit, until the flesh is exposed. Working over a bowl, cut the segments of fruit away from the membranes, letting the fruit and juices fall into the bowl.

Lay the bananas in a pan just large enough to accommodate them in a single layer. Strain the rum sauce over them and then scatter the orange segments and juice over all. Broil, basting frequently with the pan juices, until the bananas are soft and the juices are thick and browned, about 5 to 7 minutes. Serve with dollops of sour cream.

# Grilled Pineapple with Gin, Juniper, & Lime

When it comes to grilled desserts, pineapple is a natural, since the fruit really benefits from high heat, whether it's the browned pieces of pineapple on top of a ham or the caramelized sweetness of pineapple seared on the grill. This dessert calls for strong flavors to stand up to the grilled fruit, so I use a gin and juniper syrup inspired by traditional fruit sauces usually served with game. The piney, earthy flavor of juniper is a nice foil for the bright acidity of the pineapple and lime, and the effect is refreshing and simple yet very flavorful.

Juniper berries are not hard to find, but the dish is worth making even if you don't have them—just leave them out.

SERVES 4 TO 6

**1 lime**
**¹/2 cup plus 2 tablespoons sugar**
**¹/4 cup gin**
**5 juniper berries, lightly crushed (see Note)**
**1 vanilla bean, split lengthwise**
**1 ripe pineapple, peeled, cored, and sliced ¹/2 inch thick**
**Vanilla ice cream and/or berry or tropical fruit sorbet for serving**

Light the grill. Grate the zest from the lime and then juice it.

In a saucepan over medium heat, combine ¹/2 cup of the sugar with 2 tablespoons water, the lime zest and juice, gin, and juniper berries. Scrape the seeds from the vanilla bean into the pan and add the pod. Bring to a simmer, stirring until the sugar dissolves. Simmer until thickened, about 5 minutes.

Sprinkle both sides of the pineapple slices with the remaining 2 tablespoons of sugar, then use tongs to lay them carefully on the grill. Cook, turning once, until caramelized, about 5 to 8 minutes per side.

Pour the lime syrup over the pineapple and serve with ice cream and/or sorbet.

NOTE  Juniper berries are available at many supermarkets, or you can mail-order them from Penzeys Spices, (800) 741–7787.

# Toasted Farmer's Cheese with Honey & Dried Fruit Compote

This recipe is a combination of a traditional Jewish baked farmer's cheese and a sweet my Lebanese grandmother often served, in which dried fruit is reconstituted in tea and honey and served over labneh, the Middle Eastern yogurt. I only began to like my grandmother's dessert when I was a little bit older, but then it came back to me when I wanted to develop a dessert using some wonderful farmer's cheese that we had at the restaurant. I drizzle the creamy cheese with honey and surround it with a compote of dried fruits, orangey Earl Grey tea, and bright citrus zest, and then the whole thing gets caramelized in the oven. It's a creamy yet light dessert that's warm and comforting and perfect when there aren't a lot of fresh fruits in season. Serve this with crisp cookies.

SERVES 6 TO 8

**5 teaspoons loose Earl Grey tea or 5 tea bags**

**I lemon**

**I orange**

**I cup dried sour cherries**

**I cup dried apricots, quartered**

**$^1/_2$ cup dried figs, stemmed and quartered**

**$^1/_2$ cup pitted prunes, quartered**

**$^1/_2$ cup golden raisins**

**$^1/_4$ cup dates, sliced**

**I pound farmer's cheese**

**$^1/_2$ cup honey**

Bring 3 cups water to a boil. Place the tea in a heatproof bowl or teapot and pour the water over it. Let steep until very strong, about 5 minutes, then strain.

Use a vegetable peeler to remove strips of zest from half of the lemon and half of the orange. Grate the remaining zests and place them in a covered container in the refrigerator.

In a large pot, stir together all the dried fruit and the strips of orange and lemon zest. Pour the hot tea over the fruit. Over medium heat, bring this mixture to a simmer and cook, covered, for 5 minutes. Let cool, then refrigerate for at least 4 hours or overnight. *(continued)*

Remove the fruit compote from the refrigerator and let it come back to room temperature, about 30 minutes.

Preheat the broiler.

Place the farmer's cheese in the center of a wide, shallow gratin or baking dish. Pour the honey over the cheese and top with the grated orange and lemon zest. Broil until the honey bubbles and the cheese begins to brown on the edges, about 2 to 3 minutes. Using a slotted spoon, place the compote around the cheese and serve in bowls.

# Chocolate Angel Food Cake with Roasted Brandied Strawberries & Chocolate Sauce

Angel food cake was always my favorite while growing up, and my mother made it for all my birthdays. Much later, when I realized that I could play with recipes, I added cocoa powder and chocolate chips to make it richer and chocolaty. I still consider it angel food, but maybe for angels with a dark side. In this version I make it even better by serving toasted slices of cake with chocolate sauce and strawberries that have been roasted until their juices are syrupy and almost caramelized. I find that all red berries work well here, their fresh fruitiness and concentrated sauce complementing the chocolate for a relatively light, summery dessert. And of course, you can't go wrong by adding a dollop of whipped cream or a scoop of ice cream. (The cake can be made 2 days ahead.)

SERVES 8 TO 10

**For the Cake**

1 $^1/_2$ cups sugar

$^3/_4$ cup all-purpose flour

6 tablespoons unsweetened cocoa powder

10 large egg whites

1 $^1/_2$ teaspoons cream of tartar

$^1/_4$ teaspoon fine sea salt or kosher salt

1 $^1/_2$ teaspoons vanilla extract

$^1/_2$ cup mini chocolate chips

Ice cream, berry sorbet, or crème fraîche for garnish

**For the Strawberries**

3 pints fresh strawberries, hulled

6 tablespoons sugar

1 $^1/_2$ tablespoons brandy

1 tablespoon unsalted butter

**For the Chocolate Sauce**

1 cup heavy cream

$^1/_2$ pound bittersweet chocolate, chopped

2 tablespoons unsalted butter

1 tablespoon Grand Marnier

*(continued)*

Preheat the oven to 350°F. To prepare the cake, sift ³/4 cup of the sugar with the flour and cocoa and set aside.

In the bowl of a mixer fitted with the whisk attachment, beat the egg whites with the cream of tartar and salt until soft peaks form. Sprinkle the remaining sugar over the egg whites, 2 tablespoons at a time, beating after each addition. Beat until stiff peaks form. Fold in the vanilla. Gently but thoroughly fold in the dry ingredients in 3 additions. Fold in the chips.

Pour the batter into an ungreased 10-inch angel food cake pan and bake until the cake is tall and lightly golden and the top springs back when touched lightly, about 45 minutes. Cool the cake upside down by inverting the pan on a long-necked bottle for 1 ¹/2 hours. Slide a thin spatula around the sides and then the bottom of the cake to loosen it before turning it out onto a plate.

Preheat the oven to 450°F.

In a bowl, combine the strawberries, sugar, and brandy. Spread the berries in a single layer on a rimmed baking sheet and dot with the butter. Roast, tossing once, until the syrup is thick and bubbling, about 10 minutes. Let cool.

---

*Individual Chocolate Chip Angel Food Cakes* These make an elegant presentation. Prepare the batter as directed and bake in 18 regular or 12 jumbo muffin tins for 20 to 25 minutes. Let cool in the pans (prop the muffin tins upside down on glasses so the cakes don't lose height as they cool). To serve, halve the cakes horizontally and toast both sides.

---

To make the chocolate sauce, in a small pot over medium heat, bring the cream to a boil. Place the chocolate and butter in a heatproof bowl and pour the boiling cream on top. Let sit for 5 minutes, then whisk until smooth. Whisk in the Grand Marnier. Keep warm.

Preheat the broiler, light the grill, or use a toaster oven. Slice the cake gently with a serrated knife and toast or grill the slices on both sides. Serve the cake with chocolate sauce and strawberries, garnished with ice cream, berry sorbet, or crème fraîche.

# Chocolate Pizzas with Fruit Variations

This is a dessert that appeals to adults yet is also perfect for a make-your-own-pizza children's birthday party. And I can pretty much guarantee you'll be the only one on the block making these—at least until word gets out. The crust is decadently brownielike, which makes the idea seem less far-fetched, and the fruit toppings are fun and colorful. If you're aiming for a pizza look-alike, the strawberry ricotta pizza is the most convincing. If you are trying to decide on which chocolate to use, keep in mind that while white chocolate looks the most like melted mozzarella cheese, milk and dark chocolates have more pronounced flavors.

MAKES FOUR 10-INCH PIZZAS, SERVING 16 TO 20

$1^1/2$ teaspoons active dry yeast

$2^1/2$ tablespoons sugar, plus additional to proof yeast

$3^3/4$ cups all-purpose flour, plus additional for dusting

$^1/2$ cup plus 2 tablespoons unsweetened cocoa powder

3 tablespoons vegetable oil

$2^1/2$ teaspoons fine sea salt or kosher salt

---

## TOPPINGS (each makes enough to top 1 pizza)

### Caramelized Pineapple-Raspberry

Four $^1/2$-inch-thick pineapple slices, cored

2 tablespoons sugar

2 tablespoons raspberry jam

$^1/4$ cup raspberries

$^1/4$ cup grated white, milk, or dark chocolate

### Apricot-Peach

2 tablespoons apricot jam

1 large peach, thinly sliced (about 1 cup)

$^1/4$ cup grated white, milk, or dark chocolate

### Ginger-Mango

2 tablespoons ginger marmalade or preserves

1 cup thinly sliced peeled mango

$^1/4$ cup grated white, milk, or dark chocolate

## Strawberry-Ricotta

**2 tablespoons strawberry jam**

**1 cup thinly sliced strawberries**

**$^1/_2$ cup ricotta cheese**

**2 teaspoons sugar**

**Honey for drizzling**

**Fresh mint leaves for garnish**

Warm $^1/_2$ cup water to 110–115°F (it should feel warm to the touch). In the bowl of an electric mixer fitted with a dough hook, mix the yeast with the warm water and a pinch of sugar. Let sit for 15 minutes. If the yeast is not foaming, discard it and begin again with fresh yeast. Add the flour, cocoa, oil, salt, remaining sugar, and another cup of water to the foaming yeast and mix on medium speed until the dough is smooth and elastic and springs back when pinched, about 15 minutes. Cover the bowl with plastic wrap and let rise in a warm place until doubled in bulk, about 1$^1/_2$ to 2 hours.

Meanwhile, preheat the broiler or light the grill. To caramelize the pineapple, sprinkle the slices with the sugar.

*In the Oven*  Lay the pineapple on a rimmed baking sheet and place it as close to the heat source as possible. Broil, turning once, until the slices are browned, about 5 to 6 minutes per side.

*On the Grill*  Lay the pineapple on the grill and cook, turning once, until the slices are browned on both sides, about 5 to 8 minutes per side.

Place a pizza stone or an inverted baking sheet on the lower rack of the oven and preheat it to 500°F or add more charcoal to the grill if necessary.

Press the risen pizza dough down and turn it onto a flat, lightly floured surface. Lightly knead the dough a few times. Divide the dough into 4 equal balls. Roll out each round on a piece of parchment paper to $^1/_4$-inch thickness (they will be about

10 inches in diameter). Slide the rounds, on the paper, onto cookie sheets or upside-down rimmed baking sheets.

For the pineapple-raspberry pizza, slice each pineapple ring into 6 pieces. Spread the jam evenly over the top of the dough to the edges and arrange the pineapple over it. Scatter the raspberries between the pineapple pieces and sprinkle the chocolate over all.

For the apricot-peach pizza, spread the jam evenly over the top of the dough to the edges and arrange the peaches over it. Sprinkle the chocolate over all.

For the ginger-mango pizza, spread the marmalade evenly over the top of the dough to the edges and arrange the mango over it. Sprinkle the chocolate over all.

For the strawberry-ricotta pizza, spread the jam evenly over the top of the dough to the edges and arrange the strawberries over it. Drop teaspoon-sized dollops of ricotta evenly over the pizza and sprinkle the sugar over all.

*In the Oven*   Trim the parchment paper around the pizzas, leaving a narrow border around the dough. Slide the pizzas on the paper onto the pizza stone or baking sheet, one at a time, and cook until the bottom is browned and crisp, about 8 to 10 minutes.

*On the Grill*   Chill the pizzas in the refrigerator until they are firm enough to slide from a baking sheet or board onto the grill, about 30 minutes to an hour. Slide the pizzas off the paper onto the grill and cook, with the grill covered, until the edges are crisp and the dough is cooked through, about 7 to 9 minutes.

Slice the pizzas and serve warm, drizzling the strawberry-ricotta pizza with honey and garnishing it with mint.

# Index

Calves' liver, grilled, with apple-smoked bacon and vermouth, 156

Camembert, quail with bacon, sage, and, 114–15

Capers, mustard shrimp with, 26

Carpaccio, charred tuna, with basil oil, 16–17

Carrots
roasted, with honey and black pepper, 212
roasted winter root vegetables with balsamic vinegar, 214–15
roasted winter vegetable risotto, 82–83

Cauliflower
caramelized cauliflower soup, 54–55

Celery, braised, 173

Celery root
roasted parsnip and celery root soup, 58–59
roasted winter root vegetables with balsamic vinegar, 214–15

Chanterelles, veal chops with chives and, 132–33

Charcoal grills, 7–8

Cheddar
aged, watercress salad with grilled or roasted red onions and, 40–41
apple Cheddar pie, 260–61

Cheese. See also specific cheeses
asparagus with herbs and cheese crisps, 198–99
roasted pasta shells with potatoes and, 76–77
scalloped potatoes with two cheeses, 216–17
thin-crust pizza with three cheeses and basil, 236–37
toasted farmer's cheese with honey and dried fruit compote, 269–70

Cherry tomatoes, 41
sweet tomato and bocconcini salad with scallions, 43
watercress salad with grilled or roasted red onions and aged Cheddar, 40–41

Chervil vinaigrette, wood-grilled or roasted trout with, 174–75

Chicken, 92–113
breasts, with cider glaze and grilled apples, 108–9
breasts, with grainy mustard, almonds, and thyme, 110–11
breasts, hot-smoked, with balsamic marinade and onion-parsley relish, 112–13
chili-rubbed chicken fingers with molasses and brandy dipping sauce, 92–93
chopped chicken salad with grilled or roasted vegetables, 94–95
with cipollini, 106–7
crisp spicy chicken wings, 103

garlic and egg chicken soup, 64–65
herbed chicken salad with basil-chive vinaigrette, 96–97
roasted, with ten herbs, 100–2
roasted, with tomato and tarragon, 98–99
roasted spice-rubbed chicken under a brick, 104–5

Chili-rubbed chicken fingers with molasses and brandy dipping sauce, 92–93

Chives
asparagus with herbs and cheese crisps, 198–99
basil-chive vinaigrette, herbed chicken salad with, 96–97
cremini mushrooms with chive pasta, 75
herb oil, 149
mixed herb salad with roasted tomato vinaigrette, 42
veal chops with chanterelles and, 132–33

Chocolate
bitter, loin of pork with apples and, 150–51
chocolate angel food cake with roasted brandied strawberries and chocolate sauce, 271–73
chocolate pizzas with fruit toppings, 274–76

Chowder, smoky corn and cod, 68–69

Chutney, tomato-ginger, sea scallops on rosemary skewers with, 180–81

Cilantro
-onion relish, yellow tomato soup with, 48–49
-yogurt sauce, Mediterranean stuffed zucchini with, 204–5

Cipollini, chicken with, 106–7

Citrus rub, rib steak with, 128–29

Clams
roasted, with garlic, lemon, and red pepper, 18–19
roasted shellfish stew with mussels, shrimp, linguiça sausage and, 190–91
thin-crust white pizza with caramelized onions and, 242–43

Cod
smoky corn and cod chowder, 68–69
sweet onion and thyme-glazed cod, 166–67

Compote, honey and dried fruit, toasted farmer's cheese with, 269–70

Coriander crust, loin of lamb with, 136–37

Corn
rigatoni with Roquefort and, 74
seared polenta squares with scallions and, 88–89
smoky corn and cod chowder, 68–69
smoky corn succotash, 202–3

hot-smoked chicken breasts with balsamic
marinade and onion-parsley relish,
112–13
hot-smoked salmon with spicy cucumbers, 164–65

Internal temperatures, judging doneness, 3

Juniper, grilled pineapple with gin, lime, and, 268

Ketchup, homemade, classic grilled hamburger with,
120–21

Lamb
butterflied leg of, with thyme and honey,
138–39
chops, with mint and garlic relish, 134–35
loin of, with a coriander crust, 136–37
rack or chops with black olives and lemon,
140–42
Leek relish, spicy, sea scallops on a potato disk with,
182–83
Lemon(s)
citrus rub, rib steak with, 128–29
grilled or roasted, 142
quick lemon confit, halibut with white wine and,
170–71
rack of lamb with black olives and, 140–42
roasted baby artichokes with garlic and, 224
roasted clams with garlic, red pepper, and, 18–19
shrimp with parsley, garlic, and lemon butter,
178–79
squid with white beans and, 192–93
Lettuce. *See also* Salad(s)
butter lettuce salad with red pepper vinaigrette,
44–45
lobster salad with red onion, basil, and Bibb
lettuce, 187
Linguiça sausage, roasted shellfish stew with
mussels, clams, shrimp, and, 190–91
Liver
grilled calves' liver with apple-smoked bacon and
vermouth, 156
Lobster
boiled, 189
charred, thin-crust pizza with tomatoes and,
244–45

with dill and yellow pepper-fennel slaw, 188–89
salad, with red onion, basil, and Bibb lettuce,
187

Madeira, figs with orange zest and, 258–59
Mango
ginger-mango topping, for chocolate pizza,
274
Maple and cayenne glaze, roasted winter squash
with, 213
Mayonnaise
broken, fixing, 186
tarragon, grilled soft-shell crab sandwiches with,
184–86
Meat. *See also* Beef; Lamb; Pork; Sausage; Veal
about doneness and resting time, 2–3
grilled calves' liver with apple-smoked bacon and
vermouth, 156
venison chops with spicy currant and red wine
sauce, 154–55
Mediterranean stuffed zucchini with cilantro-yogurt
sauce, 204–5
Mint
asparagus with herbs and cheese crisps, 198–99
baby eggplant with harissa and, 206
crispy stuffed onions with herbs, 208
and garlic relish, lamb chops with, 134–35
mixed herb salad with roasted tomato vinaigrette,
42
spicy cucumbers, hot-smoked salmon with,
164–65
sweet tomato and bocconcini salad with scallions,
43
Molasses and brandy dipping sauce, chili-rubbed
chicken fingers with, 92–93
Moscato roasted apricots, almond ricotta cake with,
254–55
Mozzarella
asparagus and portobello mushroom bundles with,
196–97
bocconcini and sweet tomato salad with scallions,
43
Mushrooms
asparagus and portobello mushroom bundles with
mozzarella, 196–97
creamy mushroom soup, 60–61
cremini mushrooms with chive pasta, 75
shiitake mushroom and gingered crabmeat salad,
30–31

thin-crust pizza with white truffle oil and, 240–41

veal chops with chanterelles and chives, 132–33

Mussels, roasted shellfish stew with clams, shrimp, linguiça sausage and, 190–91

Mustard

chicken breasts with grainy mustard, almonds, and thyme, 110

crispy potato wedges with thyme and, 218–19

mustard shrimp with capers, 26

roasted pork chops with cabbage and, 146–47

swordfish steaks in a mustard seed crust, 172–73

Nectarine and almond crostata, 256–57

New York strip steaks with black pepper, onions, and garlic, 124–25

Oil

basil oil, charred tuna carpaccio with, 16–17

herb oil, 149

white truffle oil, thin-crust pizza with mushrooms and, 240–41

Olives

rack of lamb with black olives and lemon, 140–42

tuna salad with potatoes, green beans, herb vinaigrette, and, 158–59

whole red snapper with baby fennel and Niçoise olives, 176–77

Onions. See also Scallions

caramelized, thin-crust white pizza with clams and, 242–43

caramelized onion and Roquefort gratin, 209–10

charred onion soup, 50–51

chicken with cipollini, 106–7

in chopped chicken salad with grilled or roasted vegetables, 94–95

cilantro-onion relish, yellow tomato soup with, 48–49

crispy stuffed onions with herbs, 208

grilled or roasted red onions, watercress salad with aged Cheddar and, 40–41

New York strip steaks with black pepper, garlic, and, 124–25

onion-bacon vinaigrette, roasted fennel and orange salad with, 38–39

onion-parsley relish, hot-smoked chicken breasts with balsamic marinade and, 112–13

red, lobster salad with basil, Bibb lettuce, and, 187

sweet onion and thyme-glazed cod, 166–67

Orange(s)

caramelized bananas with blood oranges, rum, and spices, 266–67

citrus rub, rib steak with, 128–29

figs with Madeira and orange zest, 258–59

and roasted fennel salad with onion-bacon vinaigrette, 38–39

Oregano

crispy stuffed onions with herbs, 208

striped bass with verjuice and, 168–69

Oven roasting equipment and techniques, 11–13

Oysters

roasted, with shallots and herbs, 20–21

shucking, 21

Parmesan cheese, 23

asparagus with herbs and cheese crisps, 198–99

scalloped potatoes with two cheeses, 216–17

Parsley

butter lettuce salad with red pepper vinaigrette, 44

crispy stuffed onions with herbs, 208

herb oil, 149

mixed herb salad with roasted tomato vinaigrette, 42

onion-parsley relish, hot-smoked chicken breasts with balsamic marinade and, 112–13

shrimp with parsley, garlic, and lemon butter, 178–79

Parsnips

roasted parsnip and celery root soup, 58–59

roasted winter root vegetables with balsamic vinegar, 214–15

Pasta, 72–79

basic tomato sauce, 235

cremini mushrooms with chive pasta, 75

crisp penne with ricotta, roasted tomatoes, and herbs, 72–73

rigatoni with Roquefort and corn, 74

roasted shells with potatoes and cheese, 76–77

roasted winter squash ravioli with sage and walnut butter, 78–79

Peaches

apricot-peach topping for chocolate pizza, 274

with balsamic vinegar and Roquefort, 252–53

roasted peach and blueberry cake with pan juices, 250–51

peppered tuna with shallots and, 160–61

Relish. *See also* Chutney; Salsa

cilantro-onion, for yellow tomato soup, 48–49

mint and garlic, lamb chops with, 134–35

onion-parsley, hot-smoked chicken breasts with balsamic marinade and, 112–13

spicy leek, sea scallops on a potato disk with, 182–83

Resting time, meat and fish, 2

Rib steak with citrus rub, 128–29

Ricotta

almond ricotta cake with Moscato roasted apricots, 254–55

crisp penne with roasted tomatoes, herbs, and, 72–73

strawberry-ricotta topping for chocolate pizza, 275

Rigatoni with Roquefort and corn, 74

Risotto

grilled or roasted shrimp risotto, 84–85

grilled summer vegetable, 80–81

roasted winter vegetable, 82–83

Roasting equipment and techniques, 11–13

Roquefort

caramelized onion and Roquefort gratin, 209–10

in chopped chicken salad with grilled or roasted vegetables, 94–95

endive stuffed with apples, walnuts, and, 36–37

peaches with balsamic vinegar and, 252–53

rigatoni with corn and, 74

Rosemary

flank steak with roasted garlic and, 122–23

roasted baby artichokes with lemon and garlic, 224

skewers, sea scallops on, with tomato ginger chutney, 180–81

Rum, caramelized bananas with blood oranges, spices, and, 266–67

Rutabaga

roasted winter root vegetables with balsamic vinegar, 214–15


Sage

quail with bacon, Camembert, and, 114–15

roasted winter squash ravioli with sage and walnut butter, 78–79

turkey breast paillardes with black pepper, garlic, and, 118

Salad(s). *See also* Appetizers

arugula, with crisp fingerling potato chips, 27

arugula, with crispy squid and garlic croutons, 22–23

butter lettuce, with red pepper vinaigrette, 44–45

chopped chicken salad with grilled or roasted vegetables, 94–95

endive stuffed with apples, Roquefort, and walnuts, 36–37

green apple and potato, sausage "mixed grill" with, 152–53

herbed chicken salad with basil-chive vinaigrette, 96–97

lobster, with red onion, basil, and Bibb lettuce, 187

mixed herb, with roasted tomato vinaigrette, 42

potato, spicy, with sweet and hot peppers, 28–29

red pepper and parsley, with veal chops and green peppercorns, 130–31

roasted fennel and orange, with onion-bacon vinaigrette, 38–39

shiitake mushroom and gingered crabmeat, 30–31

spicy cucumber, hot-smoked salmon with, 164–65

squid with lemon and white beans, 192–93

sweet tomato and bocconcini, with scallions, 43

tangerine and arugula, duck breasts with, 116–17

tuna, with potatoes, green beans, olives, and herb vinaigrette, 158–59

watercress, with grilled or roasted red onions and aged Cheddar, 40–41

yellow pepper-fennel slaw, lobster with dill and, 188–89

Salmon

herb-crusted, with horseradish bread sauce, 162–63

hot-smoked, with spicy cucumbers, 164–65

salmon tartare, 232

Salsa. *See also* Relish

roasted tomato and avocado, 233

tomato-horseradish, shrimp with, 24–25

Sandwiches. *See also* Bruschetta

barbecued pork, 145

grilled soft-shell crab, on English muffins with tarragon mayonnaise, 184–86

Sauce(s)

barbecue, 143–45

basic tomato sauce, 235

chocolate, chocolate angel food cake with roasted brandied strawberries and, 271–73

cilantro-yogurt, Mediterranean stuffed zucchini with, 204–5

horseradish-bread, herb-crusted salmon with, 162–63

ketchup, homemade, classic grilled hamburger with, 120–21

molasses and brandy dipping sauce, chili-rubbed chicken fingers with, 92–93

red pepper, for veal chops with green peppercorns, 130–31

spicy currant and red wine, venison chops with, 154–55

Sausage

linguiça, roasted shellfish stew with mussels, clams, shrimp, and, 190–91

sausage "mixed grill" with green apple and potato salad, 152–53

Scallions

seared polenta squares with corn and, 88–89

sweet tomato and bocconcini salad with, 43

Scalloped potatoes with two cheeses, 216–17

Scallops. *See* Sea scallops

Seafood, 148–93. *See also* Fish; *specific types*

Sea scallops

on a potato disk with spicy leek relish, 182–83

on rosemary skewers with tomato ginger chutney, 180–81

Shallots

peppered tuna with red wine and, 160–61

roasted oysters with herbs and, 20–21

Shellfish. *See also specific types*

roasted shellfish stew with mussels, clams, shrimp, and linguiça sausage, 190

Shiitake mushroom and gingered crabmeat salad, 30–31

Shortcakes, roasted summer berry, 248–49

Shrimp

and fennel soup with Pernod, 66–67

grilled or roasted shrimp risotto, 84–85

mustard shrimp with capers, 26

with parsley, garlic, and lemon butter, 178–79

roasted shellfish stew with mussels, clams, linguiça sausage and, 190–91

with tomato-horseradish salsa, 24–25

Smoking. *See* Hot smoking

Soup(s), 48–69

asparagus, with egg mimosa, 52–53

caramelized cauliflower, 54–55

charred onion, 50–51

charred yellow tomato, 48–49

creamy mushroom, 60–61

garlic and egg chicken soup, 64–65

roasted butternut squash and pear, 56–57

roasted parsnip and celery root, 58–59

shrimp and fennel, with Pernod, 66–67

smoky corn and cod chowder, 68–69

sweet potato, with spicy red pepper aïoli, 62–63

Spicy broccoli rabe, seared polenta squares with, 86–87

Spicy crisp chicken wings, 103

Spicy cucumbers, hot-smoked salmon with, 164–65

Spicy currant and red wine sauce, venison chops with, 154–55

Spicy eggplant dip, 207

Spicy leek relish, sea scallops on a potato disk with, 182–83

Spicy potato salad with sweet and hot peppers, 28–29

Spicy red pepper aïoli, sweet potato soup with, 62–63

Spinach

sautéed, with garlic, 125

squid with lemon and white beans, 192–93

Spreads. *See* Dips and spreads

Squash. *See* Summer squash; Winter squash

Squid

crispy, with arugula and garlic croutons, 22–23

with lemon and white beans, 192–93

Steak. *See* Beef

Stew

roasted shellfish stew with mussels, clams, shrimp, and linguiça sausage, 190–91

Strawberries

roasted brandied, chocolate angel food cake with chocolate sauce and, 271–73

roasted summer berry shortcakes, 248–49

strawberry-ricotta topping for chocolate pizza, 275

Striped bass with oregano and verjuice, 168–69

Succotash, smoky corn, 202–3

Summer squash. *See also* Zucchini

grilled or roasted summer vegetables, 200–1

grilled summer vegetable risotto, 80–81